WAR AND PEACE
IN THE GULF

WAR AND PEACE IN THE GULF

Domestic Politics and Regional Relations into the 1990s

by
ANOUSHIRAVAN EHTESHAMI
and
GERD NONNEMAN

with CHARLES TRIPP

ITHACA PRESS
READING
1991

Exeter Middle East Monographs No. 5

© 1991

First published in 1991 by Ithaca Press, 8 Southern Court
South Street, Reading, Berks RG1 4QS, UK

All rights reserved.
Except for brief quotations in a review, this book, or any part thereof, must not be reproduced in any form without permission in writing from the publisher.

British Library Cataloguing-in-Publication Data

Ehteshami, Anoushiravan
　War and peace in the Gulf: domestic politics and regional relations into the 1990s. – (Exeter Middle East monographs; no. 5)
　　1. Foreign relations　2. Middle East
　　I. Nonneman, Gerd　II. Tripp, Charles
　　　327.09536

ISBN 0-86372-134-6

Produced by Imprint, Oxford
Typeset at Oxford University Computing Service
Printed and bound in England by Short Run Press, Exeter

To Emma and Mariví

Exeter Middle East Monographs

Editorial board:

Nazih Ayubi
Youssef Choueiri
Anoushiravan Ehteshami
Fadia Faqir
Gerd Nonneman

The EXETER MIDDLE EAST MONOGRAPH series, which succeeds an earlier and more narrowly focused series on Middle East politics, aims to promote the publication of high-quality research on all aspects of the Middle East region and, by extension, the Islamic world, with priority given to titles originating from work done at the University of Exeter. The composition of the Editorial Board reflects the contribution of various disciplines to the study of the region, in line with the projected content of the series.

Forthcoming titles in the Exeter series include:

H. Jawad, *The Euro-Arab Dialogue a study in collective diplomacy*
E. Murphy (ed.), *1984: recent research on the early history of the Israeli state*
P. Robins, *Hashemite Power in Jordan*
B. Croydon, *Sudan and the Manchester Connection*
I. Marzouqi, *Human Rights in Islamic Law*

CONTENTS

List of Tables	ix
Foreword by Ambassador Richard Murphy	xi
Glossary and Abbreviations	xiii

Introduction	1
1 The Structure of Power in Post-Khomeini Iran	3
2 Domestic Politics in Iraq: Saddam Hussein and the Autocrat's Fallacy (Charles Tripp)	19
3 Iraq and the Arab States of the Gulf: Full Circle	35
4 The Military Balance in the Gulf: One Step Forward Two Steps Back	91
5 Defence Investment and Military Procurement Strategies of Iran and Iraq	119
6 Documents: From the 1975 Algiers Agreement to the 1990 UN Security Council Resolutions on the Kuwait Crisis	141
7 Chronology of Gulf Events 1980–1991	225
Postscript	245

Notes	257
Select Bibliography	271
Maps	275
About the Authors	277
Index	279

LIST OF TABLES

1.1	Voting patterns for the Cabinet by Majlis deputies (Iran)	6
1.2	Seven most and least popular Cabinet ministers (Iran, 1989)	9
1.3	Qualifications of the Iranian Cabinet	13
4.1	The military balance in the Gulf	93
4.2	Value of arms transfers to the Gulf states	98
4.3	Defence expenditures of Iran, Iraq and Saudi Arabia	101
4.4	Gulf military manpower	115
5.1	A survey of Iran's sophisticated airpower	125
5.2	A survey of Iraq's sophisticated airpower	130
5.3	SSMs in the Gulf	138

FOREWORD

This thoughtful volume is going to print in the midst of a conflict between an international coalition of land, sea and air forces and the armed forces of Iraq. Historians will debate whether this has been a necessary war. They will analyse the tactical skills displayed by the combatants and the role played by weapons systems never before used in warfare. They will record as well the extraordinary global sense of participation in the battle provided by the ubiquitous eye of television interpreted by a sizeable media army deployed throughout the Middle East.

This conflict, the first of the post cold war era, is being fought out on ancient lands and reflects many ancient antagonisms. It introduces the United Sates as a major combatant in the region for the first time since the Second World War. The particular value of this book lies in its careful analysis of the immediate background of the present conflict, the still fluid power structure of Iran, and the extraordinary autocracy of Saddam Hussein of Iraq. The authors describe the misjudgements widely shared in the region and beyond about Iraq's likely political course after its exhausting eight years' war with Iran, and, finally, the make-up of the military might assembled by Iraq and Iran over the past two decades.

The reader is bound to ask after reading these chapters if this war should not be enough to convince the powers who have so vigorously promoted their arms sales to this volatile region that the time has come for a new approach. Surely overdue is a high-level international effort to introduce arms control and arms reduction in the Middle East. A broad and reinvigorated diplomatic initiative to attack the region's festering political disputes will be essential. The 'new world order' is today an American slogan. Much hard work lies ahead to translate this slogan into an international reality.

Richard Murphy
Senior Fellow for the Middle East Council on
Foreign Relations, New York, January 1991

Mr Murphy served as Assistant Secretary of State for Near Eastern and South Asian Affairs 1983–89, and was US Ambassador to Syria 1974–78 and Saudi Arabia 1981–83.

GLOSSARY AND ABBREVIATIONS

ACC	Arab Cooperation Council: Egypt, Iraq, Jordan, Yemen
AFESD	Arab Fund for Economic and Social Development
AMF	Arab Monetary Fund
APC	Armoured Personnel Carrier
AWACS	Airborne Warning and Air Control System
Ayatollah	The rank of Islamic scholar above *Hojjatoleslam* (referring to the length of religious study at the advanced level)
b	barrel
Ba'th	Arabic for 'rebirth': the name of the ruling party in Iraq and Syria ('the Arab Ba'th Socialist Party')
b/d	barrels per day
CENTCOM	Central Command
EIU	Economist Intelligence Unit (London)
Faqih	Islamic legal scholar or jurisconsult
Fatwa	Islamic religious ruling
FBIS	*Foreign Broadcast Information Service* (Washington)
GCC	Gulf Cooperation Council: Saudi Arabia, Kuwait, United Arab Emirates, Bahrain, Qatar, Oman
GDP	Gross Domestic Product
Hajj	The annual pilgrimage to Mecca
Hezbollah	Iran's 'Party of God', as well as similarly named parties in the Arab world (from Arabic hizb Allah)
Hojjatoleslam	'Islamic canonist', who has studied Islamic theology at the advanced level. The title ranks between the lowest one of *Saqatoleslam*, and that of *Ayatollah*
ICO	Islamic Conference Organisation
IISS	International Institute for Strategic Studies

GLOSSARY AND ABBREVIATIONS

Infitah	Arabic for 'opening up', here used for domestic and external economic liberalisation
IPSA	Iraqi Pipeline through Saudi Arabia
IRBM	Intermediate Range Ballistic Missile
IRGC	Islamic Revolution Guards Corps
IRNA	Islamic Republic News Agency
JCSS	Jaffee Centre for Strategic Studies (Tel Aviv University)
KFAED	Kuwait Fund for Arab Economic Development
Kolahi	Non-clerical Islamic revolutionaries in the Islamic Republic
KUNA	Kuwait News Agency
Majlis	'gathering' or 'council' in Arabic and Farsi; here used for the Iranian parliament
MBT	Main Battle Tank
MEED	*Middle East Economic Digest* (London)
MEES	*Middle East Economic Survey* (Cyprus)
Mojahedin	Mojahedin Khalq Organisation (Arabic version: *Mujahidin*): an Iranian Islamic opposition organisation
Mullah	Iranian and Shi'a clergy
NLA	National Liberation Army (Iranian opposition Mojahedin)
Pasdaran	Iran's Revolutionary Guards
OPEC	Organisation of Petroleum Exporting Countries
RCC	Revolutionary Command Council: Iraq's ruling body
SAM	Surface-to-Air Missile
Shi'i	of the Shi'a, the 'Party' of Ali: the major schismatic branch of Islam, accounting for some 10 per cent of Muslims (as oposed to the orthodox Sunnis); *Shi'ism* is the dominant form of Islam in Iran. Also for a person of the *Shi'i* persuasion: a *Shi'i*
SIPRI	Stockholm International Peace Research Institute
SSM	Surface-to-Surface Missile
SWB	BBC *Summary of World Broadcasts*

GLOSSARY AND ABBREVIATIONS

UAE	United Arab Emirates: Abu Dhabi, Dubai, Sharjah, Ras al-Khaimah, Umm al-Qaiwain, Ajman, Fujairah
US ACDA	United States Arms Control and Disarmament Agency
Vali Asr	The embodiment of *Velayat-e Faqih*, the Islamic Leader of the Islamic Republic of Iran. Literally, the 'guardian of the age'
Velayat-e Faqih	Literally: 'guardianship of the jurisconsult'; Khomeini's concept of rule by a top Islamic scholar

INTRODUCTION

Crystal ball gazing is a hazardous pastime. This much should be clear from the unexpected developments that took place in the Gulf region over the year 1990 alone. Iraq invaded Kuwait, and days later accepted the re-establishment of the *status quo ante* with Iran; both events occurred suddenly and few if any observers might have expected them, yet for all that they had an impact at least equal to that of the outbreak of the Gulf War in 1980. The war between Iran and Iraq, contrary to general expectations, lasted for nearly a decade rather than for weeks, and was a major factor in transforming the balance and alignments within the region and outside it. Can the same be said of the 1990 Kuwait crisis?

The authors believe that the two conflagrations marking the beginning and the end of the 1980s, are products of a configuration of political, security and military interactions rooted in part in the power vacuum that was created in the early 1970s by the sudden British withdrawal from the area. The struggle for supremacy in the Gulf has since continued unabated between the 'three ugly sisters' (Iran, Iraq and Saudi Arabia), which have represented both distinct military powers and ideological platforms. The use of military power to maintain or strengthen such competing ideological pretensions has been a trade mark of Gulf politics since the 1970s. Repeated crises have made it difficult to distinguish between the drive towards the fulfilment of geo-political ambitions, and a commitment to ideological supremacy. In the case of Iraq, for instance, the scene has been complicated by Saddam Hussein's increasingly idiosyncratic personal hold over power and policy.

In an attempt to gain further understanding of the dynamics of events during the 1980s and, consequently, of those forces which are likely to shape the coming decade, this volume begins in Chapters 1 and 2 by analysing the domestic political scene in Iran and Iraq, the erstwhile Gulf belligerents. The internal political structures and processes of these two states have helped to determine their outlook and policies, and have therefore affected the shifting balance in the region. The political and military aspects of this balance, and the changing

INTRODUCTION

nature of regional relations, are examined in the course of Chapters 3 and 4. The fifth chapter then ties together the domestic aspects of militarisation in Iran and Iraq with its international implications. Chapter 6 provides a documentary history of Gulf conflict and international reactions since 1975: the authors felt there was a need for such a focused but comprehensive collection of documents, which had not yet been fulfilled elsewhere. This is followed by a chronology covering the 1980s and early 1991 (Chapter 7), which is intended as a reliable but user-friendly 'tool'. Inevitably the Iran-Iraq War and the Kuwait crisis account for a considerable part of this chronology; equally, however, it aims to highlight significant domestic developments in the countries of the Gulf, as well as key related events in regional and international politics.

Given the fluidity of the political and military situation in the Gulf at the time of writing the authors cannot hope to put forward definitive predictions. Rather, in presenting the above analyses, it is intended that the book may offer the reader an insight into the underlying dynamics of the unfolding drama of the world's first post-Cold War crisis. It is hoped, too, that the decision to complete this book in mid-crisis (January 1991) will add to rather than detract from its usefulness.

The authors are greatly indebted to Charles Tripp for agreeing to contribute the chapter on Iraq's domestic politics.

NOTE ON THE USE OF GULF TERMINOLOGY

While the name *Persian Gulf* has historically been used most frequently for the geographical subject area of this book, since the 1960s the label *Arab(ian) Gulf* has also gained increasing currency; among Arabs the other epithet in fact came to be rejected altogether (although they often refer to it simply as *al-Khaleej—the Gulf*). Both sides are perfectly entitled to use the name of their choice, as either will be recognised internationally as designating the same body of water. So, too, certainly in the midst of the events of the 1980s and 1990s, will the more practical shorthand label of *the Gulf*—with the added advantage, it is to be hoped, of avoiding offence: it will be the preferred name for use in the present volume.

1 THE STRUCTURE OF POWER IN POST-KHOMEINI IRAN[1]

The dismissal of Ayatollah Montazeri (March 1989) as the prospective leader of the Islamic Republic (he was to have been the *Faqih* after Khomeini's death), and the crisis that followed the Salman Rushdie[2] affair in the spring of 1989 helped to disguise a definite and secular trend that was developing towards the *Second Republic*. The Second Republic had actually begun its life almost a year earlier with the appointment of Hojjatoleslam Hashemi Rafsanjani as the Commander-in-Chief of the armed forces in June 1988, only weeks before Iran's unconditional acceptance of UN Security Council Resolution 598. The loss of the 'moderate' Montazeri was interpreted by analysts as a blow to the pragmatic/realist line prevailing in Iran at that time, and the Rushdie affair was seen as marking the ascendency of the radical elements within the Islamic Republic, enabling them to consolidate power before the Ayatollah's impending demise. But it would seem that no one school has a monopoly over the truth of the matter where the political life of modern Islamic Iran is concerned. Therefore, with the benefit of hindsight, an alternative presentation of these two events can be made, one which we would regard as advancing the cause of the realists rather than, as has commonly been argued, resulting in a setback in their programmes.

Far from weakening the hand of the realists, the dismissal of Ayatollah Montazeri helped this loose grouping in two important ways. First, it removed a potential source of political power against the Khamenei-Rafsanjani coalition *before* Khomeini's death, thus strengthening the general realist platform in the medium-term (i.e., after Khomeini's death), despite the short-term negative impact of losing a leading 'moderate' figure. Secondly, and more sinisterly, the more ambitious realists may actually have been involved in the anti-Montazeri campaign, by setting him up as the figure to draw the fire and venom of the hard-liners and other radicalist forces. In this sense his political future made him the sacrificial lamb that again united the hungry wolves around one dining table. In Ayatollah Montazeri's fall from grace all factions found a positive twist to their own fortunes. The

3

pragmatists saw in his downfall their own *medium-term* rise to power, and the 'radicals' interpreted the absence of Ayatollah Montazeri as a mortal blow to 'moderation' and as an *immediate* gain for their line.

The Rushdie affair, on the other hand, can be regarded as an aftertaste—a shock reaction—to the pace of change in the Islamic Republic's foreign relations, and to domestic indicators of accepted political behaviour. Its medium-term impact, it must be noted, has been minimal, affecting adversely and directly only Tehran's relations with one (non-Islamic) country, the United Kingdom. Domestically, the Rushdie affair has played a negligible role in the balance of forces, failing to instigate an inward rupture or, indeed, any contradictory outpouring of sentiments among the political elite.

Thus, the Second Republic, the regime of the pragmatists, was born not so much with a bang (the fears of civil war, etc. having proved groundless) as with a whimper: there was an almost totally smooth and steady transfer of all the important and decisive reins of power to the pragmatists. The hasty promotion of Hojjatoleslam Khamenei to the rank of Ayatollah and his designation in July 1989 as the *Faqih* (the Vali Asr) over the heads of many other very able and senior Ayatollahs on the one hand, and on the other the election in August of Hojjatoleslam Hashemi Rafsanjani (the speaker of the *Majlis*, or Parliament, for nine years), to the office of president (a position that Khamenei himself had held for the previous eight years), greatly consolidated the role of these individuals in the pragmatist cause of the Second Republic. Constitutional amendments proposed at the same time as the presidential elections were taking place, were carried easily by the Majlis and the electorate, and put the necessary flesh on the skeleton of the 'new' republic, which had so far been characterised only by its theatrical characters or by the events spawned by the upheavals of an unstable social environment. The loss to the Presidency of the Prime Minister's portfolio can be seen as the most fundamental structural change in the system: as a chapter in the book of the Second Republic. Other important amendments to the constitution, such as the creation of a new centralised body (e.g. the Supreme Council of National Security) are to all intents and purposes selected pages of the book. The fifty or so changes to the constitution, amounting to alterations to about one-third of the original constitution, typify the changes in power structure and institutional control, which are after all the essence of the Second Republic.

However, we must use the term 'Second Republic' with some caution. Many of the bureaucratic structures utilised and created by 'Young Turks' of the post-Khomeini era are not significantly different from those of the First Republic, or even indeed particularly distinct from the Imperial state machinery that had been partly perfected by the Shah. For example, the Expediency Council formed early in 1988 to mediate between the Majlis and the Council of Constitutional Guardians was been maintained, and its membership enlarged from the original 13 to include 20 individuals. Its new make-up was also somewhat different: President Rafsanjani chaired the Council, the members of which were appointed by Ayatollah Khamenei. Control thus remained with the 'Leader-President' coalition. Despite the presence of Ahmad Khomeini, Majlis Speaker Karrubi, former Prime Minister Moussavi and former Prosecutor-General Khoini'a, as the Old Guard hardliners, and of Rafsanjani, Ayatollah Yazdi and Mahdavi Kani as their counterweights in the Council, the 'institutional' appointments ensured a bias toward the realists' line.[3] As well as the six Islamic jurisprudence members, the heads of the three branches of government and the Minister of the Interior, in any discussion the cabinet minister and the head of Majlis committee concerned are always present. It is also notable that Hojjatoleslam Mohtashemi (the former Interior Minister) was not a member of the Council. This would appear to lend credence to the rumours that he was deliberately forced into a position from where direct political action against the consolidating Leader-President coalition would be difficult, if not impossible.

The 1989 Rafsanjani cabinet

All the members of President Rafsanjani's proposed cabinet received an unprecedented vote of confidence from the 261 Majlis deputies who were present at the Majlis session late in August 1989, thus putting the seal of approval on the realists' line despite the many reservations that were expressed by a number of deputies and by the Speaker himself. Having urged the deputies to support the proposed cabinet, Karrubi was quick to point out that the Majlis still maintained enough powers to monitor and to scrutinise the activities of the ministers and, if need be, to dismiss them from their posts: 'our hands will not be tied if a minister gets the vote', he said reassuringly in his address.[4]

Of the 22 appointments, 12 were 'new' nominees, but had already served the Islamic Republic in other capacities. One feature of the new cabinet was its technocratic/specialist character, since it included many individuals with few, if any, Hezbollahi credentials. Indeed a number of them had been engaged in political battles with the Hezbollah/hardliners for some years. Most notable among these were Mohsen Nourbakhsh (the former Governor of the Central Bank) and Iraj Fazel (the

TABLE 1.1 Voting pattern of the Cabinet and Majlis deputies, 29 August 1989

Name	Title	Post
I. Kalantari	Dr	Agriculture
A. Vahaji	Mr	Commerce—New
G. Foruzeh	Eng.	Construction Jihad
A. Torkan	Eng.	Defence & Logistics—New
M. Nourbakhsh	Dr	Economics & Finance—New
M. A. Najafi	Dr	Education
B. Namdar-Zanganeh	Eng.	Energy
A. A. Velayati	Dr	Foreign Affairs
I. Fazel	Dr	Health—New
M. H. Nezhad-Hosseinian	Dr	Heavy Industries—New
M. Mo'in	Dr	Higher Education—New
S. Kazerouni	Eng.	Housing
M. R. Nematzadeh	Eng.	Industries—New
A. Fallahiyan	Hoj.	Information—New
A. Nouri	Hoj.	Interior—New
M. Khatami	Hoj.	Islamic
A. Shostari	Hoj.	Justice—New
H. Kamali	Mr	Labour—New
M. H. Mahloji	Eng.	Mines & Metals—New
G. Aqazadeh	Eng.	Oil
M. Gharazi	Eng.	Post, Telegraph & Telephone
M. Sa'edi-Kia	Eng.	Road & Transport

Source: Islamic Republic of Iran News Agency (IRNA).

TABLE 1.1 (cont.)

For	Agnst	Abstn	Total
186	53	20	259
147	93	18	258
221	30	10	261
242	10	9	261
195	43	19	257
160	86	12	258
245	5	7	257
213	35	10	258
165	86	9	260
219	26	11	256
237	14	6	257
145	97	14	256
217	28	12	257
158	79	18	255
224	20	15	259
246	10	4	260
209	30	18	257
224	18	16	258
150	85	22	257
231	18	10	259
230	16	11	257
222	21	9	252

Note: 261 of Majlis' 270 deputies were present on 29 September 1989. Ministers had to receive a minimum of 132 votes (half of the deputies present plus one) for approval.

former Higher Education Minister). The general de-ideologisation of the machinery of government gained further momentum with such appointments, prompting many influential figures in Iran to dub President Rafsanjani's team the 'cabinet of construction'.[5]

Insofar as empirical interpretation is possible, the position of the seven most and the seven least popular cabinet ministers may, in terms of Majlis voting patterns, throw some light on the relationship between the legislative and executive branches of government in the Second Republic. But one of the points emerging from Table 1.1 is the mix of continuity and change aimed at by Rafsanjani. Continuity in the areas deemed important to the smooth functioning of the Islamic Republic resulted in continuity in the following areas: Agriculture, Foreign affairs, Energy, Oil, Construction Jihad, and the Ministry of Communications and Transport. The replacement of statists from key ministries such as Heavy Industries, Commerce, and Economic and Finance, removed the potential barriers to the liberalisation of the economy.

Looking at Table 1.2, one is struck by the significant gap that divides the ministers most popular with the deputies, from their least popular colleagues. The pro-vote of 246 for Hojjatoleslam Mohammed Khatami (Islamic Guidance Minister) contrasts sharply with that of the 145 votes for Engineer Serajaddin Kazerouni (Housing Minister)—a difference of 101 votes. If we add the abstentions to the 'disapproving' camp (the total negative vote) then Khatami's net vote would stand at 242, whereas Kazerouni's would be reduced sharply to stand at only 131, one vote below the 'pass mark' and 111 votes behind Khatami's score. The gap, however, narrows as we approach the edges of each category. For example, the least of the 'least popular' ministers (Dr Nourbakhsh) in our categorisation is only 29 votes behind the two seventh 'most popular' ministers, Hojjatoleslam Nouri and Mr Kamali.

Secondly, the seven 'least popular' ministers (votes against) also recorded fairly high abstention votes. The addition of the 'abstention' votes to the votes 'against' would therefore record a greater net loss for this category than it would for the 'most popular' tier of our segmented cabinet. An average of 11 to 13 votes can be subtracted from each minister's score in the 'least popular' category in order to arrive at the 'true' picture, whereas an additional 5 votes on average (excluding the unusually high abstention votes against Hojjatoleslam Nouri and Mr Kamali) can be subtracted from the figures of the 'most popular' ministers.

Thirdly, seven of the 12 'new' appointments appear in the data for the highest abstention rate. This can be interpreted as a warning to the

TABLE 1.2 Seven most and least popular cabinet ministers, 1989 vote

	For	Agnst	Abstn
1) Hoj. Khatami	246	10	4
2) Eng. Namdar-Zanganeh	245	5	7
3) Eng. Torkan (n)	242	10	9
4) Dr Mo'in (n)	237	14	6
5) Eng. Aqazadeh	231	18	10
6) Eng. Gharazi	230	16	11
7) Hoj. Nouri (n)	224	20	15
7) Mr Kamali (n)	224	18	16

	Agnst	For	Abstn
1) Eng. Kazerouni	97	145	14
2) Mr Vahaji (n)	93	147	18
3) Dr Najafi	86	160	12
3) Dr Fazel (n)	86	165	9
4) Eng. Mahloji (n)	85	150	22
5) Hoj. Fallahiyan (n)	79	158	18
6) Dr Kalantari	53	186	20
7) Dr Nourbakhsh (n)	43	195	19

	Abstn	Agnst	For
1) Eng. Mahloji (n)	22	85	150
2) Dr Kalantari	20	53	186
3) Dr Nourbakhsh (N)	19	43	195
4) Mr Vahaji (n)	18	93	147
4) Hoj. Fallahiyan (n)	18	79	158
4) Hoj. Shostari (n)	18	30	209
5) Mr Kamali (n)	16	18	224
6) Hoj. Nouri (n)	15	20	224
7) Eng. Kazerouni	14	97	145

Source: See Table 1.1

President; short of rejecting his first cabinet outright, the deputies were raising questions about the 'new' half of the Rafsanjani cabinet in the most subtle and least damaging style. Although the deputies were not condemning outright the new president and the re-styled presidency as such (as they had done in the past with the Prime Minister and his team), they were causing a certain concern to the greatly empowered Rafsanjani. The beating of the consensus drum by all the influential figures in the run up to the Majlis vote, which was intended to minimise the new cabinet's casualty rate, was singularly successful in reducing the dropout rate to zero, for the first time in the turbulent history of the Islamic Republic. As the abstention vote shows, however, it was unsuccessful in creating full and unconditional support for the Rafsanjani mandate. Therefore a potent source of trouble for the new leaders remained. It is safe to say that at that stage the opposition was down but certainly not beaten. The negative total vote shows that the unpopularity ratio (realistically set at about one-sixth of the cabinet) would rise to an unacceptable proportion that would engulf nearly one-third of the cabinet and register some 50 out of 261 votes cast against the ministers.

As secret balloting prevents an empirical examination of the voting pattern of each deputy, their speeches and the relative consistency in the abstention figures suggest to us that a hardcore of the deputies objected to the Rafsanjani cabinet. If this is so, then two possible interpretations can be made. First, a real anti-Rafsanjani alliance, albeit still relatively small, had emerged in the Majlis. Secondly, the massive damage limitation exercise that was undertaken by the national clerical figures worked particularly well, and—whether as a result of pressure or because of genuine concern—the majority of the deputies supported the Rafsanjani cabinet for the good of the Second Republic, recognising that in the conditions prevailing and without Rafsanjani's guidance, the serious divisions among the ranks of the clergy over the social, ideological, cultural, political and economic life of the country were likely to lead to irreparable splits in the unique Mosque-State structures of the Islamic Republic.

Let us now consider some of the important individual appointments. Even though some 130 deputies had sent a letter to the President only weeks before the Majlis vote, calling for the reinstatement of the former hard-line Interior Minister, Hojjatoleslam Mohtashemi, 224 of them supported the appointment of Hojjatoleslam Nouri as the new Interior Minister in the cabinet. He received 20 votes against and 15 abstentions, a total negative vote of 35. By contrast, Mr Kamali (who is also seventh on the 'most popular' list) accumulated a total of 34 negative votes. So, while Nouri's appointment received an overwhelming endorsement in absolute terms, in relative terms he remains the most unpopular minister of the top seven. But compared with Mohtashemi's performance in the confidence vote in the 1985 Majlis, Nouri scored much better; out of 258 votes cast in October of that year, Mohtashemi received 163 votes 'for' and 32 'against' with 63 'abstentions', a total negative vote of 95—nearly three times that of Nouri's.

Nouri's key role in the affairs of the Second Republic allows us to appreciate the need for replacing Mohtashemi as the Interior Minister in the new Rafsanjani line-up. Although somewhat of a hardliner by the standards of the new leadership and the brief of the Second Republic, Nouri moved up fast to become a senior member of the cabinet. On the one hand his ministry provided the 'Leader-President' faction with (a) direct access to the provinces outside of the Mosque network; and (b) the best instrument for implementing policy and gauging national public opinion on both policy and security matters. On the other hand, his appointment as the chairman of the newly-created National Security Council, which not only formulates and co-ordinates national security and defence policies but also directs the republic's political programme, brought the commanding heights of the state's political and politico-military structures under the direct control of the 'President's Men', and away from the influence of the unpredictable Majlis. Furthermore, Nouri's role as the Imam's representative to the IRGC (the Islamic Revolution Guards Corps, or *Pasdaran*) since early 1989 may have helped his cause: by appointing him, Rafsanjani attempted to maintain a support base—albeit indirectly—in the Pasdaran, at the same time as appeasing the militant and armed hardliners of the regime (to whose faction Nouri is said to belong). The latent support from the IRGC may become crucial for the President, particularly since formal control of the armed forces, the post of Commander-in-Chief, has been returned to the Supreme Leader. With the progressive integration of IRGC and the regular armed forces, Nouri's position as the Leader's representative in the IRGC became less significant. Therefore his resignation from that post in June 1990 did not necessarily weaken the pragmatists.[6]

As a final point in relation to the popularity ratings, it is perhaps a sign of the times that while the most popular cabinet minister remained a Mullah, he still received more total negative votes (14) than his nearest rival, a non-cleric 'Kolahi' individual, with only 12 negative votes. We also find in the 'least popular' category a Mullah whose total negative vote stands at 87—one-third of the assembly present. In essence, therefore, it can be seen that exactly one-third of the clergy-dominated Majlis either did not approve of the appointment of another cleric (Hojjatoleslam Fallahiyan) to the cabinet, or at the very least, objected to his assigned post. Thus the above analysis provides graphic illustration of the heterogeneity of the clergy in Iran, and the deep social and political differences among them.

Rafsanjani's cabinet in perspective

In tandem with other political and governmental/bureaucratic structures of the Islamic Republic, the clerics were well represented in the cabinet. Of the four Hojjatoleslams in the cabinet only one (Khatami) had served in the previous Council of Ministers. The other three did have responsible positions in the regime but none as senior or central as their new portfolios: their appointment to the posts of Islamic Guidance, Justice, Interior and Information, left the 'political' posts in the cabinet in the hands of the Shi'a clergy while the technocrats were left in charge of the 'functional' ministries. Hence, the 'Islamic' nature of the republic remained intact and the clerics continued to rule Iran as the country's 'natural' rulers.

As Table 1.3 shows, the Second Republic is repeating the same shift towards technocracy which existed in what was arguably the most authoritative and professional cabinet of the Shah's long reign, that of Prime Minister Hoveyda in 1967. Compared, for instance, with the Bazargan government, formed at the time of factional competition and grave political uncertainties in the Islamic Republic, Rafsanjani's cabinet was distinctly more technocratic—even though the calibre of personnel perhaps was not as good as that of the 1967 or the 1979 cabinets. Again, it remains to be seen whether this illustrates the move to concerted central control of the state, as there was with the Shah's 1967 cabinet.

The very basic comparisons of Table 1.3 illustrate the changes in the qualification patterns in the different cabinets. On paper the qualification standards of the Rafsanjani cabinet compare favourably with those of both the Bazargan (1979) and the Hoveyda (1967) cabinets. Rafsanjani's cabinet, however, possesses the highest proportion of 'engineers', a misleading designation since it does not represent technical expertise and modernity but is simply a title, embedded in Iran's socio-economic hierarchy, that is given to all those with a technical bachelor's degree (i.e., a BSc). Nevertheless, in social class terms a *mohandes* (engineer) is a revered title denoting high social standing, professional competence and proven ability. In this context, it is possible that Rafsanjani deliberately sought a higher proportion of 'engineers' from the pool of eligible candidates available to him, the political significance being that the Second Republic symbolises progress and modernity, and furthermore, is committed to the rejuvenation and reconstruction of the country. The placing of technical experts in technical posts is seen as a way of reinforcing the serious intention of the new leadership, and of

TABLE 1.3 Qualifications of the Iranian cabinet, 1967, 1979 and 1989

	1967	1979	1989
No. of ministers	24	23	22
Physicians; PhDs	15	9	7
Engineers	5	4	9
Without title	3	9	2
Lt. General	1	1	—
Hojjatoleslam	—	—	4

Source: *Ettala'at*, 19 October 1967 and IRNA.

Note: The 1967 cabinet had one woman minister. None of the cabinets since the revolution have had a woman minister.

the latter's efforts to promote meritocracy in the system. Thus, the division of labour between clerics and non-clerics can also be viewed as a 'natural' division between the technical and non-technical portfolios in the new cabinet. Of course, it can also be argued that the 'technical' post of Islamic Guidance Minister could only have been filled by a cleric.

Although it shows some interesting patterns, the a-historical nature of this comparison across different social settings and experiences and concrete circumstances may, in the final analysis, hide more than it reveals. For instance, Iranian society has, since 1979–80, lost a large proportion of its professional class to the outside world, so the presence of 16 'professionals' in Rafsanjani's cabinet, compared with 20 in Hoveyda's, may prove to be as historically important as the exodus of the Iranian professional middle class itself. Rather than betraying technical weakness, President Rafsanjani's appointment of so many professionals to his cabinet despite the exodus of this stratum, indicated that society was again reconstituting itself in a way that would enable it to meet its needs indigenously and without an overburdening reliance on outside intervention. It is nonetheless striking that the proportion of physicians and PhDs in the cabinet has been declining steadily in historical terms, reduced by more than half from 15 in 1967 to only seven some two decades later.

It is also important to note that, for the first time in the contemporary history of Iran, there were no military personnel appointments to the cabinet. In the context of Iran's recent turbulent relations with her neighbours, this could be interpreted as a good omen. But it could also sound the death-knell of attempts by the military machine in Iran to muscle in for power with the other social and political groups in the country. Whatever the reason, by its turning away from an historic opportunity to gain power in the 1977–79 period, the Iranian military may well have lived through the long years of war in the 1980s only to witness its own political demise in the 1990s.

Additionally, six of Rafsanjani's ministers received a Western education which meant that at least they were familiar with the Western way of life and doing things, and could take their collective experiences to the highest levels of decision-making. The presence of such individuals could be advantageous since it could help promote dialogue and also, particularly in times of crisis, enable the Iranians to attack the West more efficiently.

Two peculiarities in the clerical appointments, arising from political imperatives, should be noted. First, none of the four clerical ministerial appointments exceeded the Hojjatoleslam level in rank; thus they remained equal with the President's own religious rank. This was intended partly as a way of preventing the moral and religious authority of the highest executive power in the land from being undermined from within the governmental establishment. Secondly, the equal rank among the ministers themselves removed the factor of religious differentiation from among these ministers. This prevented the undermining of governmental by religious authority, since religious rank had, in effect, been eliminated as a distinct basis for authority within the government machine.

Finally, the exclusion of Ayatollah Montazeri and Hojjatoleslam Mohtashemi from the coalition could have been an expression of the pragmatists' intention of gaining fuller control of Iran's policy on Lebanon and its other Islamic/Arab policies. As these two individuals had played key roles in implementing 'the export of Islamic revolution', it is hardly surprising that the new leaders wished to control the foreign policy agenda as firmly as the domestic economic and political environment, in order to prevent their strategy of international reintegration being jeopardised by these forces and their allies outside Iran. The rapid rebuilding of relations with Kuwait and other Gulf states and the secret negotiations with Saudi Arabia that have taken place since the formation of the new government (see also Chapter 3), its support, albeit qualified, for the anti-Iraqi forces that were massing in Saudi

Arabia from the summer of 1990, its willingness to accept Saddam Hussein's peace proposals, and its readiness to re-establish diplomatic relations with its arch enemy, Iraq, as well as its expressed desire to establish a regional security arrangement in co-operation with the conservative Gulf states in the wake of the Kuwait crisis, all testify to the pragmatism of the Second Republic, and to the importance for the new leadership of total and unhindered access to the country's foreign policy machinery as an instrument of power.

The Second Republic in perspective

In viewing the advent of the Second Republic as a positive development, we have attempted to understand the 'new' regime without mentioning the prohibitive and repressive features of the old regime which still constrain it—a case of 'new wine in old bottles'! Certainly in the economic sphere the Second Republic is moving fast towards liberalisation and openness. Its policies are a break from the generally statist traditions of the last decade. A case in point is the appointment of Ayatollah Yazdi, the former Deputy Speaker of the Islamic parliament, who failed to win re-election to the Majlis in the 1987 parliamentary elections, but who was appointed to the Head of Judiciary instead of the former Prosecutor-General Hojjatoleslam Khoini'a. Yazdi's appointment indicates the pragmatist coalition's clarity of purpose since he is well-known for his 'moderate' stance on social issues and for advocating strongly anti-statist views regarding the economy and economic policy.

Indeed, even in the political sphere, there undeniably exists a collective consensus in the 'Leader-President' coalition which resembles a form of democracy that has been chosen by the few and for the benefit of the few. The authors fully recognise that this is a purely elitist democracy, based on paternalism and patronage. The Islamic Republic, in its 'new' form and in its second decade is a long way from social, let alone societal, democracy. Mass political participation is still limited, and subject to undemocratic 'rules of engagement'. As yet, the 'new faces' have not changed the repressive features of the Islamic Republic which still prohibits political organisation along non-'Islamic Republican' lines.

Despite the recent important constitutional changes, the exceedingly important clauses of the constitution regarding liberty and freedom still remain unimplemented, while political persecution and execution of opponents has continued unabated, both at home and abroad. The prospects for a general national consensus remain bleak and Iranian political activity continues to be sectarian. It would be unrealistic to expect a speedy and total transformation of the belligerent beast into a peace-loving beauty.

In August 1979, Ayatollah Khomeini ordered, in one day, the closure of twenty-four newspapers. Their publication, and that of many others besides, is still prohibited. Organised political action, even by those non-clerics still loyal to the principle of an Islamic Republic, is forbidden, and the repressive continuity with the past continues to be very much in evidence. In the summer of 1990, for instance, many supporters of ex-Prime Minister Bazargan were rounded up and the activities of his organisation were effectively curtailed.

The return of some anti-Hezbollah technocrats to the cabinet and the promotion of technocracy will not automatically lead to a politically freer Iran. Indeed, if technocracy equals efficiency, then, in the absence of any meaningful political change, the technocrats and their a-political style can serve as the best instruments for executing state repression. Furthermore, the continuity with the past is perhaps even better illustrated by non-cabinet appointments of the 'Leader-President' alliance, than by the lack of progress on the political front referred to above. Four appointments in particular—three clerical and one civilian—need closer scrutiny: those of Hojjatoleslam Mohammed Reyshahri, Hojjatoleslam Khoini'a, Ayatollah Lajevardi and Mr Hussein Moussavi.

Reyshahri was the head of the special military revolutionary courts; Khoini'a was the leader of the 'Students following the Imam's line' and of the student Islamic societies at educational establishments, and also the former Prosecutor-General; Lajevardi was Tehran's Revolutionary Prosecutor: these three clerics presided over the bloodiest period in the history of modern Iran (from 1981 to 1986) during which time tens of thousands of political and non-political opponents of the regime, as well as scores of by-standers, lost their lives in prisons, detention centres and on the streets of Iran's towns and cities. And yet all three have important posts in the Second Republic too: Reyshari is the new Prosecutor-General; Khoini'a is head of the recently founded Centre for Strategic Studies and a member of the Council for Determining Expediency (literally translated as the Assembly for the Discernment of What is Best); while Lajevardi is head of the Prisons Organisation.

The fourth of these appointments from the past is that of the former Prime Minister, Hussein Moussavi. A cousin of Ayatollah Khamenei, Moussavi had always formed one of the three pillars of the Islamic Republic. Along with Khamenei, as President, and with Rafsanjani, as the Majlis Speaker, he was instrumental in maintaining the cohesion of the republic in the aftermath of the repeated assassinations of its top religio-political leaders in 1981 and during the gruelling war years. The period 1981 to 1989, during which time all three individuals maintained their respective offices, can be classified as a period of astonishing continuity in the executive and legislative arms of the new state.

Under the Rafsanjani-Khamenei alliance, Moussavi and a number of his close cabinet and non-cabinet allies lost their executive powers. But the fact that the more influential figures like Moussavi have found other equally important roles in the Second Republic supports the view that a strong thread of continuity links the new leadership with the Khomeini era. For instance, Moussavi, the pro-statist, hardline former prime minister, has found himself in the role of a close adviser to the president and an appointed member of the Expediency Council, while Ahmed Khomeini, who was increasingly identified with the radicals in the republic, has also formally exercised influence in his own right; as a member of the National Security Council, he has represented the 'Leader' here and wielded both institutional and moral force in one of the republic's newest power centres.[7] Therefore, not only was the break with the past not absolute and complete but, despite the significant institutional changes, strong personal links with the Khomeini era remained. This should not be surprising since, even as they aimed to transform the Islamic Republic, the leaders of the 'Leader-President' alliance could themselves still find legitimacy only in their own past and with the system of rule which they had assisted Ayatollah Khomeini to create.

Despite the reforms so far implemented, therefore, the most distinctive feature of the Second Republic is not the way in which the Islamic Republic's 'new' leaders have broken with the past, but rather the changes that have occured in the structure of power. The constitution of the Second Republic has come to resemble much more closely the constitution of the French Fifth Republic, with the powers of the Presidency fully reinstated. In the absence of the patriarch, this constitutional change—abolition of the premiership and the transfer of power to the presidency—has resulted in a balance of power emerging between the President and the new and non-charismatic Leader. Although the roots of the competition between these two institutions and their respective representatives in the Second Republic may not have been eradicated, expediency dictates that the two must do more than tolerate each other; they must assist in the efficient implementing of policies that serve the interests of the new regime, and administer those that are designed to undermine the position of 'radicals' within their own ranks.[8] It is this single factor, assisted by the pragmatic calculations of both parties, which was instrumental in forging the alliance between Rafsanjani and Khamenei. Conversely, their 'oligopolisation' of power seems to have met its opposite outside the formal structures of power, with reports that Ahmed Khomeini, Mohtashemi, Reyshahri, Moussavi, Khoini'a, Karrubi and other hardliners have plotted against the realist/reformist line of Rafsanjani.[9]

It has now become clear that the Revolutionary Council of the Islamic Republic, which was formed in 1979, has since its inception provided the leadership for the republic. Genuine reformers and liberals like Bazargan, Qutbzadeh and Bani Sadr rose from within it to take charge of revolutionary Iran. Their failures did not put out the fire of freedom; since the heady days of hostages and political competition among and between the revolutionary forces, other figures from that same Council have risen to lead the republic, and are now taking it through its second decade. Rafsanjani, his Vice-President Dr Habibi, Khamenei, Moussavi, Montazeri and Moussavi-Ardebelli were also members of the original Revolutionary Council, but their ranks are now divided. In the absence of the great religious figures of the 1979 Revolutionary Council (Ayatollah Beheshti, Hojjatoleslam Bahonar, Ayatollah Talaghani, and of course Ayatollah Khomeini himself) and of the liberals, the inheritors of that great coalition fell out with each other and every group was now set to compete with the others.

By the turn of the decade, a second generation of reformers was in control, although clearly lacking the 'liberal' credentials of the original reformers. Alongside their substantive economic reforms, they have been taking tentative steps towards improving the socio-cultural environment in Iran. The legalisation of amateur boxing, chess and fencing may appear trivial, but they serve as examples of this trend. However, as its leaders are fully aware, it is likely to take much more than these token gestures to make the Second Republic a more attractive version of an Islamic Republic. What the realists, perhaps to their peril, do not realise is that it may yet require a complete metamorphosis before the ghost of the First Republic can be laid to rest; and this is a feat which looks as if it might be beyond the natural capacities of the children of that First Republic. One thing they do realise, though, is that if such a metamorphosis were to take place, the end-product would more than likely bear no resemblance to an Islamic Republic at all.

2 DOMESTIC POLITICS IN IRAQ: SADDAM HUSSEIN AND THE AUTOCRAT'S FALLACY

Speculation about the direction of Iraqi politics during the coming decade is as risky as speculation of any kind in the uncertainties of politics. In the case of Iraq, with its closed and secretive process of political decision-making and the furtiveness of the factions which exist within the power structure, the degree of uncertainty is correspondingly large. However, this should inculcate a spirit of due modesty in any analysis. The following is, therefore, offered in such a spirit. It attempts to assess the degree to which the methods and ends of political behaviour during the period of Saddam Hussein's presidency are likely to shape the development of Iraqi politics while that presidency endures.

In examining the structure of power in Iraq in the post-war era (1988-onwards), one must ask a number of questions. Firstly, to what extent will the structure which has ensured Saddam Hussein's absolute domination of the Iraqi state and society endure and determine the conduct and content of politics? Secondly, to what degree is Saddam Hussein likely to see the need for the reorganisation of the existing dispensation of power and what will be his priorities should he decide to set that process under way? Thirdly, in what sense do there exist in Iraq groups of people who, whilst hitherto supportive of Saddam Hussein and manipulated by him to guarantee that support, might nevertheless be said to possess a potential at least for concerted action, independent of the domination of Saddam Hussein? Lastly, what are likely to be the issues of policy choice which will preoccupy the leadership of Iraq? These may constitute areas of controversy and thereby provide the terrain either of challenges to the leadership or of the leadership's pre-emptive action.

Given the ways in which the Iraqi political system of the past decade or so has been constructed, the most important starting point for its analysis is an assessment of what Saddam Hussein believes himself to be doing. This might, at the least, give one an idea of the purposes of his political activity, as well as of the particular forms of organisation which he has developed to realize his vision of power and its ends. In some respects, Saddam Hussein has been relatively open about what he is seeking to achieve in Iraq. Whether this public rationale and the persona he seeks to project correspond to his everyday concerns or to the 'privatisation' of the political at which he has been so successful, is a moot point. Nevertheless, when he believes it is to his advantage to do so, he has not hesitated to broadcast his views about the nature of his leadership, his revolution and, therefore, his regime. As in all explanations proferred by those who hold absolute power and who are seeking to justify that absolutism, one must be duly cautious about the public rationale. However, precisely because it is such an absolutist and autocratic view of power, which does indeed correspond to the reality of power's dispensation in Iraq, there is a ring of truth to it.

Saddam Hussein's Vision of Power

In a series of interviews, subsequently gathered together and published in book form[1], Saddam Hussein held forth about the nature of Iraq, the dispensation of power in the country, its likely development during the coming decade and his own position as leader of the Iraqi state. Firstly, he claimed the unique ability to deliver the benefits of orderly government. Secondly, he claimed that he, as the focus of Iraqis obedience, constituted the definition of their political community Iraqis were to define themselves politically through their obedience to him. Lastly, he claimed the unique ability to control the apparatus of the state.

In the first instance, he made a very clear distinction between what he called *al-Hakim* and *al-Qa'id*—that is, between a mere ruler, interested in the trappings of power alone, and a leader, a historical figure who was to play a central part in the destiny of Iraq as a political community. The distinction which he wanted to emphasise was that the rulers—among whom he ranked most of the previous rulers of Iraq— were interested in power for its own sake, and were therefore by definition at odds with the people, their subjects. The historical leader, on the other hand, had a unique ability to perceive the true interests of the people and was therefore uniquely qualified to be the sole guardian of their material interests, as well as of their spiritual destiny. Unsurprisingly, this lengthy preamble was building up to Saddam Hussein's appropriation of the role of unique, historical leadership for himself. He was carving out for himself a position of unparalleled supremacy in Iraq's politics, based on his claim to be able to determine the people's true interests and to guarantee order.

At the same time, he was relatively open about some of the problems he has had to face in establishing himself as leader of Iraq. Here he pointed to the problem of the public acceptance of the political order and the legal framework of the Iraqi state. He acknowledged that, by contrast with the conditions obtaining in other, longer established states, the idea of natural, or morally sanctioned obedience to the Iraqi state had been contested until the very recent present. Nevertheless, he asserted that, once again, under his leadership and as a result of the revolution, obedience to the laws had come to be seen as the correct course of action, since it was evident—given his claimed knowledge of the people's interests—that the laws now could not help but be in the true interests of the people. Indeed, he went further and claimed that people were in fact participating in the supreme legislative function which he had himself wholly appropriated, precisely because they were obeying him. In obeying the historical leader, the people were participating, through their support, in the political system of Iraq.

Lastly, during the same series of conversations, Saddam Hussein spoke at length about the apparatus of coercion and law enforcement. He stated that these agencies were necessary to protect the revolution and to maintain public order. Nevertheless, he acknowledged that there was a danger that they would abuse their power. In doing so, he claimed, they could terrorise the people and threaten the leadership, whilst forming a barrier between the leadership and the people. He warned against their transformation into centres of power which would be unanswerable to any agency or body other than themselves. Having painted a picture of the Iraqi security services which seemed to be directly drawn from the events of 1973 and possibly of 1983[2], he went on to offer his solution to the problem. The security services and the forces of coercion should be made transparent—not to the people, but to the leadership. It was the leader's unique ability to guard the people's true interests from the threats of the coercive apparatus which would guarantee the future of a beneficent political order in Iraq. Under such enlightened leadership, Iraq would pass out of one period of its history into a new and better stage. The country would cease to become a *Dawlat al-Mukhabarat* (a police state) and would be transformed into a *Dawlat al-Sha'b* (a state of the people).

These remarks by Saddam Hussein concerning his leadership and the dispensation of power in Iraq are interesting for a number of reasons. In this particular context, however, there are two specific themes which seem to be of interest. The first, unspoken, but very much implied, might be taken to justify the second. The first, hidden current in all that Saddam Hussein was saying, is the extraordinary fragility of political authority in Iraq. This may seem curious coming from someone who has often acted on the public stage as the most over-confident of dictators. However, running through his remarks is a sense of the social rejection of the state as legal framework and as political community. This implies not only rejection of, and revolt against, the government and leadership of the day, but also the possibility of a situation 'where there is war of every man, against every man'.

It is a potent message and one unlikely to be lost on many of the inhabitants of Iraq. The potential for ethnic, sectarian, tribal and class conflict is ever present. Perhaps even more importantly, in this context, it is never far below the surface of the awareness of those who are conscious of the politics of the Iraqi state. Indeed, the familial and communal solidarities it creates have been among the organising principles of Saddam Hussein's rule. At the same time, he has taken considerable trouble over the years, especially at moments of crisis for his leadership, to suggest that Iraq's future without his guiding if firm hand would be a dire one.[3] This was, of course, precisely the message which he was seeking to convey in these remarks on leadership—remarks made at a time when he had just had to face and subdue a form of revolt, as a result of his strategic miscalculations in 1986.

The second, more obvious theme running through his musings on the nature of power—and of his power in particular—is the future structure of the Iraqi political system as he intends it to be. It is clear from his vision of himself and of the purposes of his power, that he intends to maintain a structure which will perform a number of functions: most importantly, it must give him absolute, non-responsible power. The Presidency becomes the repository of leadership powers appropriate to a figure of unique historical significance. His intimate and unchallengeable knowledge of the best interests of the Iraqi people, individually and collectively, suggests the ideological supremacy and command of the instruments of power which will ensure that those interests are best safeguarded. In addition, precisely because no-one can be considered his equal in terms of this privileged knowledge to which he alone has access, there can be no question of admitting the possibility of a replacement or substitute until he himself has physically passed from the scene. The rationale of the 'presidency-for-life' is being clearly delineated.

The corollary of this bid for ideological and administrative dominance, is the interesting portrayal of the major instruments of coercion as potential barriers between the leader and 'his' people. In most respects, this warning could be taken to apply not simply to the coercive apparatus, narrowly interpreted, but to all the agencies of government on which Saddam Hussein must rely to carry out his bidding. Saddam Hussein was consequently presenting a picture in which the leader and the people could be seen to be in league together against the wilful 'centres of power' which might coalesce within the machinery of the state—the very machinery which the leader himself had created. It was a warning to those who enjoyed positions of power in the present Iraqi dispensation that, if they failed to comply wholly with the commands of the leader, he would be compelled to 'unleash the anger of the masses', in the words he had used to threaten a similar group of provisionally powerful Iraqis.[4]

It is here that one begins to see one of the particular uses of the personality cult, so keenly and flamboyantly cultivated by Saddam Hussein. As in other similar instances throughout history, the active promotion of such cults often has less effect on the ostensible targets—the mass of the population—than on the circle of those who surround the leader. These are the people who, because of the positions of power they occupy and because of their close acquaintance with the leader, are his most dangerous potential rivals. Although immune themselves to much of the myth-making which surrounds the manufacture of public personality, since many of them will have knowingly planned the strategies to make it effective, they can be impressed by its effect, realising that the further it goes, the less likely any one of them will be to replace the person of the leader himself.

It is also in this context that one can begin to see why Saddam Hussein has been so keen to emphasise the role of the National Assembly in Iraq. In 1980 its institution could be seen as simply another move in Saddam Hussein's determination to be seen as a leader supported by the people and thus entitled to speak and to rule in their name. At the time, this had a number of very specific uses, both in domestic Iraqi politics and in Iraq's relations with Iran. By 1988, these reasons were no less valid. However, in addition, there was the service which such a body was seen as capable of performing and which accorded so well with Saddam Hussein's view of his own situation. The National Assembly would act as the President's watchdog, keeping an eye on and, if necessary, indicting the officers of state with whom Saddam Hussein has so ambiguous a relationship. That it should happen in so public a forum and as such an ostensible expression of 'the people's will' would simply reinforce Saddam Hussein's thesis of the complete accord between his own and the national interest. During the past couple of years this is a role which the members of the National Assembly—vulnerable individually and without collective identity, let alone strength—have performed with gusto. It seems likely to set the pattern for the 1990s and, thereby, to fulfil Saddam Hussein's desire to have at his disposal an instrument which can give the appearance of supporting his twin claims that firstly, the leader and the people must be jointly vigilant against the agencies of government and, secondly, that the Iraqi people under his guidance have now entered the era of the *Dawlat al-Sha'b*.

The Ba'th Party

It is significant that, in his characterisation of the state which Iraq had become or was on the way to becoming, Saddam Hussein did not even mention the Ba'th Party. Theoretically, the sole rationale for his position as head of the Iraqi state is his leadership of the Ba'th Party. That is, under the original claims of the regime which emerged from the Ba'thist revolution of 1968, the Iraqi state was a transitory affair: it was to be merely a vehicle of power for a party whose identity was pan-Arab and whose goals included the dissolution of all the states of the Arab world. Needless to say, the Ba'th Party has undergone a number of transformations since that time. Saddam Hussein has remained at the helm, but the personnel has changed, as have the organisation, the ideological definition and the political role of the party. Given the confidence with which Saddam Hussein can now pronounce on such matters—exhibited in the preceding pages—it is not surprising that a political party with an autonomous existence as an institution, generating its own legitimacy and hierarchies of power by service to the ideology its cadres publicly espouse, should have difficulty surviving intact.

The crucial factor is that Saddam Hussein has appropriated for himself both the political and ideological space once occupied by the leadership of the Ba'th Party. In his characteristic manner, he has been very open in spelling out the implications of this development:

> When you say that the people now argue with you and take my speeches and statements as evidence in their arguments, I would say that I mean it to be this way. In fact, I had meant it to be this way since the early days of the July 1968 revolution . . . I wanted to get the help of the people against you. I wanted the people to make use of my words and my conduct so that nobody would come and tell them the opposite or act in a contradictory manner, claiming that this is the line adopted by the party.

It is unlikely that this point has been lost on the members of the Ba'th. It has been no part of Saddam Hussein's intention to find himself arraigned before the bar of the party, accused of ideological backsliding. In many respects, he could be said to have become Secretary-General of the Regional Command of the Ba'th, to have taken the late Michel Aflaq (founder and Secretary General of the National Command of the Ba'th) under his wing and subsequently to have become President of the Iraqi state precisely to avoid being beholden to those in the party who held rigidly to the tenets of its formal ideology. He became President amidst a spate of arrests and executions of men who had held to the principles of socialism and of Arab unity (specifically with Syria) at a time when this was judged not to be desirable by Saddam Hussein. In eliminating these people, Saddam Hussein was not only impressing his own ruthlessness and all-powerful reach upon those who survived, but also the fact that he would henceforth become the ideological arbiter of the party.

This position was formally acknowledged by the 9th Regional Congress of the Ba'th Party in June 1982. As the subsequent report made clear, the first part of the conference was devoted to an extended paean of praise for Saddam Hussein's leading role in the organisation, strategic planning and ideology of the party. He was elevated to the role of 'Leader-Necessity [sic] . . . the man who at a certain stage represents the aspirations and basic interests of the Party and people.'[6] The 'ideology' of the Ba'th is consequently whatever Saddam Hussein determines it to be. It would be a brave and foolhardy party member who would try to stand up for the line of the party, if he thought it to be at odds with the line of the President. As the vehicle, therefore, for an ideology specific to it as a party, the Ba'th is clearly bankrupt and is likely to remain so. Instead, it has become the sounding board for Saddam Hussein—another mechanism to amplify the messages he wishes to get across at any one time, through its congresses, its newspapers and its membership.

Under Saddam Hussein's dominance, the membership also has changed. In part this is due to the fact that, as soon as the Ba'th became the party of government in 1968, the motives for joining it tended to change. Ambition to ingratiate oneself with the state authorities, or indeed to move up the ladder of state advancement, now became a prime motive for joining. It was good for one's career. Indeed it was an indispensable part of one's career, since most professions required Ba'th party membership of some kind. The ranks and grades of apprenticeship and membership were maintained, more to determine the loyalty than the ideological purity of the member concerned. Indeed, the Ba'th was becoming a mechanism for the surveillance and patronage of those who were likely to be the most politically conscious elements in Iraqi society. Rewards were distributed to those who proved themselves and the means by which they proved themselves often made them accomplices in the designs of the regime. At the same time, the formal system of scrutiny, examination, secrecy and the proving of trust, was an ideal mechanism for the extension and maintenance of those informal, regional, tribal and familial networks of patronage and trust which run through Iraqi politics and administration. The point is that in Ba'thist cadres shaped and tested in such a system, there were unlikely to be many in senior positions who believed in the mission of the party, defined differently or independently from the mission which the leader chose to give it.

During the 1980s, the party underwent another significant change, since literally hundreds of thousands of Iraqis were now made eligible for membership. Service in the war—and virtually any employment could be categorised under that heading, not simply military service narrowly defined—qualified an individual for more rapid acceptance into the ranks of the Ba'th. Once inside, the grades and levels still remained, but it was noticeable that at all levels there was a great increase in numbers. In other words, from being a party of privilege and restricted access, the Ba'th was being transformed into a party of mass membership with a corresponding potential for mass mobilisation. Here was unmistakably the imprint of the President who was convinced that the best way of securing his position was to cement a relationship between himself and 'the people'. As with the other organs of state, therefore, he would avoid becoming beholden to those to whom some power, of an administrative kind at least, needed perforce to be delegated. In the mass membership of the party, Saddam Hussein clearly believes that he has created a reservoir of 'Saddamist-Ba'thists' who may be mobilised should those who think of themselves more as Ba'thists, strictly interpreted, ever be tempted to question the authority of Saddam Hussein.

Given the way in which the Ba'th has become a mere adjunct of the 'monarchical' presidency, there is no reason why this should not continue to be the case during the coming decade. The party will continue to function as a system for the distribution of rewards for the politically loyal, as a means of mobilising people (in the sense of getting them on to the streets in the 'oceanic' demonstrations so beloved by such regimes), as another agency of supervision and surveillance and as the amplifier of the President's views on what needs to be done. In other words, the impulse for its organisation and its expression lies with Saddam Hussein: all initiative comes from the presidential palace and will continue to do so whilst the form of leadership practised by

Saddam Hussein continues to function in Iraq. As long as he remains alive, there is no reason to suppose that this style of autocracy will be dismantled.

The subordination of the Ba'th to the presidency was underlined by Saddam Hussein's sudden announcement on television in January 1989 that a multi-party system would be introduced in Iraq.[7] This was followed by the elections of 1 April 1989 for the National Assembly in which candidates approved by the security services, but not necessarily Ba'thists, were allowed to stand—and were able to win a substantial number of seats. All of these non-Ba'thists, save the members of the 'tame' Kurdish party, call themselves independents and do not claim any party affiliation. The difference between them and those who call themselves Ba'thists should not be overestimated. Nor should the label 'independent' lead one to suppose that they are in any sense free agents, answerable only to their constituents and their consciences. They are as much an extension of the President's power as all who hold public office in Iraq and thus, like all others, they are answerable to him alone and serve his purposes. In this case, the purpose is to remind the Ba'thists once again that they should not come to believe that they possess any collective identity separate from that which Saddam Hussein chooses to assign to them. The granting of equal status in the National Assembly to non-Ba'thists merely reminds them that Saddam Hussein is capable of looking elsewhere for his following and that they have no prior claim on his patronage.

The Iraqi government has heralded these moves as the introduction of a 'multi-party system'. This fiction is difficult to maintain. In the first place, there has been a good deal of confusion within Iraq about what Saddam Hussein intends—and not to read correctly the intentions of the President can be dangerous. As a result, no-one has been willing to form a party which differentiates itself ideologically from the President's line, hitherto expressed through the Ba'th. The independents have hastened to make it very clear that they are firm adherents to Saddam Hussein's ideological direction—and indeed often pose as watchdogs on his behalf, ensuring that careerists in the Ba'th do not become too forgetful of their duty to the President. Secondly, there do exist Iraqi political parties which differentiate themselves markedly from the Ba'thist ideal—whether traditionally interpreted, or represented as 'Saddam's line'. The problem is that they are banned by the government and, in some cases, membership of them is punishable by death. Thus, the Kurdish Democratic Party, the Patriotic Union of Kurdistan, the Communist Party of Iraq and the Islamic Da'wa Party must function either underground or among Iraqi exiles. They represent political programmes and movements so much at odds with Saddam Hussein's vision of Iraqi politics that they are unlikely to form part of the promised 'multi-party system'.

Consequently, whatever 'parties' do emerge outside the organisation of the Ba'th, it is inconceivable under the present regime that they would be allowed to differ with, criticise or challenge the President. The labels they may choose will not signify political identities, as commonly understood in the context of political parties. In this respect, of course, the Ba'th, as presently constituted in Iraq, is scarcely a political party in the contemporary sense of the term. It has become, rather, an extension and manifestation of Saddam Hussein's power, subject to his whims and to the apparatus of surveillance and enforcement which gives those whims reality. Its formal existence is maintained, since it serves a number of purposes, but those purposes and the ways in which the machinery that serves them is maintained flow from a very particular organisation of power, centred on Saddam Hussein, subject to his vision of politics and sustained by the informal, social formations and prejudices which form the basis of political trust in Iraq.

The Armed Forces

Reliance on the social foundations of trust applies no less in the organisation of the armed forces than in other spheres of the organisation of power. If anything, it is more closely followed in this area, precisely because of the capacity of the armed forces to use massive violence to resolve any dispute. Consequently, when Saddam Hussein contemplates the Iraqi armed forces, he not only has a vivid memory of the decisive role they have played politically in Iraq's history, but he also has a particular set of concerns. Firstly, there is his suspicion—at times a certainty—that numerous army commanders believe that they know better than he how the armed forces should be used, and possibly also how the society which funds and supports them and which they are dedicated to protecting, should be governed. His fear is that army commanders who know that they have the coercive power to enforce their will, may also believe that they consequently have the right to do so. This is, after all, the origin and foundation of his own rule. The important thing, therefore, is for him to maintain control of the cause in the name of which they exercise their power. That is, he must ensure that their loyalties are focused on his person and that he has as much control over them as over the senior Ba'th party cadres.

Saddam Hussein has asserted his dominance of the armed forces in a number of ways. Firstly, he has ensured that they are dedicated to a professional task, professionally defined. During the war against Iran—a relatively uncontroversial undertaking, at least after 1982—this was not difficult to achieve. The only visible disputes were on those occasions when Saddam Hussein's misconceived interventions in military planning seemed to compromise this very professionalism.[8] Secondly, he has ensured that a network of key commanders has been established which is related to him by blood, clan or tribal affiliation. Opportunities to extend this principle were provided in the expansion—and, after the Fao débâcle of 1986, reconstitution—of the Republican Guard. This is a formation of several battalions, the task of which is specifically to guard the President, but which acts both as an elite formation, entrusted with special duties by the President, and as a line of defence, should any other army unit be tempted to move against the President. Most of its members come from the Sunni Arab region around the President's home-town of Takrit and a significant number are from the President's tribe and clan. Thirdly, however, Saddam Hussein has seen some utility in patronising military officers from communities other than his own. This has led to the promotion of officers of Kurdish and Shi'i backgrounds, not on a very large scale, but sufficient to suggest that, in addition to those bound to Saddam Hussein by ties of kinship, he is anxious to create a circle of officers tied to him personally, since they rely on his patronage.[9] This may be a strategy designed to spare Saddam Hussein from becoming over-dependent on his sometimes unruly kin.

Each of the techniques of supervision and control outlined above, have their obverse sides. That is, they do not eliminate risk, but could be said to spread it, since each has, at times, produced challenges of a kind with which Saddam Hussein is likely to be confronted until his presidency ends—and which may, of course, eventually be instrumental in ending it. Firstly, as far as the professional tasks of the armed forces are concerned, there have been a number of developments in Iraqi strategy since the ending of the war with Iran which may have added an element of controversy into the role which Saddam Hussein expects the armed forces to play. The scorched earth policy pursued in Kurdistan both before and after the cease-fire with Iran had evidently aroused misgivings among some of the military officers responsible for carrying out operations. Whilst there is scarce sympathy for the Kurdish guerrillas or for Kurdish political aspirations in the mainly Sunni Arab senior officer ranks of the Iraqi army, some appear to have had qualms about the extreme brutality of the campaign waged against the population of Kurdistan during 1988.[10]

Secondly, the development by Saddam Hussein of Iraq's missile capability and chemical arsenal as one of Iraq's principal strategic options in the region and, specifically, in the confrontation with Israel, appeared likely to erode the position of the conventional armed forces. Indeed, this may well have been part of Saddam Hussein's intention, quite apart from the greater efficacy of such weapons, as he would see it, in pursuing the kind of regional role which he apparently thinks is his due. The deployment and control of such weapons could be interpreted as an enhancement of the President's power, since they mean fewer worries about the co-operation of specific unit commanders, the political costs of military attrition or the control of a chain of command which needs to be cultivated to do his bidding. Missile technologies allow a much more direct and instantaneous response to the President's command. Regardless of the acceptability of the final objective of these weapons, there may be professional resentment within the military that they are being, in some respects, displaced from their traditional position as the ultimate arbiters of any President's wishes.

Thirdly, recent moves, such as those against Kuwait, may be controversial in a way that the struggle with Iran was not. Again, there may not be much sympathy for Kuwait or Kuwait's recent oil policies as portrayed in the Iraqi press, but there may be a considerable sense of unease about the use of force against a fellow Arab state. Iraqi military officers can probably take in their stride that Saddam Hussein's rhetoric in denouncing the alleged 'threat' posed by Kuwait to Iraq's national security has not differed substantially from his descriptions of the very different kind of threat represented by Iran during 1980–1988. They are, after all used to this kind of presidential exaggeration. However, the use of military force to undo this 'threat', and the resulting image this creates, both within Iraq and in the Arab world, of the Iraqi armed forces must leave a certain sense of unease about Saddam Hussein's future plans for the military.[11]

These are the areas where the definition of the professional role of the armed forces may be contested. As that role develops in the 1990s beyond the apparently straightforward one of defence against Iran, such forms of contestation may give grounds for dispute between the President and his senior commanders. Ordinarily, such matters of policy dispute are not necessarily threatening to the survival of a regime. However, in a system where so much power and so many claims to absolute authority are vested in the President, contestation of his policy choices inevitably suggests contestation of his authority. Saddam

Hussein certainly treats such differences in this light and thus reinforces the trend which equates political disagreement with treason, ironically multiplying the possible number of reasons for his overthrow.

Nor does Saddam Hussein's meticulously constructed network of kin and patronage linkages necessarily make him immune to such challenges. Indeed, whilst they seem to establish within the armed forces a system of trust, they also set up countervailing forces of resentment. Thus, the particular beneficiaries of Saddam Hussein's favour may be resented individually, or as representatives of a system which necessarily excludes those unrelated by blood. At the same time, even those who qualify under all the terms which Saddam Hussein regards as constituting reliable foundations of political trust—and who have benefited accordingly—may harbour ambitions of their own, or be suspected of doing so. This makes their proximity to the centre of power potentially dangerous, especially in a situation where they see their main rivals as being too similar to themselves in many ways and thus capable of colluding with Saddam Hussein in their own downfall.

These are the dynamics of court and faction politics, characteristic of any such autocracy as that of Saddam Hussein. They are difficult to follow and there is no particular set of rules to guide their behaviour. One is left, therefore, with a series of unsubstantiated reports about dissent, purges, arrests and executions in the armed forces. There have been plenty of these during the past couple of years. They include reports of widespread arrests of officers serving in the northern army corps in October 1988;[12] reports of further arrests and executions and of an abortive coup attempt in December 1988/January 1989 (one public signal of which was the abrupt cancellation of the Army Day parade in January 1989);[13] the circumstances surrounding the death of the Minister of Defence, General Adnan Khairallah Tulfah in May 1989;[14] and the reports of arrests of a large number of senior officers in July 1990.[15]

Whatever the details or accuracy of these reports, these conspiracies, or alleged conspiracies, seem to have followed lines which suggest an underlying degree of collective resentment, based on the very identities which Saddam Hussein has used to cement his rule. Thus, there have been accompanying reports of resentment of the Takritis by officers from Mosul or Samarra, or resentment of the disproportionate influence of members of the al-Majid, Tulfah and al-Rashid families (all blood relations of Saddam Hussein) by other Takritis, or even resentment at privileges accorded to one of these family factions by those family members who have felt themselves slighted. There have even been suggestions of unrest amongst all of these groups at the favours granted by Saddam Hussein to Kurds, Shi'i and others beyond the tribal circles of the Sunni Arabs on whom all Iraqi presidents have relied in the last resort. In the sense that this gives a large number of people cause for common grievance against him, this is perhaps the most dangerous development of all for Saddam Hussein. Nor are these tensions likely to dissipate in the 1990s. On the contrary, since reliance on the networks of patronage which generate such tensions is likely, if anything, to increase, this will be a perennial source of danger for the President.

Conclusion

One of the dominant themes of Saddam Hussein's rise to power and of the consolidation of his position as President of Iraq, has been his single-minded quest for power without responsibility. To this end, he has ensured that the apparatus of power in Iraq should be anwerable to him, rather than to any larger constituency and, further, that he should on no account be answerable to those whom he must delegate to ensure that his commands are carried out. The subordination of the Ba'th Party and of the armed forces are but two examples of a process which has been in operation in all walks of public life in Iraq. It is a process which has been facilitated and advanced by the remorseless weeding out, marginalisation and, in some cases, physical liquidation, of the people who cannot be implicitly trusted by Saddam Hussein—that is of those who cannot be considered *Ahl al-Thiqa* (the people of trust). One of Saddam Hussein's major preoccupations has been to establish the criteria for those who are to count as *Ahl al-Thiqa*, as well as the machinery which will ensure that they can be supervised by others—as an insurance. In addition, he has been concerned to devise an organisation of power which will allow these people to carry out his commands, whilst denying them a power base of sufficient security to lead them to believe they can challenge him.

In a society, such as that of Iraq, where provincial origin and common family, clan and tribal membership are still among the most important determinants of an individual's sense of his social location and identity, the criteria of political trust—that is, the criteria for selecting those whom one trusts sufficiently for the delegation of political power—will tend to follow these lines. They are certainly lines which Saddam Hussein has used in seeking to create a system of undemanding obedience. At the same time, family members can begin to take a great deal for granted and may cause problems—as they have done periodically for Saddam Hussein—with their disputes, ambitions, and presumptions. Consequently, it has been in Saddam Hussein's interest to encourage, through selective patronage, members of communities other than his own, who nevertheless rely in the last analysis on his own patronage for any power or prestige they enjoy. These are the creatures of Saddam Hussein, forming another layer of *Ahl al-Thiqa*, owing their position not to blood, but to subservience. When they begin to win a following of their own, Saddam Hussein's trust in them inevitably begins to falter, since he can no longer be certain that he alone forms the only reference point of their existence or the only figure to which they feel they must answer. Ba'thists concerned about their fidelity to the ideology of the Ba'th, or who have succeeded in building up a following within the party, have tended to fall victim to Saddam Hussein's growing mistrust. The same fate has befallen army commanders who thought they knew better than he what the strategic requirements of the Iraqi armed forces were or who were able to inspire personal loyalty in the men under their command.

The problem with such a system of government is that it is both extraordinarily troublesome to maintain and potentially extremely unstable. In order to work, it relies upon Saddam Hussein's ability both to sense who can be trusted at any given time, and to protect himself should pre-emption fail and an attempt be made against his life. In many respects, the kinds of resentments it produces amongst those who have suffered under its administration, or who have felt themselves to have been insufficiently rewarded by the ruling dispensation, are self-generating. That is, they are internal to such a system and scarcely have to rely upon any very obvious external cause to set them in motion. Thus, a conspiracy of resentment could be encouraged by any particular set of policy differences—on the economy, on military strategy, on the peace with Iran, on oil policy, on the Kuwait crisis—or it could use differences with the leadership to throw into question the authority of Saddam Hussein and thus recruit others to the cause of his overthrow. It could, additionally, be galvanised into action, not by any sequence of public events, but simply by the fear that Saddam Hussein's men were close to finding out its existence.

By encouraging a limited measure of open debate about certain areas of public life, by allowing criticism of civil servants to appear in the official press and by making his government ministers answerable to the members of the National Assembly, Saddam Hussein is not only trying to create the illusion of a 'liberalising' polity, but may also be seeking to make less controversial, less a matter of life and death, certain areas of policy. Quite apart from the fact that debate about most areas of public life remains proscribed, as does investigation or criticism of all the important ministers or government servants closely connected to Saddam Hussein himself, it is in many respects a vain endeavour. Although he has systematically avoided responsibility to any institution or body of people, Saddam Hussein has regularly claimed sole responsibility for every important policy initiative. Thus, whatever the issue, there is little doubt where ultimate responsibility must lie. This is the autocratic fallacy and, generally, the undoing of most autocrats. Having claimed absolute power, they are perceived as having absolute responsibility for all developments in public life. Each issue, however small, brings with it questions not only about their policy choices, but also about their authority. Their own sensitivity encourages such a link, quite apart from the accusations levelled against them by those who may be contesting such policy choices. The process of intimidation and pre-emption which this establishes may, in turn, provide the catalyst for the attempt physically to remove the autocrat. This has been and remains the flaw at the heart of Iraqi politics. Saddam Hussein has successfully avoided its consequences during the 1980s, in the sense of having succeeded in staying ahead of the game. During the 1990s, however, the efforts made by Saddam Hussein to remain ahead, as well, of course, as the success of these efforts, will largely shape the course of Iraqi politics.

3 IRAQ AND THE ARAB STATES OF THE GULF: FULL CIRCLE

The Iraqi invasion of Kuwait on 2 August 1990 threw the whole of the region and much of the world into turmoil, and caused disarray amongst the community of government and academic analysts of Iraq and the Gulf. Indeed, most were taken unawares, having previously concluded that Saddam Hussein would prove to be essentially a rational actor in international affairs, since his recent record appeared to show both a need and an intention to continue on a moderate course. This chapter traces the original transformation of the Iraqi regime into its more moderate self of the 1980s, before considering the question of the apparent sudden reversal in the summer of 1990.[1]

Saddam Hussein, oil, and regional politics: origins of a metamorphosis

In the heady days of the 1960s and early 1970s, Iraqi foreign policy was characterised by the preponderance of the elements of socialism, revolution and pan-Arabism—witness the report of the 8th regional Congress of the Ba'th Party in Iraq, in 1974. Two of the basic considerations underlying the Party's foreign policy had a particularly ominous ring for the Gulf monarchies: (a) 'The requirements of the Arab liberation struggle and its main issues, especially those of Palestine and the Gulf'; and (b) 'the need to protect the revolution in Iraq as a fighting base for the movement of Arab Revolution in pursuit of the objectives of Unity, Liberty and Socialism'.[2] However, whereas the revolutionary and socialist strands had been dominant until the early 1970s, the element of pan-Arabism gained in relative weight from 1974, as Saddam Hussein's domination of the formulation of ideology and decision-making grew into a monopoly. Indeed, over the following years one finds a definite evolution in the Ba'th's position. Linked with this was an emphasis on non-alignment (rather than alliance with the Soviet Union). This, it was argued, was not only desirable in itself but constituted the only sensible way of handling the changing global system that was gradually becoming multi-rather than bi-polar.[3] This combination of Arab perspective and non-alignment was compatible with a more pragmatic approach to international relations, and was in fact partly prompted by the latter. The main source of this pragmatic line was Saddam Hussein. Although the Ba'th's ostensibly 'revolutionary' orientation was not immediately dropped, developments from the mid-1970s made it clear that the regime in fact desired normal relations with the other Arab states of the region. In addition, an injection of pragmatism was necessary in order to allow Iraq to assume the more active and leading role in the Arab world and in the Third World, which was regarded by Saddam as the country's logical task.[4] It becomes particularly clear, with hindsight, that the personal factor was equally important in this respect: one of the driving forces was Saddam's desire to manoeuvre himself into the position of 'a, if not *the*, leading Arab statesman'.[5] In the report of the Ninth Regional Congress of the Ba'th Party, held in 1982, this shift is explicitly recognised, and, implicitly, the coinciding of this evolution with Saddam's formal take-over of the reins of power is laid out for all to see. The report stresses the strong development of participatory activities in Arab and Third World affairs beween July 1979 and the beginning of the war (as well as subsequently). Even on the political level the 'fight against imperialism', was relegated to the background, with the stress shifting to the economic: it was argued that, with the world recession and higher energy prices, the main danger for Third World countries had become economic, and thus economic help became the prime necessity.[6]

However, Iraqi foreign policy behaviour from the mid-1970s was not determined solely by the party line as described above. Indeed, Saddam himself pointed out that the positions of party and state do not necessarily always coincide: 'the state has to adapt to changing circumstances and conduct day-to-day affairs; the party does not'.[7] As Saddam was effectively the main ideologue in the party, the party line came to include an array of pragmatic attitudes that made it easier to defend elements of Iraqi foreign policy behaviour as ideologically sound. The 'pure' Ba'th line, progressively dominated by the issues of non-alignment and Arab nationalism, was, for instance, visible in strong opposition against the Soviet invasion of Afghanistan, the diversification of arms imports sources, the assumption of a central role on the Palestine issue, and—as regards the Gulf—in resistance against Persian domination of the region and against the apparently unquestioning alliance of the Gulf monarchies with the United States. In addition, two other categories of elements influenced the foreign policy behaviour of the Iraqi state. First, there were pragmatic but ideologically 'sound' considerations. These included the change in attitude that allowed Iraq to assume its logical leading role in the non-aligned movement and the Arab World, and a shift in the stance on the Palestine question for tactical reasons. Considerations of strategy and *raison d'état* were put forward to justify new policies in terms of 'defending the revolution in Iraq'.

Secondly, one can identify a number of domestic motives which help explain the shift to 'moderation' and towards the West. On the one hand, and having in the wake of the oil price hikes of 1973–4, acquired sufficient funds to speed up development at an unprecedented rate, Iraq needed the West to sell it the building blocks for that development and for later imports of consumer goods. Not all of these could be provided by the Soviet Union. The shift to moderation was an element that helped draw the West closer. The acquisition of oil wealth also gave Iraq the financial independence and economic freedom to opt for a shift to the West. On the other hand, the improved domestic security of the regime against external as well as internal plots, particularly after the 1975 Algiers agreement, meant that it was no longer so dependent on a revolutionary posture in order to dismiss rivals and opponents. Moreover, the regime understandably felt that it could gain enormously in domestic prestige from an enhanced position in the non-aligned movement and the Arab world, which could be achieved only by moderating its policies. In addition, having realised the potential importance of having allies to rely on in the event of renewed tension with Iran, the Iraqi leadership had a further motive for building bridges.

More recently, yet another element in Iraq's changing attitude was becoming obvious, confirming this apparent evolution and giving it a long-term character. Particularly from 1979 onwards, a policy of economic liberalisation was adopted, which gradually introduced a degree of *infitah* and privatisation. Springborg has convincingly argued that this was at least partly a reflection of Saddam's efforts to enhance his grip on power by weakening the hold of the Ba'th over the economy through the encouragement of the private sector, and that this paved 'the way for the emergence of a new, as yet amorphous group rather than class, upon which an increasing amount of the President's political base and legitimacy rests'.[8] This ties in with the work of Isam al-Khafaji, who has presented evidence for the existence of an alliance of the ruling group around Saddam with the Iraqi commercial bourgeoisie.[9] As indicated, this adds to the general contextual change behind Iraqi foreign policy.

Clearly, then, Iraq's foreign policy had by 1980 acquired a substantially different character. This was illustrated in the 'National Charter for the Arab States' which Saddam put forward on 8 February 1980. This document stressed strict non-alignment, peaceful means of solving problems between Arab states, Arab mutual defence, the adherence to international law, and Arab economic integration. Most remarkable, perhaps, was the implied recognition of the existing Arab state system.

Iraq's behaviour towards the Gulf Arab states before the war evolved within the parameters of the government's changing overall foreign policy. To an extent, of course, the changing circumstances in and around the Gulf—and the policy alterations which these required—can be assumed to have influenced Iraq's overall foreign policy orientation. The implications for the Gulf of the pan-Arabist and non-aligned strands of Ba'thism have been noted above. It would appear, as Niblock has argued, that frictions between Iraq and the Arab states of the Gulf before the war resulted mainly from the interaction between (1) the Iraqis' insistence on keeping the non-aligned as well as the Arab character of the Gulf (the latter implying the importance of Iraqi influence); (2) the Gulf Arab states' attitude towards Iraq, the West and Iran; and (3) the Iranian attitude. The principle of the Arab character of the Gulf and the necessity of an Iraqi role in the Gulf meant opposition to Iranian (i.e. to non-Arab) influence and, because of the degree of Iranian control over the Shatt al-Arab, also necessitated some Iraqi control over the Kuwaiti islands Warba and Bubiyan, which 'blocked' the approach to the second Iraqi port, Umm Qasr. With the Gulf states sticking to a staunchly pro-Western line and preferring Iran rather than Iraq as an ally, there is a case for arguing that 'the Ba'th's 'subversive' role . . . may have been more the effect than the cause of the problems in Iraq's relations with the Arab states of the Gulf'.[10] It goes without saying that, apart from possessing an 'ideological' rationale, the Warba/Bubiyan issue was of major strategic significance for Iraq.

The crucial factors, therefore, which, in practical terms, influenced Iraq's behaviour towards the Gulf Arab states were (a) Iran, and (b) the orientations of the Gulf states themselves. There were several dimensions to this. First, strategic, in that Iranian control over the Shatt al-Arab (coupled with Kuwaiti sovereignty over Warba and Bubiyan) jeopardised Iraq's military capacity in the Gulf; second, economic, in that the Shatt al-Arab and the Gulf constituted one of Iraq's main outlets to the world; and third, ideological, in that non-Arab and pro-Western Iran's influence had to be curbed. Fourth, and more broadly political, Iraq's position and influence in the region had to be strengthened.

IRAQ AND THE ARAB STATES OF THE GULF

As already indicated, events in the Gulf itself seem to have had a major impact on the overall direction of Iraq's foreign policy. One may note that the shift towards international pragmatism coincides roughly with the Algiers agreement of 1975, and the further shift in 1978–79 with the Iranian revolution. In the Gulf, the Algiers accords temporarily ended the perception of Iran as a direct rival and a source of threats. Differences with the Gulf Arab states on this account thus diminished. The Iranian revolution re-introduced the Iranian threat, but this time the Gulf monarchies felt equally threatened and therefore objectively and subjectively ended up (or remained) in Iraq's camp. For Iraq, the new configuration also heightened the need for the construction of pro-Iraqi *axes*, to include all anti-Iranian forces.

Following consultations from early 1978, a mutual internal security agreement was signed with Saudi Arabia in February 1979; Iraq declared it would defend the Kingdom against any infringement of its sovereignty. This was broadened on 6 February 1980, when the Iraqi Information Minister declared: 'Any attack on any of the Arab Gulf states is a direct aggression against Iraq'. Relations with Kuwait had also warmed considerably (although a round of security talks did not lead anywhere at that stage), and when the Kuwaiti heir apparent came to Baghdad in May 1980 to discuss economic co-operation, he was given a very warm welcome.[11]

During the last months before the war, Iraqi diplomatic activity further intensified. Pro-Iraqi Shaikh Saqr of Ras al-Khaimah was invited to Iraq and was received by Saddam. Renewed border demarcation discussions were suggested to (and accepted by) Kuwait in early July.[12] Then, of course, there was Saddam's much commented-upon surprise visit to Saudi Arabia on 5 August, when he and a top delegation met with King Khalid, Prince Fahd and Prince Sa'ud al-Faisal for talks on 'the current situation in the Middle East and the Gulf region', during which at least the possibility of tackling the Iranian threat by military means was discussed. The joint communiqué focused discreetly on the threat of sanctions against states recognising Israel's annexation of Jerusalem—but even here it is telling that the position on the Palestine question was very moderate in comparison with earlier Iraqi declarations.[13] Furthest among the Gulf states from Iraq had been Oman, where the rebels of the Popular Front for the Liberation of Oman had received support from Baghdad until the early 1970s. But diplomatic relations were established in 1976 and a subsequent further warming of Iraq's attitude towards the Sultanate was indicated by the reception given to Qays al-Zawawi on his visit in late May 1980, when Iraq is reported specifically to have promised to send troops to Oman in case of a South Yemeni attack.[14]

However, it was not all plain sailing. The above mentioned determinants also explain why some points of friction or disagreement remained. Warba and Bubiyan retained their strategic and economic importance (and Kuwait remained unwilling to share control). Iraq continued to oppose any regional 'bloc formation' outside the Arab League, although willing to contemplate non-aligned regional security arrangements if it was included. And it kept trying to woo the Gulf Arab states away from their *de facto* alliance with the West. Particularly where Oman was concerned these last two issues remained problematic. The 1980 Iraqi proposal for a Gulf security arrangement that would include the six Gulf states and Iraq itself, was, according to Ramazani[15] 'largely designed to counter the plan of Oman', which the Ba'th's mouthpiece *Al-Thawra* described as 'a new imperialist alliance'. The Iraqis, notes Ramazani, 'did everything to discredit it among the Arab states'. The Omani plan centred on the security of shipping through the Strait of Hormuz, and implied accepting financial and technical aid from major oil-consuming nations.

Next, let us consider the view from the Gulf Arab states themselves. Among the main determinants of Saudi foreign policy which concern us here is the fact of the absolute primacy of national and regime survival, while a second crucial determinant lies in the Kingdom's very weakness. Judged by most standards, Saudi Arabia was no match for the other major actors in the Middle Eastern arena except financially. The country's oil wealth and installations, moreover, are highly vulnerable; hence the need for manoeuvring towards a moderate Arab consensus, and for keeping open channels towards as many actors as possible. Added to this is the need always to take into account the effect that certain policies will have on domestic legitimacy—a particularly relevant consideration as regards Islamic and Arab legitimacy. Quandt has summed up well the overall consequence of these determinants for the nature of foreign policy: 'Pushed and pulled in various directions, [the Saudis] will try to find a safe middle ground, a consensus position that will minimise pressures and risks'. This is exacerbated by another determinant of Saudi foreign policy output, *viz.* the decision-making process. Whereas King Faisal was able to put his very personal stamp on foreign policy, decision-making became more diffuse after his assassination. In addition to those of King Khalid and subsequently King Fahd, decisive voices have been those of the senior princes Abdullah, Sultan and Na'if, each with somewhat differing backgrounds, views and sympathies. As Quandt points out, consultation and consensus are key words in such a context: 'decisions may be postponed or compromises forged to preserve the facade of consensus'.[16]

The policy output in the regional arena has been marked by a tendency for *raison d'état* to assume greater importance than Islamic and anti-communist ideology. This became marked as the progressive Arab regimes on their part began to show pragmatism, and was reinforced when in that same period, after 1975, Crown Prince Fahd became the Saudi regime's strong man—even if this was not to the extent of controlling foreign policy. This links with a second characteristic, already referred to above, namely the preparedness to co-operate with the Arab 'radicals' if that would lessen intra-Arab tensions and improve the chances for a moderate consensus. Thirdly, the Saudi leaders have taken care never to move too far away from the main body of Arab governmental opinion. A fourth characteristic has been the use of the country's oil wealth where this could help smooth relations, reduce radicalism, or reduce over-dependence on the Soviet Union. Fifthly, with a view to its Islamic credentials, Saudi Arabia has tried to maintain good relations with all the major Islamic countries, including the Islamic Republic of Iran. Iranian verbal attacks after the revolution were initially played down by the leadership in Riyadh.[17] However, when they later concluded that the Iranian regime had become a real threat to stability and security in the region that would not be subdued by conciliatory gestures, some assertive reaction, using Islamic symbols, became justified. Finally, as already indicated, the nature of the decision-making process has meant that Saudi foreign policy has often suffered from indecisiveness. A related result has been that a degree of apparent inconsistency has crept in from time to time.

Before moving on to a brief appraisal of the attitudes of the Gulf Arab states towards Iraq before the war, it is worth considering some of the constraining factors on the foreign policies of the smaller Gulf states. The most important point is that they are small and weak. None of them can escape the significance which their location in and around the vital oil and shipping region of the Gulf has for bigger powers; their utter vulnerability only serves to increase this realisation. Nevertheless, actual international stances can diverge—as illustrated for example by the positions of Kuwait and Oman. In Oman, which was virtually locked away from the rest of the Arab world until twenty or so years ago, Arab nationalism does not have the same legitimising force as elsewhere. Conscious of Western support, Sultan Qaboos has very much gone his own pragmatic way. Even so, this has still implied a need to maintain the bridges with the moderate Arab majority, and, at the same time, to give careful consideration to the vulnerabilities related to the geopolitics of the Strait of Hormuz. Kuwait, on the other hand, is characterised by (a) its position next to Iraq, and (b) a relatively more politically articulate population. Both of these led it to adopt a more distinctly Arab nationalist stance and a more genuinely non-aligned foreign policy. The other Emirates occupy a middle position. The five states cannot afford to ignore either neighbouring Iran, in part because of their sizeable Shi'i populations, or Iraq, partly because of the salience of Arab nationalism as a legitimising factor. For the UAE there is the additional factor of lively trade relations with Iran, as well as joint management of some oil fields, and Bahrain and Qatar have also had a significant trade with the Islamic Republic. All five, of course, also have to take some account of Saudi positions.

Although one can easily observe a legacy of distrust in the attitude of the Gulf states towards Iraq during the second half of the 1970s, they were nevertheless ready to enter into economic co-operation with it.[18] In the case of Saudi Arabia, there was an interplay between the opening-up of Iraqi foreign policy as described earlier, the Saudi desire to respond to any such overtures, and the growing pragmatism under the influence of Fahd. Although the two still competed for influence over the smaller Gulf states, improved relations with Iraq provided the Kingdom with a welcome counterweight against Iran. When Iraq seemed, after Camp David, to be on the way to capturing at least a central role in Arab politics, the Saudis had an even stronger motivation for cultivating their Ba'thist neighbour. After the radicalisation of the Iranian revolution, both the Gulf monarchies and Iraq all found that they had a similar perception of the threat which this presented. For the Gulf six, an alliance with Iran as no longer an option. Iraq's general moderation and its growing coolness towards the Soviet Union, played a further important role in the changing attitude of the Gulf states towards Baghdad. Finally, the Soviet invasion of Afghanistan, apart from speeding up change in Iraq, directly influenced the other Gulf states' view of regional security: one Gulf official was quoted as saying that it had made Iraq 'the second line of defence for protecting the region's oil producing areas'.

As a result, the Iraqi opening up was mirrored in Gulf attitudes, and all of the Gulf states except Oman quickly expressed support for the 'National Charter' which Saddam had proposed. In the period leading up to the war (especially after Iraqi-Iranian tension started to mount during April 1980), the position of the Gulf Arab states shifted further as the Iranian threat of exporting the revolution became more clearly spelled out.[19] The conservative regimes of the Gulf increased their diplomatic activity towards Iraq from May 1980 onwards.[20] Oman even sent its foreign minister to Baghdad, and Salalah radio quoted him as saying that Oman wished to initiate co-operation with Iraq and to 'remove any misunderstanding that might have arisen as a result of certain political opinions'. Zawawi belatedly expressed Oman's support for the National Charter (although claiming later that there was no radical change in Oman's policy).[21] Overall, governmental and press attitudes in the Gulf Arab states became decidedly more pro-Iraqi.[22] As has been argued elsewhere,[23] it is very likely that Saudi Arabia at least, and probably the other Gulf states as well, was informed in advance of Iraq's plan to invade Iran, and that Saudi Arabia at least had given the green light, probably on the occasion of Saddam's visit to Riyadh in August. All six, we believe, showed varying degrees of support for Iraq's initiative, after having come reluctantly to the conclusion that there appeared to be no effective alternative. Iran was not thought to be able to put up a serious battle, and the consensus was that a *Blitzkrieg* could cut the revolutionaries down to size. Among the seven emirates of the UAE, Dubai and Sharjah were the main exceptions to this general stance.

The economic aspect of the relationship between Iraq and the Gulf Arab states became increasingly important after 1975. Apart from other considerations, this ties in with Saddam's more explicit emphasis on interlinking the Arab economies as a prerequisite for Arab unity.[24] By 1980, this had led to a structurally higher level of relations, both governmmental and private, accompanied by the improvement of the physical infrastructure linking Iraq to the six. It is worth noting that Iraq was a participant in a whole range of pan-Gulf organisations, ministerial conferences and joint projects in the agricultural, industrial, service, banking, health, educational, information and cultural sectors, and in the field of labour and social affairs. Nevertheless, trade on the whole remained low. Yet a fairly dramatic expansion of economic relations took place with Kuwait, especially from 1980, with some major contracts in Iraq being awarded to Kuwaiti companies. In addition there was the revival, in the wake of the May 1980 visit by Crown Prince Shaikh Sa'd, of the projects involving the piping of water from the Shatt al-Arab to Kuwait and the linking of the two countries' electricity grids, as well as a major increase in Kuwait's importance as a transit port, with special facilities, because of congestion at Basra and Umm Qasr. It should be noted that UAE ports were increasingly being used for transshipment as well. A final point to be made here is that on several occasions during 1980 Iraq appears to have co-ordinated its oil pricing policy with those of the other Gulf states.[25] This could be interpreted as a further sign of the co-operation in strategic economic matters that was now evolving between the ostensible former 'revolutionary' and 'reactionaries'.

The Iran-Iraq war and its impact on Gulf Arab relations

The Gulf monarchies were effectively on Iraq's side at the beginning of the war. Only the Emirates of Dubai, Sharjah and Umm al-Qaiwain did not fit this picture. A large proportion of Dubai's population is of Iranian origin and of Shi'i persuasion; to a significant extent, they fulfil key functions in the Emirate's economic life. In addition, Dubai has long had important trade links with Iran, both official and otherwise. Sharjah, and to a lesser extent Umm al-Qaiwain, have since the early 1970s had a large stake in Iranian co-operation in the exploitation of the off-shore oil field around the Tunb islands; a considerable portion of Sharjah's income derived from this. From the start these three insisted on, and succeeded in, keeping good relations with the Islamic Republic. The other camp was formed by Abu Dhabi, Ras al-Khaimah, and presumably Ajman and Fujairah. Among these, Ras al-Khaimah appears to have been the staunchest supporter of Iraq, and its ruler Shaikh Saqr is thought to have backed the idea of an Iraqi invasion of Abu Musa and the Tunbs. Abu Dhabi was more cautious, and declined co-operation in such a raid, although reportedly offering shelter to Iraqi planes and ships.[26]

There were differences in the extent to which support for Iraq was expressed, but the basic picture remains the same, nor was it fundamentally affected, initially, by Iraq's changing fortunes. Although the Gulf states all hastened to express their official neutrality after the first Iraqi *Blitz* had failed to produce the expected quick win, and after Iran had started threatening them because of their co-operation with Iraq, they remained effectively on the side of the latter. In the period of stalemate in the war, from November 1980 to late September 1981, very tangible support for Iraq was given by Saudi Arabia (with transshipment of military as well as civilian supplies, in addition to $6 billion by April 1981 and another $4 billion during the remainder of the year) and Kuwait (transshipment facilities and $4 billion by April). The UAE provided between $1 and $3 billion in financial assistance, and Qatar probably some $1 billion.[27] It was also in this period that Saudi Arabia agreed in principle with Iraq on the construction of a crude-oil pipeline to the Red Sea (to be called the IPSA-pipeline). In the Gulf conflict, therefore, the Kingdom was effectively allied to Iraq. Kuwait's vital support did not extend to giving in to Iraq's demand for a 99-year lease of Bubiyan Island. This phase witnessed another important development, following a near-clash between Oman and the Iranian navy in late 1980 after a naval accident. This led Sultan Qaboos to devise a *modus vivendi* with Iran in Gulf waters. Although remaining politically part of the pro-Iraqi camp, Oman from then on became more and more 'actively neutral'.

In this period, the whole pre-war configuration underlying the initial policies of the Gulf states changed. There was no longer any pressing need for the war, as the aim of denting Khomeini's aura had been achieved. At the same time, they had never wanted a long drawn-out conflict, with its implications of economic drain, military spill-over and superpower involvement. The need to avoid these dangers was more important than anything which could be gained from further bleeding the two combatants. Their main concern therefore became to end the war—a point on which Iraq, particularly from the spring of 1981, was very much in agreement. The second imperative was to prevent an Iranian victory; hence the active support given to Baghdad. However, the Gulf rulers' traditional suspicions of Iraq had not evaporated completely. In the security discussions that led up to the creation of the Gulf Cooperation Council (GCC) in May 1981, Iraq was never thought of as a potential partner, and the council's creation confirmed the republic's status as an outsider.

Meanwhile, Iraq was growing increasingly dependent on its conservative allies; this was reflected in the gradually diminishing importance of ideology as a factor that might unsettle its relations with these states. Examples of this were its eventual, and grudging, acceptance of the GCC, and the expulsion of the Baghdad representatives of the Popular Front for the Liberation of Oman. However, friction with Kuwait over Bubiyan remained.

In the period of the Iranian counter-offensive, from the end of September 1981 to June 1982, Iraq's 'sensitive' attitude towards the Gulf states developed further, and there was not much overt criticism of some of the latter's careful stance. The GCC, for its part, had now clearly profiled itself and Iraq acquiesced in the fact of its exclusion. The tone of the organisation's declarations, urging the end of the war, was neutral, but this covered differing attitudes on the part of its members. The attempted coup in Bahrain in late 1981 was blamed on Iran by the Bahraini and Saudi governments. Subsequently, and on several occasions, Prince Na'if bin Abdul-Aziz, in particular, stated the Kingdom's support for Iraq, urging other Arab states to follow the Saudi example. Na'if, always one of the more outspoken members of the Al-Sa'ud in criticising Iran, was quoted repeatedly as calling Iran 'the terrorist of the Gulf'. In the wake of these developments, the final border agreement between Saudi Arabia and Iraq was signed. Further considerable financial aid was also forthcoming from Riyadh. Kuwait added another $2 billion to its assistance in December 1981. This came after the Iranian missile attacks on Kuwaiti oil installations on 1 October, leading to the recalling of Kuwait's ambassador from Tehran. The remaining three states, Qatar, Oman and the UAE, kept very much a low profile.[28]

During the renewed period of semi-stalemate, until the Spring of 1984 (during which time, however, Iran carried the war into Iraq, attacking Basra and capturing Majnoon), Iraq was highly conscious of its dependence on its Gulf supporters. The GCC's communiqués remained rather bland, although Iran was reprimanded for having crossed the border. Individually, though, the Saudi position, both stated and in substance, amounted to an effective alliance with Baghdad against Iran. This was reflected in Iraq's attitude towards the Kingdom. Having previously rejected the initial Fahd plan on Palestine, for instance, the Iraqi regime approved the 'face-lifted' version at the resumed Arab League summit in Fez in September 1982. Kuwait of course had reason to feel threatened by Iran's thrusts into southern Iraq. Consequently the official neutral stance was strengthened, while at the same time material support for Iraq was maintained. Although there is no firm evidence of significant financial flows for the period 1983–1985, Kuwait and Saudi Arabia began giving some 330,000 barrels/day (b/d) of crude oil for sale to Iraqi customers ('war relief crude') from February 1983. Nevertheless Kuwait was determined to show it would not relinquish Bubiyan, and indicated this by speedily constructing a bridge between the mainland and the island in 1983. The other four GCC members, although temporarily prodded into taking some action by the Iranian incursion, soon reverted to their previous state of low profile and official neutrality. It is interesting to note that Qatar no longer appeared willing to follow the Saudi lead; nor is there much evidence of any pro-Iraqi bias on the part of Abu Dhabi.[29]

The period from the Spring of 1984 to January 1986 may be called one of internationalised conflict and stalemate, in which Iraq's siege of Kharg and of Iranian oil outlets and tankers was countered by Iranian retaliation against Arab ships and tankers carrying Arab oil. Iran's repeated threats against Saudi Arabia and Kuwait prompted these two states to persuade the GCC explicitly to criticise Iran by sponsoring a UN resolution that condemned Iranian attacks. Iran's verbal assault on the Gulf states was also stepped up in this period, which heightened Gulf antagonism. However, in May 1985, Iran switched to a policy of trying to mend fences with the six, which resulted in a mellowing of

Gulfian attitudes. Prince Sa'ud al-Faisal went to Tehran at the invitation of the Iranian leadership, although the Saudis did not give up their effective support of Iraq. The GCC's November 1985 summit communiqué was more even-handed towards Iran and Iraq than previously, but continued to insist on basing peace negotiations on two UN Security Council resolutions, even though Iran had rejected them. Nor, when Iran's Foreign Minister Velayati visited Riyadh in December, did the talks produce any agreement on ways to end the Gulf War.[30] Likewise, accounts of occasional secret negotiations between the two sides from 1984 reveal that while the Saudis were eager to reduce tension and were not wedded to Saddam's leadership, they were by no means prepared to drop support for Iraq, and were constantly irritated by Tehran's intransigence and demands.[31]

Kuwait was similarly open to any improvement in bilateral relations, and welcomed the changing Iranian attitudes from May 1985. But because the Emirate did not reduce its assistance to Iraq, criticism and threats from Tehran soon resumed. Members of the ruling family, followed even more stridently by the press, made their support for Iraq explicit. Following several previous efforts, the National Assembly succeeded, in 1985, in stopping the annual KD100 million subsidy to Syria, on the grounds of the latter's support for Iran, although this necessitated a compromise that would allow the government more funds to disburse to friendly countries at its own discretion.[32] Friction with Baghdad over Warba and Bubiyan continued, however. The islands had become even more strategically important to the Iraqis than before, but although Saddam Hussein now reduced his previous demands by asking only for a 20-year lease of part of the islands, the Kuwaiti leadership did not budge on the issue, and rather pointedly transformed Bubiyan into a military island.[33] The island and border issues thus remained a serious irritant in Kuwaiti-Iraqi relations.

As for the southern Gulf states, they had by the end of this period—and with gentle encouragement from Iran—come to accept that neutrality was their best option and it might even help to improve possibilities for peaceful resolution of the conflict. Iraq had come to acquiesce in this reality. Even so, in the framework of the GCC, they still tilted collectively towards Iraq, and it can be argued that it was the understanding stance adopted by the Iraqi regime that helped to avoid possible strains on the relationship between Iraq and these Gulf states.

THE FAO DÉBÂCLE AND ITS AFTERMATH

The shape of the Gulf War was transformed in the second half of the 1980s with the capture of Fao by Iranian forces on 9 February 1986, with the further escalation of the tanker war, and with the plummeting of oil prices which placed Iraq, as well as Iran, under grave financial pressure. Riyadh and Kuwait strongly and explicitly attacked Iran, and the GCC as a body issued a strong condemnation of Tehran's actions. Nevertheless, even Saudi Arabia still showed a willingness to opt, if possible, for a diplomatic approach and conciliation. Kuwait stands out from the start of this period in that both government and press took an unequivocally pro-Iraqi stance. The authors believe that from around this time, and following a three-year lapse, direct financial assistance to Iraq was once again forthcoming both from the Kingdom and from Kuwait.[34] Although government and press in the other Gulf states also condemned the Iranian moves, they nevertheless remained more restrained, and in no case was criticism of Iran as pronounced as in Kuwait. Meanwhile, Iraq's dependence was further heightened and highlighted, thus reinforcing its accommodating attitude towards the Gulf states.

Continuing Iranian pressure, combining the carrot and the stick, gradually succeeded in again reducing the UAE, Qatar and Oman to effective neutrality, and although the GCC umbrella continued to provide cover for the expression of more pro-Iraqi sentiments, these appeared by now to be little more than words urged upon them by Saudi Arabia and Kuwait. Indeed, it is believed that in August, when the latter two countries pressed their GCC partners to extend the AWACS patrols over the entire Gulf, Qatar, the UAE and Oman refused. On their part the Kingdom and Kuwait are thought to have extended another $4 billion 'loan' to Iraq in the second half of 1986, while Saudi Arabia is reported to have allowed Iraqi planes to land and refuel following strikes on the Iranian oil facilities in the southern Gulf.[35] The general 'camps' within the GCC on relations with Iraq and Iran, which were to endure until the end of the conflict, were now clearly crystallising. They featured the neutral camp of Qatar, the UAE and Oman—working above all towards good bilateral relations with Iran while claiming this had nothing to do with their attitude towards 'sisterly Iraq'; and the basically pro-Iraqi camp of Kuwait and Saudi Arabia, cautiously supported by Bahrain. The latter's position may be explained by its experience of Iranian-inspired protest (most importantly the 1981 coup attempt), and the island economy's high degree of dependence on Saudi aid, oil supplies, and military protection.

This configuration did not imply rigidity, however. For example, Oman, which stuck firmly to its pro-Western line, was severely criticised by Iran for hosting the British 'Operation Swiftsword' in November, while on the other hand—and for our purposes more importantly—Saudi Arabia was by no means implacable towards Iran, being still ready to respond to overtures, and especially keen to co-operate with the Islamic Republic on oil issues. This stand highlighted the friction with Iraq that was apparent during late 1986 and early 1987. Although it should be stressed that there is no evidence that the Saudi authorities officially knew about, or approved of, the shipments of Saudi refined products to Iran after mid-1986, revelations about them must have inspired grave misgivings on the part of the Iraqis. When King Fahd tried in December to convince Iraq to co-operate with OPEC's efforts to control production and thus firm up prices, Saddam Hussein refused, demanding instead a doubling of Saudi and Kuwaiti war relief crude supplies in return for more flexibility, and reportedly even refusing to answer the King's telephone calls. Iraq also insisted that the Saudis stop putting 'technical obstacles' in the way of the free flow of Iraqi crude through the IPSA-1 pipeline, (which had been completed in 1985). This had served as one way of reducing the volume of crude being poured on to the market while simultaneously exerting pressure on the Iraqis. Indeed, the Kingdom reportedly reduced the flow even further in the face of Iraqi bullying, which apparently resulted in Iraq's losing some $1 million a day in revenues around the turn of the year. It took a late February visit by a high-level Iraqi delegation (led by Taha Yassin Ramadhan, the first Deputy Premier), to obtain the Saudis' grudging agreement to allow through 500,000 b/d—double the average for the first two months of 1987.[36]

In March, Saudi efforts to find a face-saving formula to end the war proved fruitless, and the Saudi Foreign Minister let it be known that his country would ask the UN Security Council for sanctions against Iran.[37] This was probably provoked by Saudi exasperation with Iran's inability to deliver as a consequence of its internal divisions.

From now on, Saudi-Kuwaiti solidarity in supporting Iraq and confronting Iranian threats was once more clearly established. Bombings in Kuwait during April, May and June 1987 served to reinforce this position: Kuwait's government and press generally blamed the violence on Iran. They received severe threats from Tehran in return, and warnings that plans to reflag Kuwait's tanker fleet would not make it any less vulnerable to Iran's wrath. Iran subsequently seized several Kuwaiti speedboats, and in June started deploying Silkworm missiles on the Fao peninsula, directly threatening Kuwait. It may be worth noting that in the days after an Iraqi aircraft struck the *USS Stark*—accidentally or otherwise—there was no comment in the Kuwaiti press. The Saudi position was possibly even more striking: a request from the

AWACS personnel for Saudi planes to intercept the approaching Iraqi aircraft had been handled too slowly to prevent the strike; nor was there any official comment on the event.

Bahrain's Foreign Minister expressed approval for the reflagging operation—which implied a larger presence of foreign naval military strength—although he argued rather implausibly that the (mainly) American military presence should not be seen as a direct challenge to Iran because 'we do not want confrontation with Iran'. He also tried to reassure Tehran that Bahraini military bases would not be used as a springboard for attacks against the Islamic Republic.[38]

The other states, however—and particularly the UAE and Oman—were making more of an effort to be on friendly terms with Iran, guarded criticism from Baghdad notwithstanding. UAE president Shaikh Zayid stated in May 1987 that foreign protection was not needed for the UAE's ships, and the Iranian Deputy Minister of Foreign Affairs, Mr Besharati, singled out the UAE's 'wise attitude'. Iranian sources subsequently suggested that Kuwait might not have informed the UAE about the decision to invite the superpowers into the Gulf. The Iranians capitalised on this mood by sending Foreign Minister Velayati on a tour of the southern Gulf states in late May/early June in a clear attempt to drive a wedge between Kuwait and the others, specifically over the reflagging issue with all its implications. It is probably indicative of Bahrain's continuing suspicion towards Tehran that Velayati cancelled his visit there and sent an aide instead.[39] However, such hesitations were no longer part of Oman's policy. Qaboos sent his Foreign Minister to Tehran in May for discussions that resulted in an agreement on economic cooperation and in follow-up visits, the most striking of which was Velayati's visit in mid-August. Nevertheless, although the Omani government, in its official statements, agreed with Iran on the need to avoid superpower interference, the Sultanate did in fact stick to its view that Kuwait had a right to secure passage of its tankers through the Gulf.[40]

All six members subscribed to the GCC Foreign Ministers' communiqué on 8 June which supported peace moves but also stressed anew the principle that an attack on any member state would be considered an attack on all. They condemned 'terrorist and sabotage acts' against Kuwait and supported the latter's measures to secure its economic and commercial interests. Although some of this must be ascribed to heavy Saudi and Kuwaiti pressure, it would also seem to indicate that there were limits to the extent to which Iran could divide the Gulf six.

July 1987 marked the beginning a new period in the war, as well as in Iraqi-Gulf-Iranian relations: at a press conference on 20 July, Kuwait's Crown Prince Shaikh Saʻd came out explicitly and strongly in support of Iraq, and the following day the reflagging operation started. On the same day the UN Security Council issued the famous Resolution 598, which called for a cease-fire in the war, and for a step-by-step resolution of the conflict. Only ten days later, hundreds of pilgrims died in Mecca, in the chaos and violence that had erupted following political demonstrations by Iranians. This followed seven weeks of exchanges of Iranian threats and Saudi warnings about demonstrations during the Hajj.[41]

Iran's continued attacks on Arab shipping, its rejection of Resolution 598 (which Iraq had accepted), and its perceived responsibility for the Mecca riots, all helped to worsen the atmosphere. Relations between Riyadh and Tehran consequently soured further (a Saudi diplomat dying after an attack on the embassy in Tehran, and Rafsanjani calling for the Al-Saʻud to be uprooted from the area), and would continue to decline until the break in Saudi-Iranian diplomatic relations in April 1988. Referring explicitly to Kuwait, Velayati threatened that Iran would no longer show restraint in retaliating against countries supporting Iraq, thus strengthening Kuwait's enmity. The Emirate positioned itself squarely behind Saudi Arabia, and Bahrain, too, condemned Iran over the Mecca events. Qatar remained virtually completely silent, while the UAE and Oman, as before, tried to steer a neutral course, the UAE refusing Iran's offer to help in clearing mines after the British supply vessel *Anita* was sunk in mid-August, and the Omanis claiming in August (while receiving the Iranian Foreign Minister) that a powerful Iran was a source of pride for the Gulf, even though they supported Kuwait's right to reflag. Baghdad's irritation with the two countries at this point flared up, and the Baʻth Party mouthpiece published a piece criticising those who were receiving 'enemies of the Arabs . . . Islam . . . and humanity'.[42]

At the meeting of the Arab League's Foreign Ministers in Tunis in August, Saʻud al-Faisal called the Iranians 'terrorists' and urged sanctions. The meeting stopped short of calling for a break in relations with Iran, but issued a stern warning to Tehran that Resolution 598 should be accepted. Oman and the UAE were among those arguing most forcefully against a break. The contrast with Saudi Arabia, where the press for the first time was now given *carte blanche* to attack Iran,[43] could not have been greater.

In September, after a missile attack from Fao, Kuwait expelled five Iranian diplomats, and Bahrain again openly condemned Iran, calling for international sanctions if Tehran failed to accept Resolution 598. Further evidence of the firm support from Iraq's three Gulf allies may perhaps be sought in the fact that Baghdad felt at liberty to resume the tanker war in late August, and its further strikes on economic and oil targets in September. Saudi Arabia's stand is illustrated by the signing (on 20 September) of the contract for the second phase of the IPSA-pipeline which would, on completion, enable Iraq to export another 1.65 million b/d across the Kingdom. In addition, Saudi Arabia and Kuwait are believed to have contributed in excess of $1 billion during 1987, although one unconfirmed report has the Kingdom giving Iraq an outright grant worth $2 billion in the wake of these developments.[44] Bahrain's attitude was recognised by Tehran for what it was, and the commander of the Revolutionary Guards remarked in October that as the island was 'US-occupied', it was fair game for attacks on the Americans. Oman, meanwhile, stated explicitly its desire to see international even-handedness towards Iran and Iraq. The Sultanate was clearly establishing itself as a go-between between the pro-Iraqi camp and the West on the one hand, and Iran on the other.[45]

In the face of such a lack of support from Oman, the UAE and Qatar, Saddam Hussein adopted a diplomatic and pragmatic line, informing the Kuwaiti press that while GCC support stopped short of his aspirations, a GCC state that refrained from harming Iraq was better than one that did—although one that helped Iraq would be better than either.[46]

After two tankers (one US-flagged) were hit in mid-October by Iranian missiles in Kuwaiti territorial waters, the US retaliated by striking and virtually destroying two Iranian oil platforms used by the Revolutionary Guards, an action justified by the press in both Kuwait and Saudi Arabia. The Iranians, in turn, hit a Kuwaiti oil terminal on 21 October, which not only kindled Bahraini protest, but also proved to be a 'last straw' in the process of swinging large sections of public opinion in the Gulf against Iran. As one observer noted, 'for most citizens, the Iranian revolution ceased to mean anything more than war against the Arabs'. In Kuwait, 'big Shi'i families went so far as to put ads in local newspapers dissociating themselves from the [Iranian and Iranian-inspired] violence'.[47] However, official policy in Qatar, the UAE and Oman stayed neutral. Though they subscribed to the strongly-worded statement from November's Arab summit in Amman, which condemned Iran and gave clear support to Iraq, these countries were not quite as anxious to blame Iran. Sultan Qaboos indeed stated his desire to maintain good relations with the Islamic Republic—these relations being 'dictated by history and geography'—and commented that in the Gulf War *both* sides should observe the cease-fire order. Omani-Iranian economic co-operation, meanwhile, was developing further.[48] It is worth noting that, prior to the GCC summit of late December, Saddam Hussein sent messages with Tariq Aziz and Sa'doun Shakir to all the Gulf states except Oman. There was no doubt about the continued support of Kuwait and Saudi Arabia: the contract to supply war relief crude oil (which had in fact expired in January 1987 but which had run on because of previous under-lifting) was renewed in November.[49] Nevertheless, pressure mainly from the UAE and Oman (and probably also Qatar) influenced decisions at the summit. The leaders noted with regret 'Iran's attempt to procrastinate on the implementation' of Resolution 598. Even so, and a personal attack by King Fahd on Iran notwithstanding, the Kingdom and Kuwait acquiesced in the desire of the neutral partners to try to keep channels to Iran open. Shaikh Zayid of the UAE was designated to lead the GCC dialogue with Tehran, in the hope that the Iranian leadership might be persuaded to accept the UN Security Council resolution.[50]

1988: TOWARDS A CEASE-FIRE

The message from Iraq in response to these GCC intentions came loud and clear: no such dialogue was acceptable except on Iraq's terms. Nevertheless, from the beginning of 1988 some movement in the GCC's position was discernible. During January it became clear that, in addition to the three 'neutrals', Bahrain also favoured the principle of dialogue with Iran, although it remained very wary. Manama rather played down a failed coup attempt in February that was at least indirectly Iranian-inspired. The Syrian government indicated that it too was playing a role in getting the dialogue on the road. Iraq was adamant that there should be no such exercise if Iraq was not a party to it or was not satisfied with it. In Kuwait, although newspapers derided the proposal, the official mood also turned more pliant. Saddam had sent Izzat Ibrahim, the vice-chairman of the RCC, to Kuwait as well as to Riyadh, in anticipation that agreement in principle to a dialogue might be announced. But the Kuwaiti Foreign Minister said on 25 January that contacts with Tehran had never ceased, and that the Kuwaiti embassy in the Iranian capital would be reopened.[51] Baghdad's anger at this was expressed through the state-controlled press, with the regime claiming that the GCC overtures to Iran were a flagrant violation of the Amman summit resolutions, and that Syria's hand could be seen in it.[52] Although Kuwait and Saudi Arabia appeared to be excluded from these accusations, the subsequent statement by the Kuwaiti minister indicated that in fact only the Kingdom was still holding out. It is worth noting, too, that the rulers of Oman, Qatar and the UAE had all made known their opposition to an arms embargo on Iran.[53]

Saddam responded by exhorting Arab countries to stand by him in the name of Arab nationalism, while at the same time making it clear that his brand of Arab nationalism was not a threat to any Arab regime. This can be seen as confirming the evolution in Iraq's position that we have noted earlier.[54]

Following the flare-up in February of the 'war of the cities', in which Tehran and Qom were both hit, the press in Kuwait and in Saudi Arabia supported Iraq. The other countries were more circumspect. But Shaikh Zayid warned Iran not to force Kuwait to seek defence aid from abroad, and the Assistant Secretary-General of the GCC, Sayf Hashid al-Maskari, from the UAE, indicated in March that it was now up to Iran to show there was substance to its proclaimed principle of good-neighbourliness.[55] It should be noted in this context that around this time, Oman's assistance to US operations in the Gulf was openly acknowledged by Secretary of State Shultz.[56]

The improvement in Iranian-Kuwaiti relations received a setback when a number of Iranian patrol boats attacked Bubiyan Island at the end of March (interestingly, the UAE condemned Iran for this) and when a Kuwaiti airliner was highjacked en route to Mashad on 5 April. In both instances probably only a minority faction in the Iranian regime was involved, and Kuwait initially hoped that these hitches could be overcome. Yet the outcome of the highjacking led both the Kuwaitis and the Saudis to accuse Tehran of complicity.[57] Bahrain reaffirmed its position in the pro-Iraqi camp in a different way, when Shaikh Khalifa bin Salman went to Baghdad for top-level talks, described as 'supportive', on 12 April. Iran continued its own public relations offensive, sending envoys to Oman, Qatar and the UAE to present them with evidence of Iraq's use of chemical weapons against its Kurdish population in Halabja.[58]

This phase of the war effectively ended in mid-April 1988. The escalation of America's military confrontation with Iran more or less coincided with a string of military successes on the part of Iraq. In this last phase of the war, Iran experienced mainly reverses, culminating in Iraq's recapture of the Majnoon islands on 26 June, while the eventual acceptance by Iran of Resolution 598 was to be followed on 6 August by Iraq's agreement to a cease-fire.

In April Iran accused Kuwait of allowing Iraq to use Bubiyan in its successful counter attack and recapture of Fao. The Kuwaiti government denied this, but Iraq's success was hailed by officialdom

IRAQ AND THE ARAB STATES OF THE GULF

and press alike. The same fulsome praise was forthcoming from Saudi Arabia.[59]

In a gesture aimed as much at bolstering his own legitimacy in Islamic terms as at acknowledging the Al-Sa'ud's supportive stance, Saddam Hussein, accompanied by a top-level Iraqi delegation, went to Saudi Arabia on 19 April to perform the *Umra* (or little Hajj) as well as to visit King Fahd. He strengthened Iraq's 'moral' position by the immediate offer of a cease-fire, and only a few days after this latest show of solidarity (on 26 April) the Kingdom severed diplomatic relations with Iraq's adversary, having failed to convince the Iranians to accept a quota of 45,000 persons for the 1988 Hajj, ostensibly for reasons of construction work in the holy cities. Saudi fears about the numbers and activities of Iranian pilgrims at that year's Hajj, and the Iranians' total intransigence on the subject, indeed appear to have been the most important reasons behind the break—although it did of course occur only after months of mutual recriminations. Taha Yassin Ramadhan could on 7 May describe Saudi and Iraqi viewpoints as 'identical', and King Fahd himself, in his *Id al-Fitr* message nine days later, heaped praise on the Iraqi leadership for having successfully withstood the onslaught of 'oppression and tyranny'.[60]

In the wake of the Saudi-Iranian break the Kuwaiti press argued strongly for following the Kingdom's example, urging the other GCC states to do the same, even though Shaikh Jabir's government appears never to have considered this option very seriously. As regards Oman and the UAE, their essentially unchanged position was illustrated by continuing high-level contacts with Iranian emissaries.[61]

Meeting in the first week of June, the GCC Foreign Ministers congratulated Iraq on its military successes (Salamcheh had been recaptured on 25 May), and appealed yet again to Iran to accept Resolution 598. As usual, the wording was somewhat tempered by the 'neutrals', although Prince Sa'ud al-Faisal's accompanying remarks were not. Bahrain's Minister of Defence, Shaikh Hamad bin Khalifa (in a move which, although surprising, was consistent with the state's basic position) actually visited the newly-liberated areas of Fao and Salamcheh on an official visit to Iraq on 20 June, being now clearly undeterred by Iran. In a further show of determination, Manama jailed nine Bahraini members of the Tehran-based Islamic Front for the Liberation of Bahrain because of their dealings with Iran.[62]

The crucial turning point in Iran's attitude (which remained possibly *the* determining factor for the GCC states' attitudes) came on 2 June, when the pragmatic Hashemi Rafsanjani, Speaker of the Majlis, was appointed acting Commander-in-Chief of the armed forces. He immediately stressed the need for Iran to start making friends.[63] This was an illustration of the increasing strength of the pragmatic element in the Iranian leadership. The move towards acceptance of a cease-fire was hastened the very next day when an American warship shot down an Iranian Airbus aircraft. This incident also provided the excuse for a gradual and tentative *rapprochement* with Kuwait and Saudi Arabia. Kuwait immediately expressed its 'deep regret and sorrow' and extended its condolences to those affected, stressing at the same time the need to end the war: Iran sent its thanks in return. Saudi Arabia reacted two days later, but also expressed regret for the loss of innocent lives, and called for an end to the war (although the Saudi press still showed little sympathy).[64]

When Iran announced on 18 July that it accepted Resolution 598, there was jubilation in Kuwait, expressed by government, press and public alike. The Saudi reaction was less exuberant and rather more sceptical, while in Bahrain, the Iranian decision was welcomed, and a cautious optimism prevailed. The UAE saw the decision as 'a turning point' and a message from Shaikh Zayid to the Iranian President spoke of Iran's courage in taking the decision; similar reactions were forthcoming from the Omani and Qatari governments and press.[65]

Nevertheless, when Iraq—dragging its feet over the issue of a cease-fire—pushed on and into Iranian territory, several newspapers in Kuwait and Saudi Arabia supported the Iraqi position. The Saudi-funded, London-based *Al-Sharq al-Awsat* even went so far as to advocate the removal of the Iranian leadership. We can assume, however, that all the GCC states, including Saudi Arabia and Kuwait, were eager for Iraq to show some flexibility, and for the outstanding obstacles still impeding the long-awaited cease-fire to be minimised or removed. There were reports claiming that Riyadh was pressing the Iraqi leadership on this, and the official Saudi denial, on 2 August, cannot quite be taken at face value. Iraq did its best to convince its Gulf neighbours of its own views, by sending top envoys round the Gulf at the beginning of August, but its case was now much weakened.[66]

On 4 August, the Saudi Information Minister was sent to Baghdad, to put the case for implementing Resolution 598 as it stood, and thus for immediately accepting a cease-fire. Having decided at least as far back as 1981 that the costs of a continuing situation of war outweighed the benefits, the Saudis could no longer see any convincing reason for continuing to bankroll Iraqi military adventures once Iran had sued for peace. It must have been as clear to the leadership in Riyadh as it was to the pragmatists in Iran that the Islamic Republic did not really have any alternative to peace. When the Iraqis did a U-turn on 6 August, and accepted the cease-fire, this followed consultations between Saddam Hussein and Prince Saʻud al-Faisal, among others, the Saudis (through their ambassador in the US, Prince Bandar) having been closely involved in the UN negotiations before (and indeed after) the Iraqi decision. While on the one hand this illustrates their closeness to Iraq, there can be little doubt, on the other, that they did apply pressure on their ally, particularly before Saddam's 6 August decision. At the same time, the outcome served as another indication of Iraq's dependence on its Gulf backers.[67]

Iraq and the Gulf states, between cease-fire and Kuwait crisis

It did not seem likely that the end of the Gulf War would bring a return to Iraq's erstwhile radicalism. The war itself had done nothing to counter most of the factors which had brought about the pre-war shift toward moderation in the country's foreign policy: Saddam's domination of policy-making had increased further; his interest in building an alliance with the commercial bourgeoisie and giving more opportunities to private capital remained (as was indicated by the further expansion of economic liberalisation policies); the 'new' brand of Arab nationalism, with its pragmatic overtones, remained in place and was in fact made more secure by the direction of Arab politics as a whole; and Saddam's concept of using the international balance of forces for Iraq's benefit was merely reinforced during the war. Some of the financial/economic independence which had made the original shift in the 1970s possible was of course lost during the war. But the fact that it was lost to the conservative Gulf states in effect reinforced the pre-war evolution. It appeared, therefore, that Iraq's foreign policy stance by the end of the war was a result of the combination of indigenous factors with war-time pressures. Some assurance that it would persist was thought to come from another important, global development that had occurred after the outbreak of the war, though unrelated to it: this was the 'Gorbachev-effect', or Soviet international pragmatism translated into pressure on friends to behave likewise. The specific factors that concerned the Gulf states were the fear of Iran and, in Iraq, the importance attached to obtaining Gulf Arab investment—shifting to aid and financing during the war. Although the first element may have become less powerful following what was in effect an Iranian defeat, this can only be temporary. Moreover, the positive outcome of the war for Iraq was largely due to Gulf assistance and to the goodwill of the international community—both, it was presumed, having proved to be gains that were too precious to be put at risk. The existence of points of friction, such as occasional displays of Iraqi irritation with the lack of support from what we have called the 'neutrals', or even Baghdad's anger at the willingness of the GCC (including Saudi Arabia and Kuwait) to enter into negotiations with Iran; none of these seemed to detract from the apparent existence of a 'bottom line' of good relations. The evolution in economic relations and Iraqi domestic policy appeared to confirm this. Throughout the war, economic links between Iraq and the GCC states (particularly Saudi Arabia and Kuwait) developed further, even if the financial pressures of the last six years of the war were translated into temporary constraints in some areas such as trade and construction. The economic and socio-cultural links, both bilateral and with the GCC as a whole, fitted well into a foreign policy concept that viewed them in a long-term framework.[68] In addition to Iraq's many organisational and functional links in various fields with the GCC, other outstanding examples of practical links were the IPSA pipeline that carried Iraqi crude across Saudi Arabia to the Red Sea, and the gas pipeline connecting southern Iraq with Kuwait, that had since May 1986 brought some 200 million cubic feet per day of gas to the emirate.[69]

Iraq's gradually accelerating turn towards economic liberalisation, on both the domestic and the international level (each with its own strong long-term rationale, as indicated earlier), also implied a long-term commitment.[70] None of this was compatible with a renewed 'radical' attitude towards the Gulf Arab states. Admittedly, one of the main causes of the acceleration of economic liberalisation after was the pressures of war, and the consequent reconstruction. Yet this was a matter of degree, not of principle, and even these developments of degree and speed tend to have a momentum of their own.

The relationship with Kuwait is a special case, because it contains the border and the Warba/Bubiyan factors. Although a very clear alliance developed between the two states with respect to the Gulf War, potential for friction over the islands remained. The issue was indeed made even more salient by the war, and acutely so after Iran's capture of Fao. Nevertheless, the Iraqi leadership seems to have played the issue down during the last two years of the conflict, in the face of Kuwaiti determination and Iraq's need for Kuwaiti help. Clearly, however, the issue was not about to disappear with the end of the war, grounded as it was in strategic facts.

On the part of the GCC states, the trend towards friendly relations with Baghdad, which had developed before the war, was essentially maintained, in spite of Kuwait's apprehensions, and even though Oman, the UAE and Qatar—when faced with Iranian carrots and sticks—risked irritating Baghdad for remaining on good terms with Iran. This was due largely to the change in Iraq's own foreign policy and domestic character. All the states, including Kuwait and Saudi Arabia, remained intent on reducing tension with Iran when that was possible, but these two were not prepared to reduce their support of Iraq to achieve that aim. Because of Iran's attitude, this caused outbursts of animosity, exacerbated in the case of Saudi Arabia by the Hajj issue. To a large extent, it was the powerful antipathy towards the Al-Sa'ud amongst Iranian radicals and on the part of Khomeini himself, which—translated via political condemnations and tangible acts—eventually pushed the Kingdom into an uncharacteristically tough anti-Iranian stance, that was reflected in a stridently pro-Iraqi position.

Indeed it was Iran's behaviour that remained a key factor in determining the attitude of the GCC members towards their larger Gulf neighbours. Essentially they all want a predictable, non-threatening environment and thus they are quite willing to ignore differing points of view if bilateral and regional stability can thereby be maintained or achieved. They were therefore likely eagerly to accept Iran's outstretched hand when offered at the end of the Iran-Iraq war. This would not necessarily have implied a conscious opting for cooler relations with Iraq—although it could of course be interpreted by the latter, and indeed was, as somewhat of a slap in the face. In any case, Gulf leaders remained uneasy about the prospect of being bullied by an Iraq that felt itself victorious.

It was not surprising, then, that Iran's continuing 'charm offensive' which was aimed at all the Gulf states except Saudi Arabia, resulted in a rapid improvement of their relations with the Islamic Republic. Oman, already on good terms, sent its Foreign Minister to Tehran twice during August and September, the second visit apparently as a result of the GCC Foreign Ministers' meeting on 4–5 September, at which a desire for 'friendship between all the peoples of the Islamic nation' was expressed. It is believed that the GCC decided to probe the possibilities of upgrading relations with Iran, and to send envoys to both Iran and Iraq in an attempt to break the deadlock in the Geneva peace talks. Iranian radio even quoted the Omani Minister as saying that the GCC 'saw no obstacles in the way of a GCC session being held including Iran and Iraq, after the main differences between (them) are resolved'. The Sultanate also signed a wide-ranging economic agreement with Iran, and in a mid-December interview Sultan Qaboos implicitly took Iran's side when suggesting that 'forces' should withdraw behind their own borders. The country continued its vigorous policy of expanding its links with the Islamic Republic.[71]

Qatar maintained its own very quiet pragmatism, although an Iranian claim in March 1989 to part of the gas field off Qatar, is likely to create difficulties. The same problem may surface between Iran and the UAE.[72]

The UAE continued meanwhile to develop economic relations with the Islamic Republic without any grand announcements, though in some instances it indicated support for Iraqi rather than for Iranian positions, such as over the question of raising the Iraqi production quotas in OPEC in September 1988, when it came out in favour of output parity. In Bahrain, the Foreign Minister confirmed that relations with Iran would be resumed at ambassadorial level. The Iraqis were considerably irked by the GCC's haste to mend fences with Iran—especially so in the cases of Kuwait and, to a lesser degree, Saudi Arabia. A Kuwaiti official told the *Washington Post* on 28 September 1988 that his government was prepared to resume friendly relations with Iran, making the point that they did not need to consult Iraq before doing so.[73]

The gap between Iran and Saudi Arabia was less easy to bridge, given the legacy of the Mecca riots and Iranian intransigence on the issue of the Hajj, which had led to the rupture in diplomatic relations. This appeared partly to be a reflection of Riyadh's support for Baghdad. Yet Saudi-Iraqi relations were less smooth than the leaderships wanted them to appear, as will be illustrated below. The reasons for the animosity of the ruling Al-Sa'ud towards the regime in Tehran had been the threatening implications of the war; Iran's behaviour towards the Kingdom; and most specifically the Iranian attitude to the Hajj, which, if left unchecked, would have created a serious security risk—both directly, and also indirectly by eroding the regime's Islamic legitimacy. With the end of the hostilities the first point had disappeared. As to the second and third, a pragmatic, accommodationist foreign policy had become evident in Tehran since July, and there was reason to believe that at least some elements in the Iranian leadership might be willing to come to an understanding on the Hajj issue.

Saudi Arabia's conciliatory statements towards Iran from October 1988, and the halting of its press attacks on Tehran, received a positive response. In December Rafsanjani expressed his belief that relations would be normalised 'in the not too distant future', and King Fahd called on the rich Arab states to help both Iran and Iraq in their reconstruction efforts. Negotiations of some kind over the Hajj issue continued into 1989.[74]

IRAQ AND THE ARAB STATES OF THE GULF

One may assume that the GCC members, and particularly Bahrain, Saudi Arabia and Kuwait, remained throughout wary of Tehran's unpredictability: relations could not become relaxed as long as Iran's internal divisions remained unresolved. When Salman Rushdie's book *The Satanic Verses* exploded on to the Islamic scene and Ayatollah Khomeini issued his *fatwa* of 14 February calling for the author to be killed, it soon became apparent that the voices of moderation were, at least temporarily, being drowned. Even Rafsanjani had to swing into line behind the renewed radicalisation in Iran's foreign policy stance. Yet for the GCC states, Iran appeared to pass the test at least to some extent. Tehran's renewed animosity towards the West notwithstanding, it became clear that there was no change in Iran's attitude towards the southern side of the Gulf. At the Islamic Conference Organisation (ICO) meeting in Riyadh in March 1989, accommodation prevailed once more and a compromise over the Rushdie case was reached, that allowed both Iran and the moderate countries, led by Saudi Arabia, to come away without loss of face.[75] Whereas relations between the five smaller Gulf states and Iran therefore continued on a reasonably even keel (particularly so for Oman and the UAE), the Hajj question eventually soured the Saudi-Iranian relationship once more. The Iranian side, driven by Khomeini's virulent hatred of the Al-Sa'ud, refused to budge on the issue, while the security implications were too important to allow the Saudi leadership to give in from their side. From April, statements on the question became more aggressive and critical of the Saudi regime, with the Iranians insisting on their right to send 150,000 pilgrims to Mecca and once again accusing the Saudis of the 1987 'massacre'. In this atmosphere of mutual recrimination, Saudi Arabia tried hard to sound reasonable, stressing quite explicitly that it was eager to maintain good neighbourliness and that, provided the Hajj was not disturbed, it would still welcome the quota of 45,000 Iranian pilgrims which the ICO had adopted.[76]

Gradually, however, attacks on Iran became more frequent in the Saudi press. The implacable enmity against the Saudi regime, which was revealed in Ayatollah Khomeini's will, and which, apart from expressing the feelings of at least part of the Iranian political elite, also forced the Iranian pragmatists to stay their hand for the time being, did not leave the Saudis much incentive to continue their active goodwill policy. Not surprisingly, therefore, Riyadh maintained a complete silence on hearing the news of Khomeini's death on 3 June 1989. The other GCC members sent bland messages of condolence to Tehran, and some junior officials attended the funeral.[77] The leaders in all six Gulf Arab states were no doubt relieved at the Ayatollah's passing, and the emerging new partnership of Khamenei and Rafsanjani as leaders augurs well for continuing pragmatism. But the still somewhat tenuous nature of their hold on power, as well as the difficulty of shaking off Khomeini's legacy on Saudi Arabia, continued to be causes for concern.

The 'neutrals' could feel fairly comfortable. However, even in Oman, government sources indicated that without some solid evidence of Iran's intentions, they were not keen to give Iran everything at once.[78] Qatar and the UAE were doubtless shocked by Iran's claim to part of their oil and gas fields—although at the time of writing neither had reacted officially. Both Kuwait and Bahrain remained wary of the Islamic Republic, although relations were restored to their previous level.

Against this background, Iraq's own political offensive took place; focusing in particular on Kuwait and Saudi Arabia, it did not neglect the other Gulf countries, although it had to accept the inevitability of Omani neutrality, as well probably as that of the UAE and Qatar. According to an Iraqi official 'familiar with the government's planning', quoted in the *Washington Post* after the cease-fire had come into effect on 20 August, Iraq's Gulf policy would take shape as follows: Iraq would do everything in its power to block any quick restoration of diplomatic relations between Saudi Arabia and Iran; it would seek to establish a new Arab axis with Saudi Arabia, Egypt and Jordan; it would compete with Iran for regional influence; economic development would be one of the main foci; and Iraq was unlikely to join the GCC.[79]

Addressing Arab Information Ministers in Baghdad in early September 1988, Saddam Hussein reassured the other regimes once again that the eagerness of 'some' to bring down existing political structures in order to establish Arab unity was a thing of the past.[80] The Iraqi president clearly had the six Gulf monarchies in mind as his specific audience for these remarks (mentioning Kuwait and the UAE by name), and his oblique admission of Iraq's own past mistakes gave extra credibility to this new statement of policy. The following week, Saddam's long-awaited Arab solidarity appeared to come alive after the US Senate had voted to impose sanctions on Iraq for its use of chemical weapons against the Kurds. The Kuwaiti press immediately came out in full support of Iraq, followed by the governments and the press in all the Gulf states except Oman. As a sop to official Arab opinion, the Sultanate's Foreign Minister said he thought the issue of Iraq's use of chemical weapons had probably been 'inflated a bit'.[81]

Nevertheless, Iraq's campaign for the 'Gulf's ear' was not in the end particularly successful. Some of the positive results with regard to Saudi Arabia can equally be ascribed to Iran's behaviour, as illustrated above. The Iraqi leadership appeared not to expect too much either from Oman, the UAE and Qatar, although it hoped that they could at least be persuaded to support the Iraqi position in the peace negotiations with Iran under the umbrella of the GCC, as well as to support parity in oil output between Iraq and Iran within OPEC. In pursuit of these objectives, Taha Yassin Ramadhan and other top members of the leadership were sent on a major diplomatic offensive around the GCC states during the last four months of 1988. In the event, the UAE did explicitly support Iraqi output parity, but Iraq's claims to have encountered 'identical stands' to its own, appear to be more the result of 'diplomat-ese' or wishful thinking than of substantial policy. Oman's Under-Secretary for Foreign Affairs has since explained that the Iraqis were 'sensitive' about the country's dialogue with Iran, but that they accepted that it had been 'kept at exactly the same level' with both countries.[82] The three 'neutrals', in effect, remained just that: accommodating both Iran and Iraq, while making some allowance for Iraq's Arabness, on occasions such as the US sanctions vote, or in the framework of the GCC.

Bahrain's Sunni leadership, still suspicious of an unpredictable Iran, and in concert with the Al-Sa'ud, stuck to its position of supporting Iraq while maintaining the 'medium' profile it had adopted earlier. It certainly did not want to jeopardise the rebuilding of relations with the Islamic Republic. After assuming the chairmanship of the GCC, Bahraini government statements were more circumspect, and after the GCC Foreign Ministers had agreed in March 1989 to help in mediating between Iran and Iraq, Bahrain contacted both sides. Nevertheless, the rather closer nature of Iraqi-Bahraini links was illustrated by the visit of the Iraqi Interior Minister for discussion on ways 'to co-ordinate bilateral co-operation in the field of security' in early April. This is particularly significant given the mainly Shi'i, and often Iranian-inspired, nature of the Bahraini security threat. If any further confirmation was needed, it came in mid-May in the form of a three-day official visit to Iraq by the Emir and a large, high-level delegation.[83]

Iraq's relationship with Kuwait and Saudi Arabia remained of a much higher profile, both from the point of view of co-operation and in the evidence of clashes. Both had been allies of Iraq during the war, and links had been firmly established, particularly in trade and commercial activity between Kuwait and Iraq, transshipment from both Kuwait and the Kingdom, the gas link with Kuwait, the IPSA pipeline carrying Iraqi crude across Saudi Arabia, and the massive debt—most of which was effectively, though not officially, written off—incurred towards the two states. At the same time there remained several issues of contention. One was the desire of the Gulf states to make up with Iran, which corresponded to their basic needs and foreign policy limitations. A second was Iraq's indebtedness. Baghdad wanted further help for reconstruction and indicated that the aid already received should be considered largely as a contribution to the struggle which Iraq had fought on behalf of the Gulf states. A third issue was Iraq's stance in the peace negotiations with Iran. At times Kuwait and Saudi Arabia felt, with reason, that the Iraqi side presented too arrogant and inflexible a front: peace was the first imperative, but a peace which dishonoured Iran would only sow the seeds of renewed conflict. Additionally, there was Iraq's wish to participate in some way in the GCC. Failing an Iranian counterweight, this was unacceptable to all of the six member states. In the Levant, there was Iraq's enmity with Syria, and the consequent disagreement with most other Arab states over Lebanon—not least with the Saudis, who had sponsored the new Lebanese settlement which was being rejected by Saddam's protégé, General Aoun. A final and continuing issue between Iraq and Kuwait was the question of the islands and the border.

KUWAIT

Having offered profuse congratulations to Saddam Hussein and the Iraqi people following his acceptance of the cease-fire, the Kuwaitis wasted no time in broaching the border issue with the Iraqi Interior Minister on 7 August; these talks probably re-emphasised the existing differences over the question of the islands of Warba and Bubiyan, about which Baghdad had, as far as one can ascertain, kept a virtual silence for the previous two years.[84] A certain continuing closeness between the two sides was illustrated by the joint missions to Moscow and Beijing undertaken in August by Shaikh Sabah and the Iraqi Minister of State for Foreign Affairs Sa'doun Hammadi on behalf of the Arab seven-man committee empowered to follow up the peace negotiations; Kuwait also condemned American sanctions against Iraq over the chemical weapons issue. But in addition to Iraq's demands on the border question there were other causes for growing friction. The war relief crude oil arrangement, under which some 310,000 b/d was still being supplied for Iraqi customers (125,000 b/d from Kuwait's share of the Neutral Zone production), was terminated in the wake of the cease-fire.[85] Another sore point was Kuwait's improving relations with Tehran, of which Iraq was critical: Kuwait, of course, had its own imperatives on this matter, and undoubtedly felt some irritation with

Iraq, as the remark made in September 1988 by a Kuwaiti official and quoted earlier, indicates.

In December Kuwait's Crown Prince reiterated his congratulations to the visiting Izzat Ibrahim on the outcome of the war, but the strength of feeling among Kuwait's leadership over the border issue became evident when plans were revealed in January 1989 for the construction of a 30-km long causeway at a cost of $1 billion across the Bay of Kuwait to Subiya, a new city located in the north, just opposite Bubiyan Island.[86] In terms of urbanisation there was some logic to the building of the new city (with a projected population of 100,000, it was to house the new Kuwait University campus) but the plans, which included the huge engineering project of the causeway, left the Iraqis in no doubt as to the commitment of Kuwait to total sovereignty over its northern territories.

February 1989 brought the spectacle of barely disguised Iraqi-Kuwaiti bickering, as well as revealing divisions within the emirate itself. Both were brought into the open over the visit to Iraq of the Kuwaiti Crown Prince, Shaikh Sa'd. Shaikh Sabah, the Foreign Minister, appears to have opposed the visit, but Shaikh Sa'd went ahead regardless, confident that something could be extracted from the Iraqis in return for Kuwait's support during the war. The Foreign Minister, who was busy leading the Arab committee on Lebanon, was attacked harshly in the Iraqi press at the time of this visit, for having failed to label the Syrian troops in Lebanon as 'foreign' (which would have implied the necessity for their withdrawal). The Crown Prince's own talks in Baghdad from 6 February, produced little more than bland statements and made no progress on the border issue. This failure, which gravely disappointed Shaikh Sa'd, is all the more stark when viewed against the background of the confident forecasts made before the visit in the Kuwaiti and Saudi press. In Kuwait, the press's attitude was, at least partly, a conscious attempt to browbeat the Iraqis, by implying that nothing less than a settlement was expected from Iraq because of Kuwait's unstinting support during the war. From 8 February, they were in turn attacked: whether this reflected emerging difficulties in the talks, was a reaction to Kuwait's stand on Lebanon, or simply highlighted a Kuwaiti-Iraqi disagreement that was there from the start, the Iraqi press insisted that the border issue was more intricate than the Kuwaiti papers had claimed. Through the media Iraq's leadership reminded the Kuwaitis that they should speak not only of Kuwait's support for Iraq, but of Iraq's solidarity in fighting the war on behalf of the Gulf states, stressing that flexibility should not be expected to come from Iraq alone.[87]

A further attempt at negotiation was made in September 1989. An announcement that senior delegations would soon exchange visits to discuss the issue, was followed in mid-September by the Kuwaiti Emir's visit to Baghdad. But while the border question had initially been listed as a key topic, this was denied by the Kuwaiti government spokesman at the time of the visit.[88] Official declarations merely served, rather ineffectually, to conceal the underlying deadlock, and no further progress was made until—in the middle of the following year—Iraq upped the stakes by launching a sweeping political attack on Kuwait over all the issues of oil, money and territory, following this with the invasion of 2 August 1990, of the State of Kuwait.

SAUDI ARABIA

The Kingdom's support for Iraq in the face of the Iranian threat was never in doubt. But after Iraq's string of military successes, and particularly after Iran's switch to the pursuit of peace, several points of friction became evident. These persisted after the cease-fire. Saddam Hussein indicated his disappointment that aid from Saudi Arabia and Kuwait had fallen off considerably after the Fao victory.[89] Iraq would have wanted previous levels of assistance—presumably including the oil counterpart sales—to continue in view of the country's reconstruction needs, and it repeatedly reminded its backers that the war had been fought to a large extent on their behalf. However, given that the question was no longer one simply of survival, the exigencies of the oil market and more generally the Kingdom's own economic constraints, dictated otherwise. As a result the war relief crude oil arrangement was stopped in the wake of the cease-fire, and, as we have seen earlier, Riyadh made it clear to the Iraqis that it would not finance further military moves by Iraq in the absence of a genuine pursuit of peace. This was indeed another key point of friction: the Saudi insistence on some flexibility in the peace process on Iraq's part, seen against the backdrop of Riyadh's tentative warming towards Tehran.

The Paris-based *Actualités Arabes* in its September 1988 issue reported an 'open crisis' between Iraq and Saudi Arabia.[90] Evidence of this is also provided by an editorial in the *Saudi Gazette* on 12 September, which directly attacked the Iraqi leadership by criticising the nation which 'convinces itself that it is negotiating from a position of strength and should have its demands conceded by the other party'.

Nevertheless, Saudi Arabia gave full support to Iraq after the US had voted for sanctions over the chemical weapons accusations, 'denouncing' and 'expressing its deep regret for' the move by the US Congress. The Kingdom also supported Iraq's demand for quota parity with Iran in OPEC, and was then accused by Iran of sabotaging OPEC agreement with non-OPEC producers for the sake of supporting Iraq. One should view Iraqi-Saudi frictions in the light of these latter positions. Although substantial, they tended to sink back again following a flare-up. An official Saudi source in November 1988 dismissed the *Actualités Arabes* report as 'calumnies and machinations'. It is significant that Riyadh maintained the official line that the outcome of the war was an Iraqi victory: as King Fahd remarked, 'a victory scored for the entire Arab Nation and a source of pride for future generations'.[91] This basic leaning towards Iraq, though it was wary and often critical, can largely be explained by the perception of Iran as being unreliable/unpredictable, and of Iraq as having undergone a genuine change away from its erstwhile leftist radicalism.[92]

BAGHDAD, RIYADH, THE ARAB COOPERATION COUNCIL AND THE GCC

On 25 February 1989, Taha Yassin Ramadhan went to the Saudi capital to explain the nature and aims of the Arab Cooperation Council (ACC). The ACC, which had been openly mooted since late 1988, was officially set up on 16 February between Iraq, Jordan, Egypt and North Yemen, whose leaders stressed that it was an economic, not a political, grouping, and that it was open to any other Arab country. Congratulatory messages were received from most Arab countries, as well as from the GCC, and King Fahd gave the ACC the Kingdom's blessing.[93] Nevertheless, several observers saw these congratulations as less than heartfelt. It was suggested that Saudi Arabia might not have been particularly pleased at the emergence of this new bloc as a potential rival to the GCC, especially since it included the erstwhile regional bully Iraq, and because the presence of North Yemen, traditionally in the Saudi sphere of influence, could be seen as evidence of a 'pincer movement'. Official Saudi sources strongly rejected reports to this effect, and in this particular case, the official Saudi position was probably close enough to the truth. Certain apprehensions notwithstanding, it is likely that on the whole the Kingdom and the other Gulf states were rather pleased with the creation of the ACC, not least because it drew Iraq into the framework of a moderate organisation (thus holding in check Saddam's unilateral Arab leadership ambitions), and away from its attempts to join the GCC.

Even so, the ACC's ostensibly economic rationale should not be taken at face value. The much-vaunted complementarity of the participating countries is in fact not at all impressive, and during the first year of its existence few significant economic decisions were taken. In any case, the *political* aspects were acquiring just as much importance. The preamble to the group's statutes speaks of Arab support for Iraq in the Gulf War, while 'co-ordination' of foreign policy was agreed in July 1989, and Iraqi concerns were addressed prominently in the ACC's Alexandria summit in June 1989.[94] But the new grouping should not be seen as an anti-Saudi alliance. It was, certainly, a means for Iraq to shine on the Arab stage again, and for the further glorification of Saddam Hussein. Yet it was essentially limited to just that: he was opting for a new channel, having realised that further integration with the GCC was unlikely. The gist of this would have been made clear by Ramadhan to senior members of the Saudi government during his February visit, and eventually accepted by them. In view of the renewed souring of Riyadh's relations with Tehran, as earlier described, ties with Iraq were once more consolidated as being basically friendly and mutually supportive, although the alliance was less clearcut than previously. This is illustrated by the positive response to Iraq's request for help in the reconstruction of Basra. It also appears that Baghdad negotiated exemption (as it did with Kuwait—see above) from repaying the 'loans' obtained from Riyadh during the war. In addition, of course, Iraq could continue to benefit from its throughput through the IPSA pipeline across the Kingdom to the Red Sea: the integrated system with a capacity of 1.65 million barrels per day became operational in September 1989.

It is in this light that the Saudi-Iraqi non-interference pact of 27 March 1989 must be seen. Although it is true that King Fahd's trip to Cairo at the end of March was at least partly inspired by a desire to secure bilateral commitment to good relations, as well as gratitude for Saudi economic assistance from the Egyptians—in an attempt to cut across any hidden ACC agenda—the visit to Baghdad en route to Cairo was not a panic reaction. Rather, it was a convenient way for Iraq to maintain, and be seen to maintain, a clear formal link with the Kingdom, and thus with the GCC, that would be sealed by a pact, notwithstanding its participation in another grouping. In its stipulation of non-interference and peaceful settlement of disputes, the agreement was similar to those that Saddam Hussein had signed with the ACC members individually, and which he had argued should be signed with all Arab states—i.e., as a bilateral expression of the principles of the 'National Charter' proposed in 1980 and already enshrined in the Arab League Charter. For Saudi Arabia, it set a welcome seal on Iraq's oft-repeated promise not to interfere any more in others' internal affairs.[96]

IRAQ AND THE ARAB STATES OF THE GULF

THE FALSE SECURITY OF ECONOMIC LINKS

As indicated earlier, one of the factors which appeared to confirm the expectation of improved relations between Iraq and the Gulf states—especially Kuwait and Saudi Arabia—consisted of the expanding set of economic links. Of special interest was the issue of Iraq's debt to its Gulf backers. In the course of the war, Saudi Arabia gave some $25 billion in financial aid, while about $10 billion was received from Kuwait, in addition to $1 billion from Qatar and $2–4 billion from the UAE.[97]

Iraq also received the proceeds of some $14–15 billion in oil counterpart sales. This brought Iraq's total indebtedness to Saudi Arabia to around $34 billion, and to Kuwait to about $15 billion. However, the conversion of at least the financial part into gifts rather than loans had long been assumed. There was no doubt, too, that Iraq wanted the oil swap debt recognised as a contribution to its efforts in protecting the Gulf against the Iranian threat. After the cease-fire both Saudi Arabia and Kuwait provided further aid, albeit of a more limited kind. In addition to governmental contributions to the reconstruction effort, there were the right sort of signals to banks and funds to help Iraq out. Iraq, realising that further financial aid from the Kuwaiti and Saudi governments would fall short of its expectations, approached the Arab development funds for assistance with reconstruction. The Arab Monetary Fund (AMF) had already agreed in December 1988 to extend a $112 million loan, and in January 1989 the Funds, in the framework of the Co-ordination Secretariat, agreed in principle jointly to provide a loan for some $1 billion over five years. The AMF and the Islamic Development Bank (IDB) subsequently gave further, smaller loans.[98]

The rationalisations of Arab aid institutions and banks for lending to Iraq, went against much of Western bankers' feelings about Iraq as a risky proposition. Even several Arab bankers were reported to 'privately believe that the economic risks of committing large amounts of funds to Iraq remain too high'. In contrast, the official line at the Arab Funds, and even at the Gulf International Bank (GIB), was that 'Iraq is a good risk'. As was the case during the war, this showed a degree of solidarity with Iraq on other than economic grounds. Iraq itself was of course an important member of the multilateral funds, and governmental hints are certain to have been forthcoming. Another interesting development was the establishment, by the AMF and AFESD, of a special fund for countertrade for Arab countries. According to Yusuf Abdul-Latif Al-Hamad, then AFESD's

Director-General, Iraq, with its massive reconstruction needs, was to have been a major recipient.[99]

The links with Kuwait and Saudi Arabia were also consolidated through a number of major projects. With Kuwait, these were the gas link, and the new water supply project. Under a deal which had come into effect in May 1986, Kuwait had been receiving 200 million cubic feet per day (cfd) of gas. The water supply project was a clear beneficiary of the cease-fire in the Gulf War: the idea of piping fresh water from the Shatt al-Arab to Kuwait had been conceived long before (it was first suggested in 1953), but had been delayed by the hostilities. During his visit to Baghdad on 14 March 1989, Kuwait's Minister of Water and Electricity signed an agreement for an initial supply of 550 million gallons per day (mgd) of river water, (350 mgd of drinking water, 200 mgd for irrigation purposes). The 290-km pipeline to bring the water from the Shatt al-Arab would be financed by Kuwait. The project's cost was estimated at KD400 million ($1.4 billion). On the same occasion, the idea of merging the Basra and Kuwait water supply schemes was welcomed, and it was agreed to link the two countries' electricity grids.[100]

The most striking tangible link with Saudi Arabia is, of course, the IPSA pipeline connection, which carries Iraqi crude to the Red Sea across Saudi territory. The completion of the second stage of the scheme in September 1989 brought Iraq's export capacity to 1.6 million barrels per day (bpd). Meanwhile, the start of the experimental stage of the project to link Iraq and the Kingdom by a microwave telecommunications net was due in 1990, the project, described as 'strategic' by the Iraqi authorities, having been agreed upon in September 1988.[101] The transshipment function of the Gulf states—especially Kuwait and Saudi Arabia—continued. Even though Iraq was aiming for a speedy restoration of its own port capacity in the Gulf, these channels retained their strategic importance.

Although the potential for trade between the Gulf states and Iraq remained limited by Iraq's cash-strapped position and, from a more long-term perspective, by the limitations of what the Gulf states had to offer, governmental efforts to develop trade and economic links continued after the cease-fire in the Gulf War. For example, in February 1989 Iraq and Kuwait signed joint trade minutes that included a long-term contract to export Iraqi barley to Kuwait, promoted the idea of barter deals, and encouraged 'Kuwaiti investors to utilise the opportunities presented by Arab Investment Law no. 46 of 1988'. Iraq issued the law after the cease-fire in August that year.[102]

Gulf Arab investors in Iraq were granted a tax-free period of up to five years for new ventures, and could remit 25 per cent of their profits in hard currency. This concession, which was part of Iraq's overall opening-up to private investment, combined with the expectation of reconstruction-related contracts, did kindle interest lower down the Gulf. By the end of November 1988, a high-powered GCC business delegation had already visited Baghdad to meet ministers and industrialists and to find out more about Iraq's needs and their own potential role, and this visit was followed by the announcement, in March 1989, that the GCC and Iraq were planning a $500 million joint venture for industrial and trade projects—the Gulf Iraq Investment Holding Company. Muhammad Abdullah al-Muʿalla, the Secretary-General of the Federation of Chambers of Commerce of the GCC, indicated that the initiative would take advantage of the policies of liberalisation which Iraq was implementing in order to revive its economy.[103] However, even before the Iraqi invasion of Kuwait, there was no tangible evidence of any follow-up; this indicated a continuing mistrust on the part of the Gulf private sector as well as their unease with the financial and exchange restrictions that still remained in Iraq.

The Kuwait Crisis[104]

After the Iraqi invasion of Kuwait in August 1990, it became fashionable to argue that academic and government observers should have seen it coming: after all, said the commentaries, the bully in Saddam had always been likely to surface again to look for new prey after the Gulf War; and, more specifically, a number of signals should have provided ample warning.[105] Although there is truth in the latter point as far as the two months or so preceding the invasion are concerned, it will be clear from the foregoing that, significant tensions with Kuwait notwithstanding, such a take-over of the emirate was, until very late in the day, always the least probable of a number of alternatives. At any rate, this was the picture if one assumed Saddam was still the brutal, yet rational, actor that he had shown himself to be during the previous fifteen years.

THE BACKGROUND

Reliable sources close to the Iraqi-Kuwaiti border discussions indicate that months before the invasion, the talks had already become extremely problematic. In addition, 1990 saw an increasing divergence between Iraq on the one hand, and Kuwait and the UAE on the other, over oil policy.[106] During the war Iraq, along with the big Gulf Arab producers, had ended up in the camp of those OPEC members who had opted for a market share confrontation with the non-OPEC producers by raising production and allowing prices to drop temporarily. They were accused by Iran of depressing the oil price on purpose in order to harm the Iranian war effort. The oil ministers of Iraq, Kuwait and Saudi Arabia had been holding regular meetings to co-ordinate policy: the last of these meetings took place on 3 March. The divergence was rooted in two factors. First, the post-cease-fire environment and the glaring need for cash led the Iraqi leadership to review its own stance on oil prices; secondly, the general feeling that the demand-supply situation over the following five years or so would evolve steadily in OPEC's favour, had given rise to complacency among most producers (Kuwait's oil minister even called for the abolition of the quota system, as it was becoming 'irrelevant'): as a result, quotas were being widely exceeded, which was bound to drive prices down again. In February 1990, the UAE, Kuwait and Saudi Arabia, the worst overproducers, were together pumping 1.6 million barrels per day above quota, so that by the time of the March meeting, the divergence was clear: Iraq wanted the reference price to be raised at least to make up for inflation since 1986, and sensibly suggested that output restraint might well be necessary to achieve this in reality; Kuwait wanted the official $18 mark to be retained for at least another three years, and Saudi Arabia took a middle position. During the remainder of the month the inevitable slide in prices began, taking the OPEC basket price from $19/b to $14/b by mid-year.

As every $1 drop in the oil price meant a loss of approximately $1 billion for the Iraqi treasury, the Iraqis upped their campaign for output restraint. Most other OPEC producers came to view some restraint as necessary as well, and the Geneva agreement of 3 May imposed a three-month cutback, which would require Kuwait to return to its 1.5 million b/d quota, and the UAE to cut 200,000 b/d from its output. Saudi Arabia from that point onwards showed itself a firm convert to production discipline, immediately reducing its production to below quota. However, Kuwait and especially the UAE continued to over-produce that month, pumping 1.75 million b/d and over 2 million b/d respectively.[107]

THE OIL STRUGGLE

This is the context in which Saddam Hussein made his dramatic decision to turn up the pressure—initially, however, behind the closed doors of the Arab summit in Baghdad on 30 May. The summit was concerned publicly with a strengthened stand against Israel and in particular the influx of Soviet Jews. But in his closing speech to the gathered heads of state, the Iraqi president issued an astonishingly direct warning to Kuwait and the UAE. Linking losses suffered by Iraq as a result of falling oil prices to those losses incurred by the Arab world as a whole, he berated the overproducers for having allowed this to happen, and put the blame squarely on a lack of a clear (Arab) nationalist vision. The bombshell followed immediately:

> I wish to tell those of our brothers who do not seek war, and those who do not intend to wage war on Iraq, that we cannot tolerate this type of economic warfare ... God willing, the situation will turn out well. But I say that we have reached a state of affairs where we cannot take the pressure.[108]

During a visit by the OPEC conference president, Mr Boussena, to Baghdad on 22 June, Iraq's Oil Minister Mr Al-Chalabi for the first time sharply criticised the UAE by name, labelling it 'the only country ... that did not abide by the Geneva decisions'.[109] In the last week of June, Saddam Hussein followed this up with urgent messages to the rulers of Kuwait, Saudi Arabia, the UAE and Qatar. Iraq's Deputy Prime Minister, Sa'doun Hammadi, who was delivering the messages, publicly criticised both Kuwait and the UAE by name for the overproduction and consequent price slide. At the same time, however, the outlines of a solution were being suggested by Al-Chalabi, who proposed that while OPEC's production ceiling could not be raised until prices reached an increased reference price, an amendment could be made to accommodate the UAE with a quota of 1.5 million b/d.

Saudi Arabia then invited the other four main Gulf Arab producers to Jeddah on 10–11 July 1990, and an agreement along precisely those lines was reached. Both Kuwait and the UAE committed themselves to stick to quotas of 1.5 million b/d each. At the same time it was agreed that the quotas would not be raised further until a higher reference price was reached—although that price was left to be discussed later. King Fahd exerted a great deal of personal pressure to achieve this result.[110]

It looked, therefore, as if the Jeddah agreement had defused the situation. This explains the sense of shock that was felt when Iraq once again denounced Kuwait and the UAE: in a memorandum submitted to the Arab League on 15 July by Tariq Aziz, the Iraqi Minister of Foreign Affairs, the oil policy of these states was equated with military aggression against Iraq. Equally ominously, they were accused of effectively being part of an 'American-Zionist plot' (see Chapter 6). Even if it had been possible to interpret the move as a way of frightening Kuwait and the rest of OPEC into adopting the Jeddah proposals at the general OPEC conference later that month (and adhering to them) the rest of the memorandum made it abundantly clear that the other issues of friction with Kuwait had now taken on the quality of head-on confrontation. Adding little else in the way of grievances against the UAE, the document accused Kuwait of having stolen oil from the Rumaila oil field (the southern tip of which straddles the border) and having encroached on Iraqi territory. Iraq demanded a reversal of oil policy, repayment of the 'stolen' oil (put at $2.4 billion), a write-off of the loans obtained during the war, and, implicitly, concessions on the border dispute. Two days later, Saddam Hussein again accused the overproducers of supporting American imperialism.

Kuwait rejected the accusations in a reply to the Arab League on 19 July, pointing out that it was in fact Iraq which had a record of encroachment, and suggesting that the boundary question should be put before an Arab League tribunal. It also drew attention to the fact that the oil it produced from the Rumaila field was from wells 'far enough from the international borders to conform with international standards' (for the document see Chapter 6). Envoys were immediately despatched to all the other Arab countries to drum up support for the Kuwaiti position, with particular attention paid to Saudi Arabia and Bahrain—both of which had signed a non-aggression agreement with Iraq—and to Egypt, which was Iraq's largest fellow member in the ACC. Shaikh Zayid of the UAE also contacted President Mubarak over the Iraqi threats.

Official and media reaction throughout the Arab world was cautious and intent on avoiding an escalation of the conflict. In the Gulf states, the only paper to report the facts of the confrontation was the Sharjah-based *Al-Khaleej* on 19 July. The rest of the Gulf press remained silent, avoiding any mention of the Iraqi threats or the issues concerned. Nor were any details released in Kuwait itself either, although editorials were published that implicitly rejected the accusations contained in Tariq Aziz's letter. King Fahd telephoned both the Kuwaiti Emir and the Iraqi president, and Jordan's King Hussein cut short a visit to Yemen to fly to Riyadh, with an offer to mediate. President Mubarak also became actively involved, keeping in touch with both sides and releasing a statement on 20 July that called for 'brotherly dialogue' between Iraq and Kuwait. The leaders were now focusing on the confrontation which seemed most likely to escalate, *viz.* that between Iraq and Kuwait: Kuwait's geographical position, the outstanding areas of dispute with Baghdad, and the contents of both Saddam's speech and Tariq Aziz's memorandum left little doubt that it was Kuwait rather than the UAE which was being targeted. Several members of the Kuwaiti government at this point took seriously the possibility of an Iraqi military move.[111]

ARMED INTIMIDATION

This perception was confirmed on 24 July, when two Iraqi armoured divisions totalling some 30,000 men—outnumbering the Emirate's total armed forces by three to two—were moved close to the border with Kuwait. In the run-up to the OPEC conference which was due to take place in Geneva two days later, most observers interpreted the move as sabre-rattling to frighten Kuwait into giving up claims to a higher quota, and OPEC into setting a higher reference price. Nevertheless, it was serious enough for the United States to issue a statement reminding Iraq that there was 'no place for coercion and intimidation', and that the US remained 'committed to supporting the individual and collective self-defence' of its friends in the Gulf. It was announced later that joint US-UAE manoeuvres had begun in the Gulf. The same day President Mubarak left for Baghdad, Kuwait, and Jeddah, with the aim of organising a summit meeting between himself and the rulers of these countries.[112] A number of Western and Arab press agencies and newspapers, as well as Egyptian officials, subsequently confirmed that Mubarak had been assured by the Iraqi president of his commitment to a peaceful solution.

The Iraqis, however, further hardened their position on the following day by rejecting Arab arbitration over the border dispute. Tariq Aziz also told the Iraqi news agency that 'Kuwait's rulers should study carefully Iraq's memos to the Arab League and repair the damage described therein, without beating around the bush ... , distance themselves from the circles of conspirators, and distance the conspirators from decision-making circles'.[113] In effect, he was accusing the Kuwaiti foreign minister of being a conspirator with the 'Imperialist-Zionist' plot, calling for the minister's removal, and demanding total concession to Iraq's demands.

Nevertheless, hopes of a settlement were raised by Mubarak's announcement, following his lightning tour, that Iraq and Kuwait had agreed to hold high-level talks on 28 July, while media attacks were to be halted as from 26 July. The latter condition was fulfilled, and it also appeared that Kuwait was ready to grant most of the points which Saddam had listed to the Egyptian president as being a basis for settlement: the Egyptian press reported that Kuwait had told Mubarak that it would stick to its quota; that it had not demanded the repayment of the old war-time loans; and that it was willing to provide further financial support to other Arab states. A senior Jordanian official was also quoted as saying that the Kuwaitis were intending to cancel Iraq's debts in return for security guarantees in the form of an agreement on the *de facto* Iraq-Kuwait border: he confirmed that the debts were not expected to be repaid by either side, but as long as they remained on the books they were affecting Iraq's credit-worthiness.[114] The sticking point, of course, remained the territorial question with its components of the Rumaila oilfield and Warba and Bubiyan islands.

An indication that the troubles were far from over came in an Iraqi government statement on 27 July, informing Crown Prince Sa'd of Kuwait that he must 'know that those [i.e., Sa'd himself] who are coming to meet us must be prepared to wipe out the harm and aggression done to Iraq and respond to Iraq's legitimate demands'. Moreover, the number of Iraqi troops on the Kuwaiti border was approaching 100,000. Yet the OPEC conference which had begun the previous day again provided some relief. Although Iraq had started out from a $25/b reference price suggestion, which Kuwait's new Oil Minister Rashid al-Amiri had labelled 'unreasonable', deft manoeuvring by Saudi Arabia on the second and closing day brought about a compromise figure of $21/b. The Jeddah agreement was in essence retained, raising the UAE's quota to 1.5 million b/d, and OPEC's overall production ceiling to 22.5 million b/d. Iraq's Oil Minister Al-Chalabi said he was 'very happy with the agreement'.[115] The tension in the region had in any case already raised prices to around $20/b.

There was hope, therefore, that the talks between Kuwait's Crown Prince and Izzat Ibrahim, the Deputy Chairman of Iraq's Revolutionary Command Council, which were hosted by King Fahd in Jeddah on 1 August, would stave off further conflict. The Kuwaitis were prepared to compromise on the financial issues, and a number of local and other Arab sources indicated that a lease on part of one of the islands would also be open to discussion.

THE IRAQI INVASION: THE GULF TRANSFORMED

Subsequent events have made it clear that the Jeddah talks were never intended to be more than a distracting side-show—except in the unlikely event of Shaikh Sa'd's having simply given in to every single Iraqi demand (which would have been tantamount to admitting guilt on all counts and signing away Kuwait's sovereignty). Although the talks were inconclusive, further sessions were expected in the following weeks and Shaikh Sa'd and his delegation returned home the same evening. Only hours later, around 2 am on 2 August, Iraq's tanks rolled across the border. By midday Kuwait's independent territorial existence had been extinguished. The armed forces were taken by surprise and were in any case no match for the invaders. The Emir and most of the royal family and the government escaped to Saudi Arabia, but up to 200 people died before the day was over. Sporadic resistance continued, but the take-over was a fact, with the number of Iraqi occupying troops soon swelling from about 50,000 to around 140,000.

Iraq portrayed the action as having been invited by a 'Provisional Free Government of Kuwait' formed by a group of young revolutionaries who were said to have overthrown the royal family. However, this ethereal body came into being only two days later, and was then composed of individuals who were unknown in Kuwait: most probably they were Iraqi officers. Leading members of the Kuwaiti opposition have since confirmed that they were approached to form the new government, but none accepted, and all the indications are that the invasion effectively united even the most vociferous critics of the regime in defence of Kuwait's independence under the Al-Sabah family. In the face of international condemnation, Saddam Hussein said that his troops would pull out within a week, as soon as the situation had settled and when the Free Provisional Government requested it. But the return of the 'corrupt Al-Sabah regime' would not be accepted.[116]

The United States immediately condemned this 'naked aggression' and began to draft a Security Council resolution proposing sanctions. On the same day the Security Council passed Resolution No. 660, which condemned the invasion and demanded an immediate and unconditional withdrawal. The Soviet Union cut arms shipments on the day of the invasion and sent a message to Saddam Hussein to the effect that he should withdraw. Iraqi and Kuwaiti assets were frozen in the US and in Italy, and blocked domestically in France, while Britain froze Kuwaiti assets—all with the aim of preventing Iraq or its puppet regime from gaining access to them. On 3 August, the US and the USSR issued an historic joint statement that reiterated condemnation of the invasion and called for an immediate withdrawal. Arab League Foreign Ministers, gathered in Cairo for a meeting of the Islamic Conference Organisation, remained silent, apparently at a loss as to how to proceed. The Gulf Cooperation Council waited until the day after the invasion to react officially, at which time its Foreign Ministers demanded 'an unconditional and immediate withdrawal', and asked the Arab League 'to take a united Arab stand . . . to end this aggression'. That same day, 14 members of the League complied, and, following President Mubarak's lead, approved a resolution condemning the invasion. The Palestine Liberation Organisation, Jordan, Mauritania, Libya, Djibouti, and of course Iraq, did not. King Hussein, meanwhile, tried to mediate and announced on 3 August that Saddam Hussein,

Shaikh Jabir and some other Arab leaders would meet in Jeddah two days later.[117] There was, then, still some prospect of containment—as well as of the avoidance of a complete rupture between Iraq and the Gulf states.

From 4 August, these prospects disappeared. The naming of the puppet government that day was accompanied by the announcement that a new 'Popular Army', open to all Arabs, would be set up, to protect Kuwait from aggression. Conveniently, over 140,000 Iraqis were claimed to have volunteered already—about the number of Iraqi troops thought to be in Kuwait at that stage. Shaikh Jabir refused to attend the suggested talks with Saddam in Jeddah as long as Iraqi troops remained in Kuwait, and as a result the summit was scuttled.[118] At the same time, around 100,000 Iraqi troops were massing near the Saudi border.

At the insistence of the GCC states, led by Saudi Arabia, the Islamic Conference Organisation, gathering in Cairo, now joined in condemning the Iraqi invasion. The European Community did likewise, imposing sanctions that included a freeze on Iraqi and Kuwaiti assets and an oil embargo. This was followed on 6 August by the unprecedented occurrence in the UN Security Council of an unopposed vote on Resolution 601, which imposed a comprehensive economic boycott. Along with Cuba, Yemen—the only Arab member in the Council and a fellow member with Iraq in the ACC—abstained. Tellingly, in Abu Dhabi a pro-Kuwaiti demonstration on 4 August was permitted and publicised—perhaps, noted *The Financial Times*, the first spontaneous demonstration in the emirate's history.[119]

Although the Saudi media had until that time still not reported the invasion, and though the only reaction from Riyadh thus far had been to call the events 'regrettable', Saudi Arabia's action within the framework of the GCC, the Arab League and the ICO indicated the country's position. In addition, President Bush had been in touch with King Fahd from the first day, assuring him of American support. The American Defence Secretary, Richard Cheney, flew to Saudi Arabia on the day Resolution 601 was passed, to discuss the opening of Saudi landing strips to US planes, and the possibility of closing down the IPSA pipeline.[120]

The Saudis were generally acknowledged to be in a precarious position. The international economic boycott of Iraq could only really work if the pipeline *was* shut, and if Saudi oil production was raised to help make up to the world for the loss of some 4 million b/d of Iraqi and Kuwaiti oil supplies. Saddam made it clear that either action would be seen as an act of aggression, and in view of the troops massing on the

Kuwait-Saudi border, these were not empty words. In order to be able to join any international boycott of Iraq, the Saudi ruling family needed three things. The first two, pertaining to the question of legitimacy (for the regime and for the action), had already been obtained: cover from the United Nations, and official condemnation of Iraq by the GCC and the Arab League. The third requirement was immediate and massive military protection, which only the United States could provide. In the event, the consensus among the Al-Sa'ud went against the option of appeasing Saddam Hussein, as this would not guarantee security either in the short or the longer term.

On 7 August the puppet government in Kuwait declared the country a republic, while Iraq announced the merger of the two currencies. Thereupon King Fahd cut through the knot and asked for international military assistance to defend the Kingdom against the Iraqi threat, Iraq's assurances that it had no designs on Saudi Arabia notwithstanding. On the same day, the US ordered planes and troops to the country. It was only then that the Saudi press was allowed to report the invasion, along with details of the UN Security Council resolution.

Clearly, another watershed had been crossed. The previous day, Saddam Hussein had still been saying that he wanted 'normal relations' with the United States. Now the Gulf states had come down off the fence and troops were on their way. Equally important, Turkey had finally closed down the pipeline that carried Iraqi oil to Ceyhan on the Mediterranean. In response, the Iraqi president defiantly declared the annexation of Kuwait on 8 August. An emergency Arab summit was called by Mubarak and even King Hussein rejected the annexation, stating: 'we continue to recognise the emiri regime'. Britain announced that it would send troops to join the Americans in Saudi Arabia—the start of the military operation's internationalisation—and the Iranian government stressed that it could not accept any change in Kuwait's borders.[121] At the United Nations, the Security Council passed another resolution condemning the annexation, and this time Yemen voted in favour. King Fahd himself, in a speech to the nation the day after the annexation, condemned Iraq's acts in the harshest terms and confirmed the arrival of Western troops: he described the invasion as 'the most horrible aggression the Arab Nation has known in its modern history' and announced that he had asked 'Arab and friendly forces to participate' in the defence of the Kingdom. Saudi Arabia, he added, 'demands the restoration of the situation to what was before the Iraqi invasion and the return of Kuwait's ruling family under Shaikh Jabir al-Ahmad Al-Sabah'.[122]

To complete the tightening of the net around Iraq, and in order to add much-needed legitimisation to the foreign military presence in Saudi Arabia, Riyadh and Cairo used all their powers to persuade the Arab League to support the idea of a multinational deterrent force for the Kingdom. All the Arab League member states, except Tunisia, gathered for an emergency summit in Cairo, where, after much effort, Mubarak managed to push through a vote on a GCC-sponsored resolution that called for the Arab League to send Arab troops to the Kingdom: these would be stationed alongside the other forces in Saudi Arabia, to deter an Iraqi attack. The resolution was supported by 12 members, Iraq and Libya voted against it, the PLO, Yemen, and Algeria abstained, and Jordan, Sudan and Mauritania 'expressed reservations'. The result was a narrow majority in favour, and Egypt, Morocco and Syria announced that they would send troops.[123]

The authors do not intend to provide a complete record of the Gulf crisis, beyond describing the initial moves and the subsequent crystallisation of the international community's position, as outlined above. In the sequence of events as they unfolded over the following months until late November 1990, however, six developments which further affected the nature of the situation must be mentioned.

The first was the effective internationalisation of the military presence in Saudi Arabia, and the provision of facilities by the other GCC states. Two months after the invasion there were—in addition to some 130,000 American troops, and about 2,000 each from Pakistan and Bangladesh—nearly 50,000 Arab soldiers in Saudi Arabia, including some 15,000 Syrians (of which at least 1,000 were in the UAE), 20,000 Egyptians, 2,000 Moroccans, 5,000 Kuwaitis and up to 5,000 from the remaining Gulf states.[124] As well as the United Kingdom and France, Belgium, Australia, Canada and others were also sending naval forces. Further commitments followed as the crisis continued. The other aspect of internationalisation was financial: on 15 September the American Secretary of State, James Baker, could announce that his fund-raising efforts for sharing the burden of the military and economic costs involved had resulted in the following pledges: $5 billion from the exiled government of Kuwait; up to $12 billion from Saudi Arabia and the Gulf states (half of which would go towards the cost of the military operations, and the other half towards relieving the burden on those countries suffering most from applying the sanctions); $4 billion from Japan; $2 billion from the European Community; and another $1.8 billion from West Germany individually.[125]

The second new element was UN Security Council Resolution 665 of 25 August, which authorised the enforcement 'by such measures...

as may be necessary' of the UN-decreed sanctions. This legalised the interdiction of Iraqi or Iraq-bound traffic in the Gulf by (mainly) US naval forces, and, together with the subsequent approval of an air blockade, completed the sanctions network.

Three further new elements were introduced by Iraq itself. On 12 August, Saddam Hussein proposed that any withdrawal from Kuwait should be linked with the issues of the Israeli-occupied territories and a Syrian withdrawal from Lebanon. If foreign troops in the Gulf were also withdrawn and sanctions frozen, he suggested, a solution could be worked out for the current crisis. This idea of linkage, although clearly intended to regain legitimacy and support for Iraq among the Arabs, was to prove a persistent factor in subsequent developments. Even if the formal link was rejected by the West, the Gulf and Palestine had become objectively connected, both because much of the growing popular opposition against the 'American' presence was clearly directly due to the legacy of the Palestine problem, and also because of the implied threat to those regimes that were friendly to the West, if the West failed to address the issue. The Arab states, France, and eventually also Britain and the US itself, all began to stress the importance of finding a solution to the Palestine question, even while rejecting any formal linkage.

The second of these new elements was the astonishing reversal on 15 August by Saddam Hussein, when he agreed to accept Iran's stated terms for peace. This meant a return to the pre-Gulf War situation, with shared sovereignty over the Shatt al-Arab, immediate withdrawal of any Iraqi troops remaining on Iranian soil, and the release of prisoners of war. The Iranian government reacted positively, and although President Rafsanjani maintained that Iraq must withdraw from Kuwait and that the UN sanctions would be applied, it became clear within the next few weeks that Iraq no longer had to worry about an enemy on its eastern flank.

The third element introduced by Iraq was the taking of hostages. Although they were referred to as 'guests', 'detainees' or otherwise, the thousands of Westerners, Japanese, Soviets, and others who were prevented from leaving Kuwait or Iraq, were certainly used as hostages. On 17 August the Speaker of the Iraqi National Assembly announced that 'the people of Iraq have decided to play host to the citizens of these aggressive nations as long as Iraq remains threatened with an aggressive war'. In a speech two days later, Saddam confirmed this effective internment and indicated that these 'guests' would be placed near strategic installations to deter attack.[126] Gradual releases of women, children and some others did not affect the basic nature of this strategy.

At the same time, however, it became apparent that it would not substantially weaken the international community's determination to bring Iraq to heel.

The final new element to be highlighted here, is the effective break-up of the Arab League. Following the vote on 10 August to send troops to Saudi Arabia, the Arab states were essentially split into those twelve who had supported the move, and those who had not. This became evident in a number of ways. A further Arab League Foreign Ministers' meeting at the end of August was attended only by the twelve (plus a Libyan representative), and the resolution which resulted (condemning Iraq and holding it responsible for any damages and losses to Kuwait) was passed by the same twelve. On 3 September Chadli Klibi, the Tunisian Secretary-General of the League, resigned, and later that month the League's ambassador to the United States and the United Nations, the Lebanese Clovis Maksoud, also resigned. And on 10 September, the 'twelve' decided to go ahead, as had been planned well before the crisis, with moving the League's headquarters from Tunisia back to Cairo—notwithstanding a boycott by Tunisia, Iraq, Libya, Algeria, Jordan, Sudan, Yemen, Mauritania, and the PLO.[127]

Whatever else happens, Arab politics will never be the same. This is illustrated by the difference in post-invasion behaviour between the three main Arab groupings—the Gulf Cooperation Council (GCC), the Arab Cooperation Council (ACC), and the Arab Maghreb Union (AMU)—but perhaps even more dramatically so by the developments within each of these blocs. The GCC was forced into a redefinition of its own role, strengths and weaknesses; from the AMU there were as many initial reactions as there were member states; and the ACC for all practical purposes ceased to exist. Iran's position and potential role in the Gulf region, moreover, has undergone a major transformation. More specifically, in the relationship between Iraq and the remaining monarchical systems of the Gulf a drastic break with the past was made. The Gulf states and especially Saudi Arabia, showed themselves increasingly decisive in their stand against the invasion and its perpetrator, the Iraqi regime. As related earlier, initial caution was soon followed by energetic Saudi action to obtain Arab condemnation of Iraq. Nevertheless, the speech by King Fahd on 9 August was still a departure from previously established norms of diplomacy and consensus-seeking in the Arab arena. For the first time, too, the press was given free rein to attack the Iraqi president. Calling in US troops—and moreover against another Arab state—was, of course, the most dramatic break with established policy. Against the expectations of many observers, the Kingdom did cut Iraq's oil exports, raising its own production to help the world cope with the shortfall, knowing that both acts were equated with aggression by Saddam Hussein. This illustrates, however (as did the firm support given to Iraq during the Gulf War) that when it comes to the crunch, the usually slow, cautious and even indecisive Saudi foreign policy-making system *does* have the capacity to take difficult decisions and follow them through. Iraq's response will only have reinforced the determination in Riyadh and to a less outspoken extent in the other Gulf capitals to stand up to Saddam Hussein and not to give him the benefit of the doubt in future. On the day that the Arab League resolved to send troops to the Kingdom, the Iraqi President discarded the hitherto valid trappings of Arab inter-state politics, by appealing directly to the peoples of the Arab world over the heads of their governments. By calling on them to 'rebel against all efforts to humiliate Mecca' he was, in effect, urging the overthrow of the regimes aligned against him—first and foremost those of Saudi Arabia and Egypt.

All this was taking place in the context of what already amounted to a new world order—though not quite yet the order variously envisaged by 'East' and 'West'. The very fact that it made little sense any more to use these terms indicates how dramatically the state of international relations had changed by the time Saddam decided to swallow Kuwait. In turn, the Kuwaiti crisis served as an additional catalyst bringing Washington and Moscow closer together; this was evident in the early joint declaration, in the unopposed UN Security Council resolutions, and in official Soviet approval of the American deployment in the Gulf. The other obvious background factor—i.e., soaring oil prices that reached $40/b by the end of September—had not, by the time of writing, dented the international community's determination to turn back the Iraqi aggression.

As a consequence, the incidence of 'sanctions-busting' was very low. Few countries were prepared to risk becoming pariahs themselves, and this was also valid for Iran, Jordan and Yemen. The services of unofficial middlemen and smugglers were, on the whole, far too expensive to provide any significant relief for an Iraq which had increasingly little with which to pay them. Thus with virtually no exports and and increasingly scarce imports, Iraq was likely to suffer soon. Domestic agriculture was not able to produce enough for the Iraqis' own needs, and most foodstuffs were stockpiled for periods of between three and six months. Industry relied on foreign inputs of technology, spare parts and chemicals. Construction and public infra-structure was similarly dependent, often dependent on the services of many foreign experts. And the armed forces themselves relied on foreign suppliers for most of their requirements and for a continued supply of spare parts and even, for example, items like textiles for uniforms and tents (from Turkey).

The international community, then, appeared to be using its opportunities wisely, pulling the net of sanctions ever tighter, yet at the same time showing flexibility. Humanitarian food supplies were excepted from the embargo. Even the American and British leadership began increasingly to stress that a peaceful solution was preferable and that economic sanctions would be given a fair chance (although without going back on the principle that force would have to be used if nothing else worked). Simultaneously, more signals were being sent that something needed to be done about the Palestine issue. Landmarks in this respect were the speeches by President Mitterrand of France to the UN General Assembly on 24 September, President Bush's speech on 1 October, and the proposal from Douglas Hurd, British Foreign Secretary, on 4 October to convene a Middle East Peace Conference with the UN Security Council once Iraq had withdrawn. The killing by Israeli security forces of 21 Palestinians around the Aqsa mosque in Jerusalem on 8 October could have provided Saddam Hussein with a propaganda coup as he continued to whip up Arab feeling against the 'US-Zionist conspiracy'. Instead, the UN Security Council passed a unanimous resolution that condemned Israel for its involvement, and the Secretary-General was instructed to send a fact-finding mission to report back to the Council (14 October 1990).

WATERSHED: FROM SCR 678 TO 16 JANUARY 1991[128]

The debate on what happened next will continue for a long time to come. Late on 16 January 1991 a coalition of international forces led by the United States unleashed a massive military operation against Iraq, forty-six days after the initial UN decision to allow the use of force had been taken. Following considerable diplomatic efforts and cajoling, America and Britain had succeeded (just before the end of America's term in the presidency of the Security Council) in persuading their key fellow-members to support a resolution that set a deadline for Iraq to implement previous Security Council resolutions, after which members states would be entitled to use 'any means necessary' to undo Iraq's occupation of Kuwait. Resolution 678 of 29 November 1990, with only Yemen and Cuba voting against and China abstaining, had set that date at 15 January 1991.

The following day, President Bush proposed to Iraq that the Iraqi Foreign Minister Tariq Aziz should visit him in Washington while the US Secretary of State, James Baker, would go to Baghdad to meet

Saddam Hussein. This represented a major move on America's part, since previous suggestions that there should be talks *before* Iraq had commited itself to a complete and unconditional withdrawal had always been dismissed by the West and its allies. Baghdad indicated agreement to the principle, but delayed in suggesting any date for the Baker visit. Meanwhile, Saddam Hussein anounced on 6 December that all foreign hostages would be released unconditionally. Three days later, the date for the Baker-Saddam talks which the Iraqi government had at last set at 12 January 1991, was rejected by Washington as too close to the UN deadline: the delay of more than a month would mean that observance of Resolution 678 would *de facto* become impossible. However, Baghdad remained adamant, and Tariq Aziz's visit to Washington consequently fell through as well.

While peace efforts continued to be made by officials as well as individuals and other groups from various countries, Iraqi statements reiterated that Kuwait would remain part of Iraq. On Christmas Eve Saddam Hussein made the explicit threat that if Iraq were attacked Israel would be the first target. In this increasingly tense context, and in response to concerns expressed in sections of the US Administration, in European nations and in much of the Arab and Third World that Iraq should be left a ladder to climb down, President Bush proposed on 3 January that James Baker and Tariq Aziz should meet in Geneva on 9 January. This time the Iraqi side accepted. Baker carried a letter to the meeting from President Bush to Saddam Hussein that enlarged upon the message that he himself was conveying to the Iraqi Foreign Minister—*viz.* that withdrawal from Kuwait was an absolute condition for lifting the pressure on Iraq, and that the anti-Iraq alliance was prepared to use massive force if necessary. In the event and contrary to expectation, the meeting lasted over six hours, indicating that the US delegation did try to probe the real, or potential, intentions underlying Iraq's public stance. However, the Iraqi side apparently was unable to give any substantial indications that the Security Council Resolutions might be implemented; the talks consequently failed.

A final attempt was made by the UN Secretary-General, Javier Perez de Cuellar, who travelled to Baghdad on 13 January. Not only was he treated with an ostentatious lack of respect (being kept waiting for hours, for instance), but the talks themselves fared no better, and he could only indicate afterwards that he had lost any hope he might have had. Subsequent attempts by a number of countries including France to sway the Iraqi leadership were left unanswered while Iraq reiterated its determination to keep Kuwait.

Less than 24 hours after the deadline had passed—at 11 pm GMT on 16 January—Operation Desert Storm was launched.

SADDAM'S MIND

What was it that impelled the Iraqi president to risk not only the tearing apart of a diplomatic strategy carefully pursued over 15 years, which would involve confrontation with the world community, and with US firepower in particular, but also economic and possibly political ruin? Clearly, his move was based on a massive miscalculation, itself a startling departure from his previous astute manipulation of the regional and international scene.

The areas of friction with Kuwait, described earlier, certainly had explosive potential, made worse by Iraq's extremely difficult financial position: there was an urgent need for foreign exchange. Yet as we have argued, these factors by themselves could not have been expected to result in invasion and annexation. Other factors played a part.

First, the Iraqi regime faced increasing dissatisfaction among its own population. The system had never been actively embraced by the Iraqi people, but a combination of repression, foreign policy posturing, the threat from Iran, and economic performance, succeeded in keeping Saddam in the saddle. With the cease-fire in the Gulf War, Iraqis had expected an improvement in their material well-being following the years of belt-tightening. Instead, the new economic policy led to rising prices, while the financial burdens of servicing the country's estimated $80 million debt, of rebuilding the economic infrastructure and the armed forces, and of paying for the self-aggrandising projects which Saddam did not want to forgo, left the government very little with which to provide affordable food and consumer goods. The move against Kuwait—rich, weak, and considered selfish by many Arabs—offered a diversion from the Iraqis' preoccupation with their own lot. At the same time Saddam Hussein's accusation that Kuwait had in effect stolen many billions of dollars' worth of oil and revenues from Iraq, was a convenient way of offering people a scapegoat for their everyday difficulties. The political importance of gaining access to the Kuwaiti treasury funds in order to help soften the domestic situation needs no elaboration.

The second issue was that of the army which had still not been demobilised. How does one reintegrate almost a million soldiers into normal life, especially if the wherewithal to smooth the process is lacking? If it is decided that this process must be postponed, or done very gradually, how are these men to be kept occupied and under control? Again, the Kuwait adventure could serve well in this respect, especially as soldiers could expect to return with the odd consumer item, such as confiscated cars.

Thirdly, by controlling Kuwait, or at least its northern area, access to the Gulf would be secured, and Iraq's failure to extract concessions from Iran over the Shatt al-Arab (the main cause of the Gulf War) could be camouflaged.

The signals sent by the West are also likely to have played a role. Saddam Hussein's increasingly aggressive rhetoric was not firmly rebuffed in the West. Until the direct threats to the Gulf states from 30 May onwards, it was perfectly reasonable to interpret such rhetoric essentially as playing to the gallery. Certainly, after the Iraqi memorandum to the Arab League on 15 July, this was no longer true and the subsequent concentration of troops on Kuwait's border, although potentially no more than sabre-rattling, clearly did require unmistakable signals to Baghdad that any further aggressive moves would be countered with determination. In this respect, the now infamous interview between the American ambassador April Glaspie and Saddam Hussein on 25 July may have been the 'fatal sign of American weakness that tempted him over the brink', as *The Economist* interpreted the view of some observers. According to the Iraqi transcript of the interview (the US State Department did not release its own version), the meeting was amicable, with Glaspie suggesting that the Iraqi President appear on US television to make Americans understand Iraq better. She then enquired—'in a spirit of friendliness, not of confrontation'—about the reason for the troop movements. In reply, Saddam Hussein referred to his conversation with the Egyptian President: he had, he said, finalised the arrangements for the Iraqi-Kuwaiti meeting in Jeddah and had promised that he would

> not do anything until we meet with [the Kuwaitis]. When we meet and when we see that there is hope, then nothing will happen. But if we are unable to find a solution, then it will be natural that Iraq will not accept death.[129]

Although this was hardly reassuring, Mrs Glaspie appeared to consider the reply sufficient (nor have the Americans even questioned the content of the Iraqi transcript). The ambassador's message, then, was clearly not the one called for.

However, there was a fifth and crucial factor: Saddam Hussein's own perception of reality, the world, and his own place therein. With hindsight, the evidence of Iraq's domestic scene might have led one to expect that he could at any moment, particularly when under the pressures described above, leave the bounds of pragmatic rationality in international affairs (see the discussion in Chapter 2). The invasion was a sign that the Iraqi president had transferred his perception of his own role in Iraq's history (the 'necessary leader' with his three-fold unique ability) to the regional scene; the problem was that he had also transferred his belief that anyone who crossed his designs in any way was betraying the lofty aims which history, aided by his guidance, had in store for Iraq and the Arab world. Any sign of dissent or questioning on the part of those who did not have his insights, was both offensive and an offence. This is well illustrated by the wording of Iraq's attacks on Kuwait in the President's May speech and the subsequent letters to the Arab League: their complete intemperateness, the equating of a straightforward inter-state dispute with military aggression, and the glaring assumption that it was the duty of any of the other Arab recipients of the messages to take Iraq's side (not to mention the negotiating stance that the Kuwaitis had to be serious about satisfying Iraq's demands)—all these factors showed Saddam Hussein playing Iraqi politics outside his own borders. And with it, he showed that his megalomania had finally caught up with his undoubted shrewdness and adaptability.

The argument has since been put forward that perhaps the move *was* calculated rationally. The suggestion then is that Saddam Hussein would have planned all along to overthrow the present state system, to derive his support directly from the people, and therefore to emerge as the Leader of the Arab world without the need to have recourse to the methods of his previous diplomacy. Even if this were true, it would have been at best an enormous gamble—without an escape route. That it is no more than a spurious *post-factum* rationalisation is indicated by the fact that well after the invasion, the Iraqi President was still trying to use the old channels and institutions to obtain support or acquiescence among the other Arab states; moreover, until 6 August he was still calling for 'normal relations' with the US. Only when it became clear that the GCC, the majority of members of the Arab League, and the international community at large were determined to oppose him, did he turn to his new strategy.

Saddam Hussein did not envisage the total opposition that his take-over of Kuwait would encounter both regionally and in the world at large. Nor did he realise how his designs for an increased role for Iraq in the Arab and the non-aligned world, along with access to arms, technology and consumer goods from East and West, would as a result be destroyed. While he was no doubt counting on the other Arab leaders' fear of confronting him, Saddam Hussein also looked to the quasi-alliance which had come into being with the ACC, and to the non-agression pacts with Saudi Arabia and Bahrain that had recently been signed. But there was little reason to suppose that any of these governments would have felt bound by such agreements and understandings, after Saddam himself had trampled on many of the most important principles that underpinned the existing Arab system (not to mention the broken promise made to President Mubarak shortly before the invasion, that he would not use military force).

By his actions, the Iraqi President lost the option to use—as a basis for legitimisation or suport—either United Nations or Arab League rules of conduct, or the principles that were set out in his own National Charter for the Arab States. He lost any reliable allies in the event of any future conflict with Iran, and he risked direct confrontation with both of the superpowers. The expected economic benefits did not materialise—rather, the reverse was true. Nor was there much probability of a general collapse of the regimes opposed to him taking place before his own time ran out. This assessment confirms that Saddam Hussein, like so many dictators before him, had indeed taken his leave of reality. Both the origins and the consequences of this development were in no small measure due to the power structure in the Iraqi polity. Since no-one around him had either the position or the inclination to confront him with this reality (see Chapter 2), the international community had no other sound option but to treat him as dangerously unpredictable. This was the case *a fortiori* for the regional states.

The new Saudi foreign policy posture was one sign that this had been recognised. Iraqi-Gulf relations had thus come full circle, and subversion was again the order of the day. Contrary to the position two decades previously, however, no Iraqi regime that contained Saddam Hussein or any of his major allies could now hope to regain the lost trust of the Gulf states. In future, any words or diplomacy that are used will be devoid of credibility. It should be stressed that in large measure this also applies to the attitudes of those Arab states which stayed outside the group of twelve: nowhere will the present regime's assurances be taken at face value any more.

Whatever course military action takes, Saddam Hussein (and consequently his regime) is likely to suffer gravely, or even to be defeated altogether, by a combination of domestic, regional and international factors—if not immediately, then very probably in the medium term. In the Gulf itself, as in Egypt or Morocco, opposition to the Western military presence was not of a breadth or depth to bring about the fall of these regimes. At the time of writing, regimes elsewhere, except perhaps in Syria, were taking an attitude that was sufficiently flexible to avoid the risk of a major popular revolt (without, however, condoning Iraq's actions): none of them was, or was likely to become, an actual ally to the regime in Baghdad. The option of attacking Israel as a way of 'regionalising' the crisis in Iraq's favour, did remain open, but the impact of missile attacks in the course of the first month of fighting was limited in both military and political terms—even though Saddam derived a symbolic 'honour' from it in some Arab and Muslim quarters.

4 THE MILITARY BALANCE IN THE GULF: ONE STEP FORWARD TWO STEPS BACK

Armed conflict, which was the most prominent form of inter-state politics in the Gulf in the 1980s, is in many ways history's ironic reply to the constant accumulation by the Gulf states over the preceding decade of ever more sophisticated weaponry. The war now terminated between the neighbouring countries of Iran and Iraq was the product *par excellence* of 'hot politics' as opposed to 'cold war', and while it lasted, it continually undermined political stability in the entire Gulf region. It can be argued that since the cease-fire the after-effects of that conflict have fuelled inter-state competition and politico-economic uncertainties to such an extent that they have drawn virtually all the Gulf states into a new crisis, bringing about the large scale military intervention of the dominant international actors in this region.

But the condition of 'no war-no peace' which prevailed between Iran and Iraq from July 1988 to September 1990, and which was perhaps more restrained than cold war, ought to have given little cause for comfort, since, as became obvious with the Iraqi invasion of Kuwait in August 1990, it was an equation that could degenerate easily and perhaps irredeemably into a 'war-no peace' situation between Iraq and other Gulf states in addition to Iran, and this time with the inevitable involvement of the superpowers and other regional and global actors. In these circumstances, the pressures to militarise, to re-arm and to modernise are as great as in the course of any actual conflict. The Iraqi invasion of Kuwait has accelerated the process of militarisation and sophisticated arms procurement in the Gulf to such an extent that even as the drama of the 'new' Gulf crisis was unfolding, major new multi-billion dollar arms deals between Saudi Arabia and its Gulf allies and the industrialised countries were being finalised.

The military balance in the Gulf—that is, the kind, the quantity, the variety and the quality of military hardware at the disposal of the Gulf belligerents—is a crucial component in assessing the security environment of any given situation. But it also has special significance, given the crisis that has resulted from the Iraqi invasion of Kuwait, and the dilemmas facing all the parties affected by the crisis. Sometimes of even more importance than the military hardware deployed at any one time, however, are the qualitative factors that also affect the military balance. Besides battle experience, a determining factor in many circumstances, there are elements within the geopolitical, ideological, political and socio-economic realm—that is, the strategic and geostrategic environments—which both assist and hinder the play of forces in their military habitat. An analysis of a combination of the military and geostrategic balances gives us a fairly full picture of the contemporary balance of power in the Gulf—an area rich in vital mineral resources, marked by ideological diversities, and quite central to the security calculations of the great and major powers alike. A concise presentation of the factors determining the balance of power in the Gulf over the past decade and now will therefore enable us to look into the crystal ball of the 1990s with a little more confidence, and perhaps allow the brave to make more intelligent guesses as to the medium-term future of the Gulf.

Geopolitics and military power in the Gulf

On the eve of the Iranian revolution two military machines dominated the Gulf region, as Table 4.1 shows: the Imperial Iranian Armed Forces and the Armed Forces of the Arab Socialist Republic of Iraq. For most of the 1960s and 1970s, and while the Soviet Union was grooming Iraq to be its power broker in the Gulf, the Western camp (led by the United States) was busy consolidating its position by continually strengthening the Iranian-Saudi Arabian 'Twin pillars'. This 'dual' Western policy, enhanced by the greater oil revenues accruing to these states in the 1970s, introduced—perhaps inadvertently—a structural element of competition into the bilateral relationship: the ruling elites of Tehran and Riyadh were encouraged by this to bid for relative supremacy (i.e., among the three Gulf powers) as well as for absolute supremacy (i.e., between each other) within the same theatre. The three Gulf powers of Iran, Iraq and Saudi Arabia thus gradually narrowed their geopolitical vision—and with it their respective definition of the 'national interest'—in consort with the established rubric of great power politics and prevailing global (zero-sum) superpower security considerations. Even Iran's grandiose vision of dominating the Arabian Sea region and of playing the counter-weight role to India in South Asia, were functions of the Imperial Army's unchallenged authority in the region on one level, and of Tehran's strategic interests in being supreme ruler in the Gulf on another.

THE MILITARY BALANCE IN THE GULF

TABLE 4.1   The military balance in the Gulf, 1978–88

	1978	1980	1982	1984	1986	1988
Combat Aircraft						
Iran	459	445	95	80	60	50
Iraq	339	332	330	500	500	500
S. Arabia	171	136	128	205	226	182
GCC	—	—	248	392	459	382
Tanks						
Iran	1870	1985	1210	1950	1000	1000
Iraq	1800	2850	2400	4000	4500	4500
S. Arabia	325	380	450	450	550	550
GCC	—	—	910	989	1155	1170
Major Naval Craft						
Iran						
A	3	3	3	3	3	1
B	4	4	4	4	4	2
Iraq						
A	—	—	—	—	—	—
B	—	—	1	1	5	5
S. Arabia						
A	—	—	—	—	—	—
B	—	—	—	4	4	8
GCC						
A	—	—	—	—	—	—
B	—	—	—	4	4	8

Source: Based on IISS, *The Military Balance* (London, various years).
Note: A = Destroyers; B = Frigates.

Likewise, Saudi Arabia has traditionally viewed itself primarily as a Gulf state, and until recently has shown little politico-military interest in developing its Levant or East African (Red Sea) roles. Incidentally, it is the only Middle Eastern state that has a geographical claim on all three important Middle Eastern theatres of conflict. It would therefore be easy to subsume Saudi Arabia into one, or a combination, of the Arab-Israeli, the Iran-Iraq (and/or Iraq-GCC) or the Horn of Africa conflicts. The fact that the Gulf Cooperation Council is by name and nature an exclusively Gulf Arab regional body merely underlines the Saudi perception of the Kingdom as being first and foremost a Gulf state, and also indicates the importance that Saudi Arabia attaches to the Gulf region for its national security.

Paradoxically, Riyadh's increased interest in its western borders in the 1980s can be attributed directly to the politico-military tensions in the Gulf. The prolonged 'tanker war' in the Gulf compelled the belligerents, as well as almost all the other Gulf states, to look for alternative routes to the Strait of Hormuz for the export of their petroleum—and, if practicable, for the importation of industrial and consumer goods as well. Iran, for instance, planned a pipeline system that would deliver Iranian crude to newly-constructed export installations along its Gulf of Oman coastline, and eagerly pursued discussions with Turkey and the USSR for the use of their territories (and facilities) for oil exports. The Iran-Iraq War underlined the importance of the Petroline pipeline (capacity 3.2 million b/d) that connects Saudi Arabia's Eastern Province to its Red Sea loading terminal at Yanbu (and, in this context, also shows the significance of the maritime dimension of the war), thus compelling Riyadh to develop a more balanced geopolitical perspective of the Kingdom's role.[1] While it provided a safe exit route for Saudi, Iraqi and Kuwaiti oil during the war, this pipeline network has been the catalyst uniting the two shorelines of the Saudi state into a single security equation. The linking of Saudi Arabia's strategic vulnerabilities in the east with the threats to its security in the west has led to the integration (and expansion) of its security calculations, and has had a direct influence on the military balance in the Gulf.[2]

The gradual spread of Saudi Arabia's industries to its Red Sea coast—which, it must be said, was partly an indicator of the endemic insecurities in the Gulf, and the direct economic linkages that were being created between the Gulf and the Red Sea, meant that the Saudi navy needed a higher profile in the latter region. The increased significance of the Saudi industrial capacity in the west on the one hand, and the emergence of the Red Sea region in general as an area of major international strategic as well as of growing economic importance on the other, has made the modernisation and strengthening of the Kingdom's Western Fleet—in line with the already well-equipped Eastern (Gulf) Fleet—a major priority. But the advantage to be derived from possessing numerous naval facilities (in the two international 'hot spots' of the Gulf and the Horn of Africa) is squarely matched by the increase in target vulnerabilities. Saudi Arabia's high territory-to-population ratio means that if its military forces are spread too thinly on the ground, monumental security vacuums are created. In purely military terms, therefore, the Kingdom is caught between its exogenous strategic strengths and its indigenous demographic weaknesses. Until this imbalance is addressed and corrected, the benefits to the Kingdom of its rapid military build-up during the 1980s will remain in question. And needless to say, the greater the emphasis on technology-intensive firepower and defence systems as a way of compensating for the inadequate supply of personnel, the more deep-rooted and structural the involvement of 'imported' technical staff and operational personnel will become for the maintenance and use of the accumulated systems.[3] Secondly, the coming to life of the Red Sea theatre has brought closer other geopolitical vulnerabilities that affect the Kingdom's standing in the Gulf. The increased strategic significance of the Red Sea region to the superpowers has resulted in a hardening of regional and extra-regional attitudes towards politico-military and ideological state orientation there. Accordingly, while Riyadh may legitimately be preoccupied with assessing the impact on its interests in the Red Sea of military developments in Israel, its major Western ally—the US—would be more interested in focusing attention on the Soviet Union's close ties with the states around the Bab al-Mandab choke-point; Ethiopia and Yemen. The crucial role of Ethiopia, and, until recently, of the PDRY in guaranteeing a viable Soviet presence in the Red Sea and East African/Indian Ocean regions cannot be over-emphasised. This is all the more so in the context of the following:

—the significance of the Red Sea as an alternative maritime passageway (to the NATO-guarded Strait of Gibraltar) for the Soviet Union;

—the pro-Western domination of the Suez canal region as the most immediate gateway to the Mediterranean (and the Black Sea);

—the formalisation of politico-military ties between three of the Red Sea resident countries (Egypt, Jordan and Yemen) in yet another politically-moderate and objectively pro-Western regional organisation;

—the presence of two staunchly pro-Western countries (Somalia and Djibouti) in the Bab al-Mandab area;

—the permanent US military presence on the island of Diego Garcia which puts a premium on any regionally-based Soviet naval access to the Indian Ocean—as facilitated by the Yemeni island of Socotra;

—the Soviet-assisted growth and expansion of the Indian army and the USSR's impressive naval expansion in the Indian Ocean in the last five years which has turned India—a close Soviet friend—into an important regional superpower, whose firepower now represents a potential threat to Western interests there. The Soviet Union, therefore, needs to remain close to the 'action' in the Indian Ocean, as well as to its long-term military and strategic investments in India;

—the importance of the Red Sea region to the US Central Command's contingency plans to mobilise thousands of troops and huge quantities of military equipment across the Levant and the Red Sea regions to meet any actual or perceived threats to Western interests in the Gulf, which means that a Soviet presence there is almost automatic.[4]

Significantly, while the tensions arising out of the situations prevailing in Ethiopia and the Horn of Africa can be easily fitted within the US-USSR confrontational framework, Riyadh and Washington diverge over how to formulate the threat that Israel poses to the Kingdom. Riyadh regards the threat from Israel as strategic, based on the imperatives of the on-going Arab-Israeli conflict and an Israeli military superiority with regard to individual Arab states, while the United States sees little cause for alarm as it eagerly—and in accordance with the requirements of the Central Command—'bunches together' Egypt, Israel, Jordan and Saudi Arabia in an attempt to form an unbroken security chain from the Mediterranean (and the Red Sea) to the heart of the Gulf. So, although America may regard the Israeli military presence in the Red Sea and the Horn of Africa as an asset, Riyadh will probably continue to view it with concern. Paradoxically, and based on other experiences (such as the 1981 bombing of the Iraqi nuclear reactor, the 1985 air raid on the PLO headquarters in Tunis, and the numerous attacks on Lebanese targets), the higher the level that they attain in military sophistication and preparedness, the more vulnerable the Saudis will feel to pre-emptive Israeli attacks. Israel's threats to neutralise Saudi Arabia's recently acquired long-range surface-to-surface missiles from China, and Riyadh's low-key justification for their deployment (which was stated to be solely in the Gulf region), clearly illustrate the latent tensions existing between Israel and its Levant neighbours, and the way in which more modern and dangerous weapons, in the process, can pose unforeseen multi-dimensional threats to non-belligerents. Thus, if questions of manpower and of the diversification of targets and possible aggressors are the primary influences on the Kingdom's military presence in the Gulf, other issues concern the potential divergence of interests between the US and Saudi Arabia over developments in the Red Sea and the Israeli military presence there.

THE MILITARY BALANCE IN THE GULF

Looking back, it is possible to discern in the late 1970s, the emergence of a three-way military tussle—rather than a stable 'balance of power' situation—between Iran, Iraq and Saudi Arabia, that could ultimately have undermined the stability of the other Gulf littoral states and disrupted the profitable *status quo* on which the two great powers and the major allies alike were capitalising. But the Iranian revolution and the overthrow of the Pahlavi regime in early 1979, the Soviet intervention in Afghanistan in late 1979, and the start of the Iran-Iraq War in 1980 halted this process, altering considerably the balance of forces in the Gulf, and inevitably transforming the landscape of local competition in the entire area.

Arms transfers and the military build-up in the Gulf

In terms of the actual transfer of arms to these three local powers in the 1970s, competition was squarely at the superpower level: Iran relied heavily and Saudi Arabia almost exclusively on the US, while Iraq relied most heavily on the Soviet Union. But European countries too were actively developing a market niche for themselves, and French, British, Italian, Czech, East and West German arms were routinely purchased by either or both Iran and Iraq, while the smaller Gulf states purchased some Western European weapons. Before the Iranian revolution, for example, while Britain was capitalising on its good relations with the Shah, France was seeking a new market for its sophisticated weapons in Iraq and the expansion of military ties with the smaller Gulf states. Thus in a sense, the experiences of the oil-boom years and the well-established ties between the major Gulf states and the important European arms suppliers served inadvertently to place the European Community's two prominent arms manufacturing countries—France and Britain—on opposing sides in a (regional) South-South conflict; this conflict had the potential not only severely to disrupt the general economic recovery of the leading advanced capitalist and newly-industrialising countries during the 1980s, and to compromise vital Western interests in a region as crucial to NATO as the European landmass itself, but also to affect adversely the Community's own fast-moving economic and political unification plans.

Although they were relatively junior partners of the major Gulf states during the 1970s, the presence of the European arms suppliers in the region symbolised the changing military relationships that were to become the hallmark of the 1980s and beyond. The military balance has, therefore, been transformed in ways that were not wholly unexpected during the 'oil decade' but which are certainly surprising as

TABLE 4.2 Value of arms transfers to the Gulf states, cumulative 1979–83 and 1982–86 ($mn)

Total	USSR	US	Fr	UK	FRG	PRC	Pol	Czech	Other
Iraq									
A 17,620	7,200	—	3,800	280	140	1,500	850	40	3,810
B 31,740	15,300	—	4,500	70	625	3,300	525	410	7,010
Saudi Arabia									
A 12,125	—	5,100	2,500	1,900	525	—	—	—	2,100
B 16,715	—	6,100	6,800	1,200	90	—	—	—	2,525
Iran									
A 5,365	975	1,200	20	140	5	230	40	—	2,755
B 8,405	240	10	40	80	—	1,200	20	30	6,785
Kuwait									
A 450	30	180	—	50	70	—	—	—	120
B 1,120	220	230	420	20	210	—	—	—	20
Oman									
A 565	—	80	20	430	—	5	—	—	30
B 890	—	70	30	525	240	5	—	—	20
Qatar									
A 765	—	10	40	310	—	—	—	—	5
B 830	—	10	650	160	—	—	—	—	10
UAE									
A 620	—	20	350	90	110	—	—	—	50
B 380	—	90	—	210	—	—	—	—	80

Bahrain							
A	120	—	10	40	—	—	30
B	135	—	70	10	5	—	10
GCC							
A	14,645	30	5,400	3,350	2,780	745	2,335
B	20,070	220	6,570	7,910	2,120	580	2,665

Source: US ACDA, *World Military Expenditures and Arms Transfers 1984 and 1987* (Washington, DC, 1984 and 1987).

Notes: The GCC figures are the authors' calculations.

The figures mentioned in this table exclude a number of significant arms transfers to Saudi Arabia, Iran and Kuwait. Since these data were compiled, Saudi Arabia has made four significant arms deals: (i) the $8 billion Anglo-Saudi al-Yamamah I of 1986; (ii) the $3.3 billion deal with China for the transfer of 60 or so CSS-2 SSMs; (iii) the 1988 $25 billion Anglo-Saudi al-Yamamah II deal, and; (iv) the 1990 $21.5 billion US-Saudi arms deal. Kuwait meanwhile had concluded a $2 billion deal in 1988 with the US. Iran had already received a consignment of weapons from China worth about $2 billion in 1987-88, and another $4 billion agreement for the supply of modern Chinese arms was reached in 1990. Iran's largest arms deal with the USSR, worth more than $2 billion was reached in 1989 after the cease-fire with Iraq.

far as the current balance sheet and future projections are concerned. Indeed, the relentless and simultaneous arming of the two adversaries throughout the Iran-Iraq War by the established arms-manufacturing and exporting countries as well as by the increasing number of Third World suppliers, is a sign of our times: we have the era of horizontal proliferation of arms industries in the world, accompanied also, and for the first time, by a definite vertical movement. In other words, not only has the number of supplier countries increased dramatically in the last 15 years, but so too have the variety and quality of military hardware indigenously developed, produced and offered for export.[5] The Iran-Iraq War provided an unprecedented market and a launching platform for many of these budding arms exporters as they attempted not only to consolidate their reputations and their positions internationally, and, of course, to pursue the logical strategy of obtaining badly needed foreign revenues for further research in the military field, but also to gain access to cheaper oil—or extra foreign currency—as a means of alleviating the burden of international debt repayments.

As will be seen later, the pattern of arms transfers changed. Initially this was at the expense of the superpowers, as the industrial countries of Europe expanded their exports to the littoral states, and was soon followed by the position of the many Third World arms producers who competed with both the superpowers and their European allies. This process has given the major Gulf states a perceptibly higher level of diplomatic leverage in their extra-regional relations, ultimately enabling just about all the Gulf purchasers to be allowed even more 'preferential' treatment.

The revolution of 1979 and the subsequent war undoubtedly took their toll of Iran's military prowess. During the course of the conflict—and particularly in the last three years of the fighting—the country's powerful and well-equipped armed forces were depleted at an alarming rate, which culminated in the loss of some $2 billion worth of military hardware to the opposition National Liberation Army (NLA) in 1988,[6] defeat in naval battles in the Gulf at the hands of the 'resident' US Navy there, and a general decline in firepower and equipment sophistication as the source of its weaponry shifted from the traditional Western (mainly American) suppliers and moved Eastwards and Southwards.[7]

Iraq and Saudi Arabia, on the other hand, have diversified the origins of their military supplies, and have at the same time significantly improved the quality of firepower at the disposal of their armed forces. The transfer in the course of the 1980s of the advanced air-superior and interdictor Tornadoes and F-15 fighters to Saudi Arabia, and of the

TABLE 4.3 Defence expenditures of Iran, Iraq and Saudi Arabia, selected years, ($mn)

	1968	1970	1972	1974	1976	1978	1979	1980
Iran	495	779	926	5,500	9,500	9,938	3,974	2,736
Iraq	252	294	310	2,701	1,417	1,988	2,328	7,051
S. Ar.	321	387	941	1,808	9,038	10,355	14,184	14,444

Source: IISS, The Military Balance (various years).

latest Soviet-made MiG-29 fighters, Su-25 attack aircraft and Dassault-Breguet Mirage F-1 and Super Etendard fighters to Iraq, epitomise this trend.[8] Saudi Arabia, of course, utilising its five AWACS aircraft, has created a complex system of ground-based and airborne early warning and defensive measures (command, control, communications and intelligence—C^3I) to complement its increased firepower.

The political turmoil of the 1970s and the military uncertainties of the 1980s in the Gulf induced similar patterns of arms procurement in the smaller Gulf Arab states. In the increasingly important field of airpower and airborne force projection, the US-Kuwaiti agreement in 1988 to transfer the advanced McDonnell-Douglas F/A-18 fighters and accompanying Maverick G anti-ship and Harpoon and Sidewinder missiles to Kuwait has been the most dramatic purchase from amongst the smaller GCC countries, somewhat overshadowing the equally significant airpower purchases of the other members. The Kuwaiti and Qatari purchases of the Mirage F-1, for instance, have been matched by Abu Dhabi's acquisition of the Mirage 2000 fighter (delivery was halted for a time because of differences, now apparently resolved, over the aircraft's avionics and airborne weapons specifications), and by Bahrain's purchases of the General Dynamics F-16 fighter and Oman's ordering of the Tornado (later cancelled and replaced with an order for the BAe-manufactured Hawk jet trainer/light fighter).[9]

Thus we see that in the military realm, four processes were occurring simultaneously:

(i) the size of Iraq's armed forces was greatly increased in the 1980s, and the quality of military equipment at the forces' disposal was improved to such an extent that the Iraqi army was now comparable to those of Israel, Egypt and Syria. Indeed it was second only to the Israeli defence Force in overall sophistication and military readiness. In addition, it remained the only Gulf Arab army with extensive offensive and defensive battle experience;

(ii) Saudi Arabia and the other GCC states increased the rate of incoming weapons transfers in absolute terms in the 1980s, and, in the process of diversifying their suppliers, raised the level of sophistication in their general procurements;

(iii) Iran's armed forces suffered in absolute and in relative terms as the depletion rate, the formidable black and grey arms market prices and the Western arms embargo began to bite. So, just as its Arab neighbours were improving the quality and quantity of weapons in their armouries in the 1980s, Iran was being forced to accept 'second best' by relying heavily, and increasingly, on older Soviet-bloc arms and military equipment originating in China, North Korea, Vietnam, Libya and Syria;

(iv) the two Gulf War protagonists, Iran and Iraq, still distantly followed by Saudi Arabia, invested heavily in military R&D and indigenous development and manufacture of weapons (including ammunition) as a means of by-passing externally-imposed embargoes, and of reducing the range of foreign purchases, and in order to obtain a more visible independence of political and military action.[10]

In sum, the military balance in the Gulf moved continuously against Iran in the 1980s, reversing the country's superior military edge of the 1970s.[11] It is this factor, coupled with the relentless improvements in the quantity and quality of weapons transferred to the Gulf Arab states, that has reduced the three-way military 'tie' of the 1970s to the two prominent Arab contenders—Iraq and Saudi Arabia. Saudi Arabia, the leading force the GCC, enjoys the support and confidence of all the Western countries. It has demonstrated an increasing independence of action in national security considerations but also in important matters of weapons purchases—the latter perhaps a function of the competition amongst the Western arms manufacturers themselves, and between them and the former Communist countries and the growing Third World arms makers—by having successfully obtained sophisticated arms from both sides of the Atlantic, as well as the 2,000+ km range IRBM CSS-2 surface-to-surface missiles (SSMs) from China.

On the other hand, Iraq continued—until the Kuwait invasion—to receive standard hardware and sophisticated arms from the Soviet Union, while also buying advanced fighters and firepower from France, and indeed obtaining Western and Third World military technology (particularly in the field of missile development) to compensate for the gaps left by its other purchases. Politically, as already mentioned in Chapter 3, Baghdad was displaying a more 'moderate' foreign policy orientation, pursuing an integrationist strategy within Arab fora (note for example its role in the creation of the ACC), and establishing improved economic and diplomatic ties with the major OECD countries during the 1980s. Ultimately it was these apparent changes in its policies which assisted Iraq in obtaining even the most inaccessible equipment, and which played a significant part in convincing its military suppliers and economic partners alike that the dreaded hardline Ba'th system of the 1970s had given way to a 'moderate' regime under President Saddam Hussein.

Thus, as far as the military balance is concerned, it is clear that while Iran was re-equipping its armed forces with much older and less sophisticated Soviet-bloc hardware in the 1980s, its Gulf neighbours were busy upgrading their armed forces with new generation weapons systems that were designed to meet the challenges of the 1990s and beyond. What are the immediate and medium-term consequences of this process? First, it is unlikely that the Gulf arms race, which began in earnest in the mid-1960s, is going to slow down now simply because the Iran-Iraq War has ended, particularly as, even before that conflict had been resolved, a new crisis—directly involving one of the belligerents—had already erupted.

Secondly, because of the absolute military superiority over Iran achieved collectively by the Gulf Arab states, and as a way of strengthening itself in the face of the new crisis and the resulting large foreign deployment in and around the Gulf since August 1990, Tehran will have no choice but hastily to re-equip both the regular armed forces and their 'Islamic' (i.e., the *Pasdaran*) counterparts.[12] Indeed the relative balance which they arrived at in the 1980s is already under severe strain. The dynamics of rearmament (replacing old equipment and upgrading ageing ones) ensures that even the best equipped army will continue to seek additions and improvements to its current stockpiles as well as to obtain yet more sophisticated arms. Furthermore, the inherent competition between Iran and Saudi Arabia on one hand and among the GCC states themselves on the other, will fuel the arms race, regardless of the status of Iran's armed forces. In addition, Iraq and the GCC states are aware that for the immediate future Iran can always draw upon the qualitative factors—its larger population, strategic advantages, and natural resources—to compensate for its (temporarily) weaker military condition.

Thirdly, political competition among the three local powers will continue, as in the past, to manifest itself in an all-encompassing arms race, notwithstanding the general recognition of the destabilising consequences and damaging effects of the Gulf War. Fourthly, Iraq and Iran will be compelled to modernise and rebuild their armed forces in order to eradicate the gaps and weak fronts in their respective military command structures and to modernise their weapon systems to meet the challenges of 'the other side' and of the 1990s at large. Fifthly, the international proliferation of arms manufacturers since the mid-1970s has made this a 'buyer's market', and has thus increased competition among the major arms producing countries to secure for themselves a healthy portion of the lucrative Gulf market. They will therefore continue to push for more contracts, in the first instance with the Gulf Arab states, and, as the political climate improves, with Iran.

Sixthly, the imperatives of *strategic interdependence* provide sufficient military and geopolitical linkages between the Gulf countries and Israel for each to be affected by developments in the other.[13] Thus, even if the local motivations were removed, the situation in the Levant, South Asia and around the Red Sea and the Arabian peninsula, and their competing interests in various countries of these regions, would still provide enough impetus for the major littoral states to maintain the momentum of their rearmament at significantly high levels.

Last but not least, the Iraqi invasion of Kuwait has affected the regional balance of power so dramatically that even if relative peace returns to the Gulf, fear and uncertainty will continue to fuel the arms race throughout the region for a considerable time to come.

One can offer examples from the 1980s to illustrate the disequilibrium of arms transfers to the Gulf states during the eighties in a pattern which is characteristic of this significant decade in the Gulf's history. By the end of 1984, Iran's airforce had lost a substantial number of the fighters and other aircraft purchased by the Shah. Of the 140 Northrop F-5E and 28 F-5F Tiger fighters only 55 remained operational; of the 177 F-4Es and 32 F-4D Phantoms a total of 45 were airworthy; of the six P-3F Orion maritime surveillance aircraft only two were functional; of the 80 sophisticated Grumman F-14 Tomcats only 12 flew, and of the 43 C-130H transport aircraft only 12 were in active service.[14] To compensate for this high rate of depletion, the Iranian armed forces had little option but to resort to equipment 'cannibalisation' and to rely more heavily on domestic military-industrial supplies, to shop among other Soviet arms-user states and to hunt out essential US-made weapons, parts and other equipment from 'neutral' Third World and Western European countries. Thus, by the end of 1986, Iran had purchased some low-quality aircraft (40 Chinese-made J-7 (MiG-21) fighters and 12 J-6 (MiG-19) interceptors), in addition to 260 T-59 main battle tanks (MBT) and a substantial quantity of SAMs from China, accounting for the bulk of its Soviet-bloc military hardware.[15] For its US-made arsenal, Iran reportedly received 18 F-14s, 18 F-5s and 46 Skyhawk aircraft from the 'grey' market and obliging Third World countries, as well as some 80 aging M-48 MBTs and over 100 M-113 APCs, attack helicopters, artillery pieces, Sidewinder missiles, and a variety of ammunition from Vietnam.[16]

In retrospect, the Islamic Republic's cancellation of the major arms ordered by the Shah, including the seven AWACS early-warning aircraft, the 160 F-16 fighters and the 400 Phoenix missiles from the US, and the 1,350 Shir-1 and Shir-2 tanks (improved versions of the Chieftain) and Rapier SAMs from Britain, considerably weakened the fighting capability of the Iranian armed forces for two main reasons: first, many of the sophisticated systems ordered by the Shah's regime found their way into the armouries of Iran's regional competitors and, secondly, the armed forces suffered directly for not having access to these advanced weapons systems, that had been due for deployment in the 1980s, in the course of the fighting.[17]

In sharp contrast to Iran's predicament, five Gulf Arab states (Saudi Arabia, Oman, the UAE, Bahrain and Iraq) were taking delivery of, or had agreed to purchase, sophisticated state-of-the-art military equipment throughout this period. By the end of 1986, Saudi Arabia was receiving of the 72 multi-role, all-weather Panavia Tornadoes it had ordered; the UAE had begun receiving 18 French-made Mirage 2000 fighters; Bahrain, the 12 F-5E/F Tigers and the 12 General Dynamics F-16C/D Falcon fighters; and Iraq, the 40 MiG-29 Fulcrums and a significant number of Su-25 attack and Su-24 Fencer all-weather strike aircraft, as well as over 30 Mirage F-1 fighters.[18] As for MBTs, Saudi Arabia took delivery of 40 M-60 A3 and over 1,000 Brazilian-made Engesa; Bahrain, of 54 M-60 A3; the UAE, of 35 OF-40 MK2. Iraq, for its part, obtained 150 T-55, T-62 and T-72 MBTs. In addition, in the same period, two Gulf Arab countries obtained some 2,100 sophisticated airborne missiles (Saudi Arabia acquired 1,800 AIM-9 Sidewinders and AGM-84 Harpoons; Oman got 300 AIM-9 Sidewinders).[19] Furthermore, among other naval equipment obtained, Saudi Arabia's purchase of eight major missile-equipped vessels, nine missile boats and three torpedo boats significantly enhanced the Kingdom's naval capability.

As already stated, the military balance had by the mid-eighties shifted firmly against Iran, with Iraq on the one hand and Saudi Arabia (and its GCC allies) on the other achieving a realistic military superiority over Iran, as well as a relative balance in levels of sophistication with each other. Since the GCC purchases were not co-ordinated at either the planning or the procurement stages the Council's operational procedures remained nationally oriented, thus somewhat reducing the value of a direct comparison between the GCC forces and those of Iraq—or indeed of Iran.

A direct comparison hides another significant weakness of the GCC military build-up in the 1980s, in addition to, and in direct consequence of, that mentioned above: national sourcing has been so diverse as to hinder any real co-ordination in, and the serious consideration of, weapons inter-changeability. In 1990 the GCC members were, for example, deploying four varieties of modern American-made fighters (F-5 Tiger, A-4 Skyhawk, F-15 Eagle and F-16 Falcon), four from France (Mirage-5, Mirage 2000, Mirage F-1 and Alphajets), three from the United Kingdom (Tornado, Jaguar and Hawk), and one from Italy (Aermacchi). MBTs were purchased from the US (M-60 A1 and A3), from the UK (Chieftain and Centurion), France (AMX-30), and Italy (OF-40 MK2) and from Brazil (Engesa). Iraq, by contrast, deployed only Soviet and French fighters, and Soviet (and captured Iranian Chieftain, M-48 and M-60) MBTs. In the 1980s Iran purchased only US and Chinese-made fighters and British, Soviet and American tanks. So, while the GCC figures may look good on paper, and the military equipment deployed is impressive, the GCC members' armed forces are far from the united fighting machine that distinguishes the northern neighbours of this group of states. In this, alas, lies the final weakness and the Achilles heel of the southern Gulf states with regard to both Iran and Iraq.

The Gulf strategic balance

The strategic balance still remains rather precarious and fluid in the Gulf. External relations, political stability and economic diversity and development greatly affect military alertness and capability. In the last analysis, therefore, factors beyond training, efficiency and military preparedness determine a regime's confidence in providing a viable deterrence, maintaining its position in regional circles, and advancing its interests in extra-regional fora. In its 1973 strategic survey of the region the International Institute for Strategic Studies (IISS) commented that 'the current willingness to supply arms [to the Gulf states] may therefore be creating the danger that potential disputes will be fuelled. Iran's growing strength, and that of Saudi Arabia, [however may have exactly the opposite effect: that of helping to bring about stability . . .'[20]

Nearly two decades later, and after a revolution and a war that shook one northern Gulf regime to its foundations and threatened to undermine the continuity of the other, only limited prospects for stability based on military might remain. Certainly the deterrent effect of a strong and well-armed military force cannot be over-emphasised, but the current willingness to supply arms to the Gulf states may result in further hostilities rather than in bolstering stability. This is primarily because, in essence, the absence of a strong and explicitly pro-Western Iran has transformed the strategic landscape of the Gulf region sufficiently to enable us to look beyond the 'Twin Pillars' strategy of the previous era, and to develop a triangular model of the contemporary balance of power in the Gulf.

The political and ideological changes in the Gulf since 1979 have created a new canvas of inter-state relations. Remarkably, of the 'ten Sheikhs, a King, a Sultan, a Shah and a radical Baathist President'[21] who ruled the Gulf countries a decade ago, only one regime—the Pahlavi Dynasty in Iran—has followed its leader to oblivion.[22] To all intents and purposes, all the other Gulf states still display many of the same regime characteristics and ideological premises that they did in the 1970s. But the establishment of an Islamic Republic in Iran has fundamentally altered the loose (conservative) monarchical/dynastical and (radical) republican regime divides that before 1979 had prevailed in the Gulf for over thirty years.

It would seem that, far from undermining its Muslim neighbours, the attitude and strategy of the Islamic Republic inadvertently initiated an unprecedented period of elite continuity, domestic stability and surgical elite control in virtually all the Gulf Arab countries. Usually synonymous with political control and a range of repressive measures, such 'stability' has increased the manoeuvrability of these regimes, enabling them to pursue their 'national' interests more assertively with regard to their neighbours and in important fora such as OPEC, OAPEC and the Arab League; it is in fact precisely the confident and unhindered pursuance of 'national', as opposed to Arab, policies by both Iraq and Kuwait (albeit with different aims after the implementation of the cease-fire agreement between Iran and Iraq) that can be said to have played a part in bringing about the final rupture between the two neighbours on 2 August 1990.

Thus, while the Islamic regime in Iran may draw strength from its domestic powerbase, its external posture during the years of the First Republic has, in many direct and indirect ways, assisted the consolidation and internal position of the ruling regimes in the other Gulf states to a degree where the two sides can confront each other at the start of the 1990s on an almost equal footing.

From the strategic viewpoint, the 1980s arms race in the Gulf was qualitatively different from the armament programmes that accompanied the first oil-boom of the 1970s. First, it occurred at a time of financial crisis in virtually all the Gulf states. Secondly, it was fuelled by war and was not run purely for prestige and competition. Thirdly, and perhaps most notably, we see, with the end to the Iran-Iraq War, three distinct identities emerging in the Gulf, each trying to function independently of the others but also to co-operate with the others to the extent that the fundamental interests of each are not threatened. Since 1979, and in particular since the GCC was formed in 1981, these three political forces—Socialist Ba'thist Republicanism, Radical Islamic Republicanism and Traditional (Islamic) Monarchies—have emerged in their own right. Ironically, while the pre-1979 alliance between Iran and Saudi Arabia against 'radical' Iraq was based simply on the 'moderate' and pro-Western position of the two monarchical systems, their politico-ideological and religious differences in the 1980s have been highlighted by their attempts to gain a monopoly over the 'word of God', a rivalry that has sometimes virtually marginalised the Iraqi dimension.[23] In addition, the arms race is, in a way, a precautionary measure taken by each in order to maximise the benefits to each arising from the transformed environment: some states, such as Kuwait and Saudi Arabia, have pre-empted the formalisation of these new structural conditions; others, e.g. Iran and Iraq must still complete their period of transition towards peace before their ideological stance for the 1990s can be confirmed, while the rest—the other GCC states—must soon begin to take stock (a) of the consequences of an end to the Iran-Iraq War; (b) of the Iraqi invasion of Kuwait; (c) of the military modernisations under way in Saudi Arabia; and (d) of the foreign military build-up (Arab and non-Arab) in Saudi Arabia.

The ideological lines have therefore been redrawn. This is the first time since the British withdrawal from the territories 'east of the Suez' that three ideological currents have converged simultaneously in the Gulf. Their differences affect the way the three counteract, and also orient themselves towards, other regional issues and forces as well as external influences. The following are a few examples:

—all three have become heavily involved in Lebanese politics, which were for so long the preserve of Syrian and Israeli intrigue: Iran assists the Muslim parties, supported by Syria; Iraq has provided military equipment and funds for some Christian forces, also supported by Israel; Saudi Arabia has been instrumental in putting together the Arab League peace plan which poses a direct challenge to Syrian (and by extension Iranian) authority, and is also against Iraq's long-term strategy against Syria and Iran in the Lebanon.

—Iran and Saudi Arabia have become direct parties to the Afghan war, although supporting competing anti-regime forces: Iran provides close military and political support for the eight Shi'i groups in the Mujahidin coalition; Saudi Arabia supports the more numerous Sunni groups, and has participated in negotiations between the Mujahidin, Kabul and the Soviet Union, even hosting a meeting in the Kingdom between the interested parties, and thus completely by-passing Iran (which borders Afghanistan and accommodates some three million Afghani refugees).

—all three have taken strong positions on the Palestine issue: Iran has opposed the PLO and its peace proposals for a 'limited' and secular Palestinian state in the Occupied Territories; Saudi Arabia has officially recognised the new Palestinian entity in the West Bank and the Gaza Strip, crediting the PLO representative with ambassadorial status (ironically doing so ten years after Iran had initiated this policy by turning the Israeli mission in Tehran into the PLO-run Palestinian Embassy); Iraq has come vehemently to support the Fatah movement's line and to accept the current PLO strategy against Iranian and Syrian opposition (again, ironically, only years after having hosted the notorious Baghdad summit which created the Steadfastness Front to oppose both the Camp David Accords and the 'direct talks and mutual recognition' policy advocated by the US and Egypt). However, since the beginning of the Kuwaiti crisis, Baghdad has again been courting the radical Palestinian factions (both PLO and non-PLO).

The political alignments in the Gulf itself have also been transformed beyond recognition since the Iran-Iraq War. Most of the GCC states developed extensive ties with Iraq, and in their continuing efforts on behalf of the Iraqi war machine (see Chapter 3), helped to sustain the Ba'thist Iraqi polity. Furthermore, the Joint Military Command set up in October 1980 by 'radical' Iraq and 'moderate' Jordan to assist the former in its war effort, as well as 'renegade' Egypt's military and diplomatic support for Iraq (in addition to Cairo's offer to protect the other Gulf Arab states), gave rise to a new Arab regional body, that was not exclusively 'Gulfian', and was certainly not as ideologically homogeneous as the GCC. The Arab Cooperation Council, established in early 1989, brought together Iraq, Egypt, Jordan and North Yemen (now a united Yemen). It could be called the 'Iraqi war effort supporters' club', and as such was readily distinguished by its anti-Iranian and anti-Syrian/Libyan bias. Although basically an economic grouping, the ACC provided Iraq with a new identity and with a regional lease of life. It also equipped Baghdad with formal support from two important Arab actors (Egypt and Jordan), thus raising its standing in the Gulf with regard to the GCC and the economic club that ties Iran to the other two important non-Arab Muslim Middle Eastern countries, Turkey and Pakistan. Also, by the virtue of belonging to the ACC (see Chapter 3), Iraq was able to claim an indirect stake in the affairs of the Arabian peninsula (through Yemen), the Levant (through Jordan) and North/East Africa (through Egypt).

The establishment in less than a decade of two Arab regional groupings that include virtually all of Iran's Gulf Arab neighbours, increased the pressures on Iran to establish firm regional alliances that would counter the force generated by this 'club-identity'. The rejuvenation of the 1975 arrangement with Turkey and Pakistan for joint military procurement and production may provide one viable solution. But it seems clear that to upgrade the current economic arrangements between these three states to a more engaged politico-military level, there will first have to be significant improvements in US-Iranian relations. Given Iran's demonstrated willingness to iron out its differences with many of Washington's Western and regional allies, this may not be an altogether impossible development.

More immediately, therefore, and as far as regional actors are concerned, Iran may have to rely on Israel and Syria (and Libya) respectively for military and politico-military support. Should Iran's bilateral ties with these countries formalise into joint policy and executive agreements, then Iraq will, at the very least, become 'routinely' vulnerable to threats from Iran and Syria simultaneously along both its western and eastern borders. One immediate impact of this military line-up would be a split in Iraqi force deployment, and subsequent reductions in the concentration of the army along the Iranian border and in the scale of resources available for the protection of Iraq's eastern flank. By the same token, even if any military emergencies develop along its western flank, Iraq will not be able (assuming that peace talks with Iran fail to lead to substantial improvements in the security environment) fully to re-deploy its armed forces for fear of opening 'windows of opportunity' for renewed Iranian military threats. Additionally, the opening of the Kuwaiti front by the Iraqis, and the virtual surrounding of this front by potential or actual enemies is likely to tie down Iraq's forces primarily to its southern and eastern borders, followed by the deployment of deterrent forces along its western and northern borders. Thus, in the prevailing circumstances, Iraq's military involvement in the Levant (whether in the form of operations against Syria, interference in the Lebanon, co-ordination with the Hashemite Kingdom, or muscle-flexing towards Israel) must necessarily remain rather limited. Again, the Gulf crisis arising from the Iraqi invasion of Kuwait could change all this: Baghdad may well choose to open another front against the UN/allied forces lined up against it either by raising its offensive military presence in Jordan or by attempting a surgical military strike against Israeli territory. The advantages of this move for Iraq would presumably be in the unification behind Baghdad of the divided Arab regimes, isolation of Egypt, Saudi Arabia and Syria (its greatest Arab competitors), increased support for its new regional agenda, the turning of Saddam Hussein into an Arab hero and, last but not least, the undermining of the American role and position in Saudi Arabia in particular and in the Middle East generally. One might note in passing how, as an element of the same equation, Iraq's neighbouring ACC partner, Jordan, would also be exposed to threats of the sort indicated above—from Syria (partly on behalf of Iran and partly due to Damascus' own opposition to Iraq), and from Israel (partly in response to Amman's formal association with Iraq, a country under great suspicion in Israel).

In strategic terms, the GCC countries may also be hostile towards such an informal (but potentially powerful) Arab/non-Arab axis, for even in purely reactive terms it exposes Saudi Arabia, their most powerful partner, to both Gulf (Iranian) and Red Sea (Israel) threats simultaneously. Indeed, from the Syrian perspective, and since it does not belong to either the ACC, the GCC, or the Arab Maghreb Union, Damascus may have little choice other than to cultivate closer strategic ties with Iran and probably to receive guidance, encouragement and material incentives from the Soviet Union in the process. Syria's military participation against Iraq in Saudi Arabia in the summer of 1990 and its simultaneous efforts to maintain close relations with Iran, illustrate well the strategic dilemmas the Syrian state is facing, as well as its related and consistent inability to consolidate single or group alliances without damaging other interests. And although Israel is conscious of the inherent fragility of such Arab fora, it will continue to be wary of the three exclusively Arab entities (with their varying degrees of military strength) that surround it. Therefore and with American approval, Israel will need to draw closer to non-Arab Iran for a modicum of strategic regional co-ordination—as has been the case in the past, *overt* politico-military co-operation need not ever occur.

In all this, there was one unlikely development that tended to preoccupy the Iranian, Syrian and Israeli military planners alike: an Iraqi-Saudi Arabian alliance. Although the 1990 Gulf crisis may have put a definite end to this scenario for the foreseeable future, such an alliance would certainly have induced serious regional consequences. For one thing, it would have united a well-equipped and battle-hardened army with another well-armed pro-Western one. It would also have resulted in a 'semi-circle' of mutually reinforcing hostilities and subsequent persistent instabilities that would have involved Israel, Syria, Iraq, Iran and Saudi Arabia. It will be apparent to the reader that a development of this sort could have paralysing consequences for the inherent problems in the region from the Levant to the Gulf, and that it would make them all the more intractable—with or without an end to the Iran-Iraq War, a 'satisfactory' resolution of the invasion of Kuwait, or the ending of the global Cold War. As things stand, however, the Iraqis have precipitated a different line-up of forces in the Gulf and in the whole region.

As discussed in Chapter 1, the death of Ayatollah Khomeini in June 1989 and the consolidation of the pragmatic/realist line in the Islamic Republic's foreign policy, which had taken shape a year earlier, will have a positive influence on the strategic balance in the Gulf by continuously strengthening the basis of the Second Republic. Marked by the absence and by the influence of the all-powerful patriarch on Iranian domestic affairs and foreign policy, the Second Republic is further characterised by the desire of its leadership to move away from the initial decade of intransigence, non-conformity and isolation towards the discovery of a new, non-confrontational, but still influential, regional identity—as opposed to a new regional role—for itself. Additionally, the Second Republic will be compelled to continue to mend fences with the Western countries, to pursue friendly diplomatic and economic (and military) relations with the Soviet Union and China, as well as to seek an improved relationship with the Arab states.

As it had no official diplomatic relations with its most powerful Gulf neighbours—Iraq and Saudi Arabia—for long periods during the 1980s, Iran remained relatively isolated in the Gulf. This isolation was compounded by the amicable relations that existed between Iraq and many GCC countries during the war. At the same time, however, Tehran has always been careful to cultivate its good relations with Oman and with a number of the shaikhdoms of the UAE. Following Iran's acceptance of the cease-fire in the war and its conciliatory Gulf strategy, the existing ties between Tehran and these GCC states have improved even further (see also Chapter 3). In this context, one notes

Velayati's well-received visit to Kuwait days before the Iraqi invasion of that country, and the continuing high-level exchanges between the exiled Kuwaiti ruling family and Iranian officials, improvements in Iraqi-Iranian relations notwithstanding. Iran can therefore use these channels both talking to Saudi Arabia and for exerting pressure on Iraq in the peace talks, and can, of course, exert influence over other regionally-based bilateral and multilateral matters. Iraq's invasion of Kuwait and the subsequent Saudi reaction has removed Tehran's previous ability to score valuable strategic points against Baghdad and the moderate Gulf states by driving a wedge between them. Saudi Arabia, still riding high on its successful initiative to isolate Iran diplomatically when required, must be conscious that its other GCC partners did not follow suit in breaking relations with Iran in 1988, and also that any warming of relations between Iran and the smaller GCC states may fracture the remarkable and durable cohesion of the Council in a period of grave crisis in the Gulf. Non-unity of purpose, and diversions in regional strategy and outlook, and level of the mutual commitment, may call into question the reason why the GCC was created in the first place, and may reduce its importance merely to that of a reactive body of small and vulnerable Arab countries afraid of being manipulated by their bigger and more powerful northern Gulf neighbours.[24] We do not, however, predict the demise and disintegration of the GCC in the foreseeable future, particularly as it also successfully manages to adapt to serve and protect the interests of its members beyond the Gulf itself. At the same time, Saudi Arabia's 'holding out' against Iran in the 1980s, established its position as an important corner-stone of traditionalist monarchism against the two other essentially competing politico-ideological currents in the Gulf.

A change of emphasis for the future?

Under the sub-heading 'The aim of war is to eliminate war', Chairman Mao Tse Tung wrote in one of his most celebrated texts:

> 'War, this monster of mutual slaughter among men, will be finally eliminated by the progress of human society, and in the not too distant future too. But there is only one way to eliminate it and that is to oppose war with war, to oppose counter-revolutionary war with revolutionary war . . . History knows only two kinds of war, just and unjust'.[25]

Chairman Mao's lofty pronouncements on war notwithstanding, the Iran-Iraq War has demonstrated more clearly than ever before that not all modern conflicts can be reduced merely to 'just and unjust', and that the 'progress of human society', far from eliminating war, can have precisely the opposite effect—of indeed prolonging it. As we have seen, in the Iran-Iraq War there was no real victor and certainly no vanquished, and very little difference between what the belligerents emphasised as right and wrong. The war produced only victims. After the border skirmishes and the initial Iraqi invasion, Iran did oppose 'war with war' but as the history of the war has shown this act did not eliminate war. On the contrary, as well as leaving behind a legacy of bloodshed and destruction, the war created an atmosphere of mistrust, tension and uncertainty in the Gulf that is likely to remain for many years to come. Add to this the additional problems that have arisen as a result of the Iraqi invasion of Kuwait, and the pitfalls in the way of those who pursue an acceptable and fair resolution of this crisis, and it should be obvious that the process of arming and rearming provides neither solutions to nor desirable preconditions for regional security. Often all that is provided are new tools for prolonging a crisis.

Under these conditions, the rush by the belligerents to rearm and the pace at which the non-belligerent Gulf states have been modernising their armouries will only provide further fuel for other confrontations and possible wars. Although it is very hard to put a value on the worth of deterrence, it is not too difficult to see how, at least in the Gulf context, the structures and rules of deterrence could be misconstrued as the preparation for hostilities. Strong armies may not rid the region of war and if another war does occur, such strength may only help to make it longer and bloodier. The acquisition of modern surface-to-surface missiles by the major Gulf states means that the next war need not even bring the hostile armies out on to the battle field; Iran and Iraq could deploy their varieties of domestically-produced and foreign-supplied missiles with both conventional and non-conventional warheads (the latter still only chemical), and Saudi Arabia could deploy its CSS-2 IRBMs armed with conventional warheads (and if required, with 'imported' chemical weapons), against virtually any target in the Gulf, the Levant, East Africa, parts of the Indian sub-continent and even some Soviet territory as well.

The military threshold is therefore rising in the Gulf and it is more than ever clear that if at all possible, political solutions must be sought for this region's problems. Following the 'second cold war', the new détente between the superpowers and their respective power-blocs has already borne fruit in the Gulf in the form of Security Council Resolution 598 and US-USSR agreements over the Iraqi invasion of Kuwait, and is prompting a new resolve to find workable and non-ideological solutions to international problems and other regional

TABLE 4.4 Gulf military manpower estimates, selected years (000's)

Country/Year	Total population	Total armed forces	As % of population
Iran			
1978	36,365	413.0	1.4
1981	39,665	260.0	0.7
1984	42,500	755.0	1.8
1987	49,900	654.0	1.1
1989	54,370	604.0	1.1
Iraq			
1978	12,470	212.0	1.7
1981	13,835	252.0	1.8
1984	14,900	642.0	4.3
1987	15,900	1,117.0	7.0
1989	17,840	1,000.0	5.6
Saudi Arabia			
1978	7,730	58.5	0.8
1981	10,395	51.7	0.5
1984	11,000	51.5	0.5
1987	11,500	73.5	0.6
1989	13,489	65.7	0.5
GCC			
1978	8,892	121.9	1.4
1981	11,544	133.3	1.1
1984	15,051	137.3	0.9
1987	15,910	163.8	1.9
1989	18,683	164.9	0.9

Source: IISS, *The Military Balance* (various years).

Note: The authors' calculations are based on the data available from IISS. All population figures are estimates.

conflicts. And yet there is little evidence of any respite in the drive by the great and major powers to 'militarise' the Third World. This is nowhere as obvious as in the Middle East. According to IISS, the

Middle East (including North Africa) spent some $63 billion on defence and defence-related projects in 1986, the GCC states accounting for at least $23 billion of this total and Iran and Iraq for a further $19 billion.[26] According to recent SIPRI figures, Iraq has, on average, spent about 25 per cent of its GDP on military expenditures since 1978; in Iran this had risen to about 53 per cent of GDP by the mid-1980s, up from about 7 per cent in 1979; Oman's has averaged about 22 per cent; Saudi Arabia's stands at about 16 per cent; and Bahrain's, Kuwait's and the UAE's at an average of 4.5 per cent, 11 per cent and 6 per cent of their GDPs respectively.[27] Discernible trends for the 1990s, furthermore, do not provide much room for optimism. The start of the decade with yet another situation of crisis in the Gulf has virtually ensured that the arms race in the Gulf and its related hinterland will continue unabated. In the aftermath of the Iraqi invasion of Kuwait, the US has rushed to equip Saudi Arabia, its closest Gulf ally, with increasing quantities of ever more sophisticated American military hardware. The 1990 Saudi-American arms deal that was reported to be in excess of $21.5 billion, and which matched the principal arms transfer agreement signed between London and Riyadh in July 1988, marks the return of the US as the largest arms exporter to the Gulf's richest arms market. The new package, which is intended to augment arms transfer deals totalling $10 billion that have been signed between the two countries since 1988, includes the sale of 24 more advanced F-15s, as well as Lockheed KC-130H tankers and C-130 transporters, 12 AH-64 Apache attack helicopters, a further 150 (in addition to the 315 already contracted for) M1 A2 MBTs, more than 350 Patriot anti-aircraft missile systems, 150 TOW anti-tank missile launchers, nine multiple launch rocket systems with 2,000 rockets, and probably four more E-3 AWACS.[28] In September 1990, Brazil's Avibras announced the sale of 10,000 rockets for the Astros II multiple launch rocket systems that had already been sold to Saudi Arabia, and France confirmed the finalisation of a $3 billion arms deal for the sale to the Kingdom of missiles and missile systems and frigates. Apart from providing a profitable outlet for the 'Cold War surpluses', the readiness of outside powers to transfer new and sophisticated weapons systems to the Gulf during a crisis situation indicates that the conflict mentality prevails in any Gulf-related diplomatic dilemmas. Iran's announcement early in October 1990 that it had started taking delivery of Soviet-made MiG-29 fighters as part of a multi-billion dollar Soviet arms transfer and training agreement that had been reached during President Rafsanjani's visit to Moscow in June 1989, indicates that the pattern of sophisticated arms procurement is a general Gulf problem (see Chapter 5). However, in view of what has already been said about the poor status of the Iranian armed forces, the procurement from the Soviet Union of sophisticated weapons systems (that are likely over the next few years to include the transfer of the Su-24 long-range strike aircraft and modern tanks and artillery systems), is not an escalation of the arms race as such, but rather is an essential part of a replenishment policy.[29] It is important to note, nonetheless, that this Irano-Soviet arms deal marks a clear departure for Tehran in arms procurement. The deal also illustrates Tehran's readiness in concrete terms to modernise and diversify its weapons sources, and its willingness to expand its politico-military relations with its long-feared northern neighbour. Conversely, this breaking into a traditionally Western-reliant market also represents a first for the Soviet Union, which is in the process of loosening its close military ties with its erstwhile allies in the Middle East (Algeria, Iraq, Libya, Syria and Yemen). The fundamental changes in the Soviet Union's foreign policy under President Gorbachev, the end to the Iran-Iraq War, and the change of government in Iran have all helped to accelerate the process of close co-operation between the two states. The Iraqi invasion of Kuwait and Moscow's response to Iraq's action are likely to put further strains on the traditional alliance between the two, thus paving the way for even closer Soviet relations with Iran and the other Gulf states.[30] If present trends continue, the Gulf will by the mid-1990s have become, relatively speaking, as militarised as the central European front had been—precisely at a time when a strong drive towards de-militarisation is in evidence in Europe!

With the tradition of competition intact, and with the problems associated with mistrust very much in evidence, the relevance to the Gulf situation of Stephen Goose's general comments about war in the post-1945 era can be easily appreciated: 'One outstanding feature of post-World War II armed conflict appears to be conflicts rarely come to a definitive conclusion; fighting may wane for months or even a year or two, only to resume at even higher levels'.[31] In the absence of negotiated peace, today's military balance in the Gulf and the disequilibrium that has resulted offers no long-term optimism and provides only a limited deterrence value to those who are currently in the lead—until the next time. The experience of the last twenty years shows that any lead in the hardware military balance acquired by one or more of the 'established' states can diminish as quickly as it appears, thus further fuelling uncertainties. The precarious strategic balance between the littoral states and their slowly emerging politico-ideological competitive structures can only encourage further intrigue in the Gulf itself, as well as in other regional hot spots: Afghanistan, the

Lebanon and the Arab-Israeli conflict are the more obvious venues. As each party tries to establish (or to create, as the case may be) a constituency outside the Gulf arena itself, this can, under both normal and emergency conditions, provide vocal support and behind-the-scenes protection; hence the opportunities for outside interference in regional matters also increase.

In spite of the rapid military build-up in the Gulf in the 1980s, the significant transformations in the military balance, an inconclusive war, an unprovoked invasion and occupation of a sovereign Gulf state and a critical regime change over the past decade in one of the key Gulf states, it is still forces outside and beyond the Gulf which ultimately determine the balance of power in this most important stretch of water and its shoreline states.

5 DEFENCE INVESTMENT AND MILITARY PROCUREMENT STRATEGIES OF IRAN AND IRAQ

In the previous chapter we discussed the regional strategic balance and the ways in which the related military balance affected relations between the belligerents themselves and with their other Gulf neighbours. The domestic context of these military relations will be considered in the present chapter. We will address primarily the position of the two belligerents during and after the Iran-Iraq War, will also and examine their indigenous arms-making capacities. Each country's military position during the war, as well as its international ties (whether of recent origin or long-established), will be shown to have played a critical part in enabling their respective ambitions to materialise.

Defence and the Second Republic

Despite the idiosyncracies in the Islamic Republic's defence strategy and in its conduct of the war with Iraq between 1980 and 1988, a constant streak of pragmatism was visible beneath the veneer of confrontationalism and rejectionism. The politico-military elite—the high-ranking military personnel and their clerical and non-clerical technocratic allies in the political establishment—was responsible not only for the planning and execution of the war effort on a daily and routine basis, but also for supervising the country's military procurements for the Islamic Revolution Guards Corps (IRGC: the *Pasdaran*) and the regular army on the one hand, and for the republic's domestic defence production efforts on the other.

The leaders of the Second Republic, from President Rafsanjani to the supreme leader Ayatollah Khamenei, have been involved in the nation's defence policies since 1980, many having served on important executive and decision-making committees and bodies. Khamenei, as the former President and the chairman of the Supreme Defence

Council was, for instance, directly involved in virtually every strategic decision taken by the country's military establishment. And the former Speaker of the Majlis, representing Ayatollah Khomeini on the same body, initiated policy at the same time as influencing critical decisions.

The transition towards pragmatism and the full control of the country's military affairs by the realists began in the mid-1980s, with the full involvement of Hojjatoleslam Rafsanjani, and culminated in his successful trips to China and North Korea. The line he championed was further boosted by Ayatollah Khomeini's decision to appoint him as the Commander-in-Chief on 2 June 1988, less than two months before Iran's unconditional acceptance of UN Security Council Resolution 598. With internal security assured, and with the justified criticisms of the populace regarding the conduct of the war (its perpetuation and its sudden end) now deflected, reconstruction efforts took on a new urgency after the death in June 1989 of the founder of the republic. In virtually all the government expenditure proposals after August 1988 and the cease-fire, defence and defence-related matters have been a top priority, destined to absorb on average one-quarter to one-third of the government's budgetary lay-outs. Indeed, until recently, Prime Minister Moussavi repeatedly pointed out that the government would continue to implement the proportional expenditures that had been envisaged for the 1984 to 1987 wartime budgets, according to which defence absorbed anything up to 50 per cent of government expenditures. Although the total amount fluctuated in tandem with the country's oil export revenues, the substantial Iranian *rial* funds that were raised through the population ensured massive domestic investment and expenditures on local procurement of defence and defence-related goods and services.[1]

Therefore, despite Iran's pressing economic problems, the Second Republic is no different from its predecessor in giving priority to its expenditures on procurement and its investment in indigenous production of arms and military infrastructure. The no war-no peace situation with Iraq (discussed in Chapter 4) that existed until the summer of 1990 added urgency to the new leadership's quest for military superiority and preparedness, thus merely reinforcing the complex domestic trend towards establishing a key role for defence in the national life of Iran. Because the formalisation of the cease-fire into a peace treaty between the former belligerents occurred at a time of renewed tensions in the Gulf, defence, defence-related matters and military preparedness are likely to continue to preoccupy the post-Gulf War leadership of the republic.

DEFENCE INVESTMENT AND PROCUREMENT

Headed by the technocrat and former director of the defence industries establishment, Akbar Torkan, the newly-created Ministry of Defence and Armed Forces Logistics has quietly diluted the national influence of the potentially troublesome IRGC by amalgamating the energies and resources of the *Pasdaran* and its separate ministry (founded in 1982) with the professional armed forces. Besides the important political implications of muzzling the 'guardians of the Islamic Revolution' and of erasing their independent military base amongst the Iranian power elite, four points are underscored by the organisation and the choice of leader for this new ministry. First, the new President chose experienced technocrats to lead the revitalisation of the armed forces. Secondly, the leadership clearly emphasised co-ordination of the domestic military production efforts of a number of institutions and bodies with a view to maximising the return on the country's investment of its precious human and material resources in the military-industrial sector. Thirdly, the post-Khomeini leadership planned to enhance the current capabilities of the military-industrial complex as a matter of priority. Finally, the new President, enjoying the confidence of the regular armed forces, aimed to re-channel the country's military potential towards the professional army.

Therefore, far from being a secondary concern of the regime, defence and related military matters are at the heart of the country's reconstruction efforts. The military sector is the inevitable beneficiary of industrial reconstruction, expanded energy production capacity, and further improvements in the country's infrastructure and other utilities. Thus, as the country's general economic condition improves, the opportunities for further military production and military-related research and development also multiply.

Iraq's military establishment

The formal transfer of political power from Hassan Al-Bakr to Saddam Hussein in July 1979 brought with it further centralisation of the decision-making process and more direct control of the armed forces. President Saddam, as both the country's premier and the Supreme Commander of its armed forces, has maintained overall control of the latter's operations for a number of years. His personalised style of rule has had a direct impact on the armed forces, affecting military strategies related to the Iran-Iraq War and the military occupation of Kuwait, military appointments and dismissals, and last but not least, weapons procurements and military co-operation with other countries.

DEFENCE INVESTMENT AND PROCUREMENT

Under Saddam Hussein's influence Iraq signed a broad border demarcation and good neighbourliness agreement with Iran in 1975, broke it in 1980, conducted a costly war with Iran from 1980 to 1988, occupied Kuwait in 1990, and arrived at what has been regarded as a capitulatory peace treaty with Iran, also in 1990. He has, since 1980, also presided over an unprecedented expansion of Iraq's armed forces, in manpower as well as in the acquisition of sophisticated weapons systems and other military equipment. As will be made clear later, Iraq's domestic arms-making capacity increased over the same period from virtually nothing to the development and modification of missiles and aircraft. The ranks of the armed forces swelled by over 100 per cent between 1980 and 1987, and this huge force regularly consumed between 40 and 50 per cent of the country's GNP in the first half of the 1980s. Thus, on average, Iraq spent some $12.5 billion a year on the military and on national security during Saddam's first decade in power.[2] This same formula has also meant that Iraq was consistently one of the world's largest importers of arms in the 1980s. For China, France and the Soviet Union this proved to be a bonanza; for many other (smaller) military suppliers it offered a most lucrative market.

A side-product of the close relationship which developed between Baghdad and Moscow following the 1958 Iraqi revolution was Iraq's easy access to Soviet arms. However, after the signing of the 1972 Treaty of Friendship between the two states, the flow of advanced Soviet military hardware to Iraq increased considerably, helped along by the post-1973 petro-dollar windfalls, eventually turning into the flood which characterised the two countries' military relations between 1983 and 1989. Some of the largest arms deals between them were signed in the 1980s, and as a result, state-of-the-art Soviet hardware systematically found its way to Iraq. In addition to the SSMs, tanks, artilley pieces, troops and personnel carriers and attack helicopters, for example, the quality of airborne firepower transferred to Iraq improved to such an extent during the 1980s that the Iraqi airforce became the first of its kind in the world outside the Warsaw Pact to deploy the Soviet-made Su-25 ground attack aircraft.

Being for a time anxious to curry favour with anti-US revolutionary Iran, Moscow deliberately reduced the flow of arms to Iraq during the first phase of the war (1980–82). But by 1983, Iranian battlefield victories and Tehran's refusal to soften its attitude towards the USSR had persuaded Moscow to revert to supporting its traditional ally in the Gulf, and so arms transfers to Iraq were renewed in earnest. During this crucial period, France and China stepped in to fill the gap left by the Soviet Union. Baghdad's long-term strategy of diversifying its military suppliers thus received an early boost. China supplied Chinese substitutes for Iraq's Soviet-made weapons, and France supplied equipment that included advanced aircraft and missile systems, as well as other military assistance.

The military relationship between Iraq and France dates back to the late 1960s, during which period each had found advantages in dealing with the other. France gained access to the rapidly expanding Iraqi economy, and Iraq cultivated the French connection as a means of gaining access to Western Europe and of reducing its reliance on the USSR. Both Giscard d'Estaing and François Mitterrand greatly expanded their country's ties with Iraq (including nuclear co-operation), capitalising on this special relationship to carve out for France the second place among Iraq's military suppliers. Although relatively limited in absolute terms, the major arms deals during the 1970s, which included military helicopters, fighters and a range of advanced missile systems and electronic equipment, laid the foundations for the much more comprehensive French arms packages of the 1980s.

China, on the other hand, when it entered the Iranian arms market, had already established military links with the Islamic Republic. Because of pressure from Arab states—mainly Egypt and some Gulf states—that were friendly with Iraq during the war years, and also because of Beijing's obsessive atempts to weaken the USSR in Third World circles (by trying in this case to drive a wedge between Moscow and Baghdad over Iraq's Soviet-made military needs), the Chinese found themselves obliged to supply Iraq with the weaponry it needed. In this fashion, they ended up arming both sides simultaneously during the war, supplying Iraq with combat aircraft (J-6, J-7 and J-8), tanks, guns and missiles, and Iran with similar—though fewer—of the same weapons.[3]

During the 1980s, Iraq's military also developed relations with other arms-producing countries, some of which led to the transfer of production technology to Iraq, although many were, by and large, straight arms deals. The Cardoen corporation of Chile, for instance, invested almost all of its resources in satisfying Iraqi requirements for ammunition and specialist needs during the war. Apparently with the full knowledge of the military government (1973–89), it assisted Iraq's arms-making industries and is known to have transferred some Western military know-how. Corporations based in some industrialised European countries fulfilled similar functions in their economic/military relations with Iraq, also apparently with the partial or full knowledge of their respective governments and other allied states. A number of other

Third World countries, the most active of which were Argentina, Brazil and Egypt, also obtained access to the Iraqi arms market and supplied its armed forces with a range of weapons, which included rocket launchers, training and anti-guerrilla aircraft, tanks and artillery pieces. The close military association between Iraq, Brazil and Egypt culminated in the assembly of some 80 Tucano EMB-312 training aircraft in Egypt in the second half of the 1980s for the Iraqi market, while the ties between Iraq, Argentina and Egypt resulted in joint research on the Condor-2 SSM project.[4]

Rearmament and arms procurement policy

IRAN

The experience of the war years has shown the leaders of the Islamic Republic that there is no shortage of international suppliers of arms, only that they may not always be able to provide the most sophisticated US-made hardware at the most reasonable price. At one time or another Iran imported arms from some twenty countries, often involving a combination of Western, Communist and Third World states. But the cruel fact was that as the war dragged on so Iran's military superiority began to evaporate. Appreciable improvements in the numbers and quality of arms in the inventories of Iraq and other Gulf Arab states merely underlined the depreciation of Iran's previously sophisticated arms inventory. This inventory was depleted at an alarming rate over the last three years of the war, making complete rearmament a necessity for the new leadership. As Table 5.1 shows, the estimated loss of Iranian military aircraft over the 1980s was substantial, and although the position of Iran's airforce, with its assortment of US-made, Chinese-made and Soviet-made combat aircraft, may have become more stable, its future development remains nonetheless rather precarious.

Throughout the 1980s, Iran was able to maintain a reasonable 'surplus' in Tiger and Phantom deployment, due largely to the generosity of Vietnam, South Korea, Pakistan and Israel in supplying parts or specialist knowledge pertaining to the complex repair and maintenance procedures for these aircraft, and in advising on the procurement or development of the sophisticated ground equipment required.[5] Without the original large supply of these aircraft, 'cannibalisation' would not have been possible, and indeed the existing stocks could not have been maintained at operative levels without substantial assistance from outside. But financial constraints and

DEFENCE INVESTMENT AND PROCUREMENT

TABLE 5.1 A survey of Iran's sophisticated airpower, 1978–90

Aircraft	1978	1988	1990
F-5E/F Tiger	168	55	70
F-4D/E Phantom	209	45	40
F-14 Tomcat	80	12	15
P-3F Orion	6	2	2
C-130 Hercules	43	12	20
MiG-29 Fulcrum	—	—	14
Total	506	126	161

Sources: Compiled from various issues of *Flight International*, *Jane's Defence Weekly* and IISS, *The Military Balance* (various years).

Note: The delivery of the MiG-29s is in progress. Apparently, none of the Su-24 Fencer aircraft reportedly purchased by Iran were delivered with the Fulcrums.

logistical difficulties encouraged the Iranians to look for cheaper, less sophisticated and more readily available alternatives for the airforce and for the air-wing of the IRGC. Thus the way was opened for the transfer of Soviet-designed aircraft and tanks to a country that historically had been reliant on Western-made, and particularly American, military hardware. Towards the end of the war Iran possessed some 40 J-7 (MiG-21 equivalent) and 12 J-6 (MiG-19 equivalent) fighters and interceptors, all of which arrived from China, North Korea and to a lesser extent Vietnam. In addition some 260 T-59 main battle tanks were received from China.

Initially, the cease-fire had little impact on Iran's procurement policy, for the path to Iran's real requirements—for advanced Western hardware—has remained blocked. Although France, amongst the Western countries, was willing to supply Iran with the sophisticated air and naval firepower it required, the fact that the Iranian armed forces were unfamiliar with French military hardware militated against the striking of any meaningful deals.

Furthermore, the fact that Iran does not start from a 'clean slate' position means that its armed forces cannot adapt quickly enough to new systems without sacrificing both efficiency and their limited human expertise and capital resources. On the other hand, the effective use of French-made weapons and support systems by Iraq against Iranian targets on land and at sea may have had a sufficiently strong 'demonstrative effect' for Tehran to consider more seriously the sophisticated French-built arms that may be available in the future. However, in the last analysis, Iran's evaluation of the French role in the war is so critical that the new politico-military leaders may wisely decide not to become militarily dependent on a country that supplied the enemy throughout the war so relentlessly and consistently—even more consistently at times than Iraq's main supplier, the Soviet Union. Nevertheless, 'supplier reliability' may encourage Tehran to cultivate the French option at a secondary level.

The all-encompassing $15 billion Irano-Soviet trade and investment agreement of 1989, known to contain a $2–4 billion military assistance component, indicates that the Soviet Union has been vigorously pursuing its 'non-ideological' arms transfer policy, and that Iran's inaccessability to Western suppliers of advanced defence equipment seems to have created the natural environment for both to capitalise on each other's needs—thus inaugurating a truly mutually-advantageous agreement between the two. Iran's familiarity with a large variety of Soviet-made weapons (largely through China, North Korea, Vietnam, Syria and Libya) makes a comprehensive arms deal between the two parties logical; as far as the trade relations between the two countries are concerned, the attractive barter arrangements embedded in any such deal makes it an imperative. Although Moscow may prefer cash deals in relation to its new arms-for-hard-currency policy, if further oil and gas agreements were signed with Tehran at the same time as the arms deals were made, the Soviet Union's need for hard currency could be satisfied by its re-sale of Iranian oil and gas in both East and West European markets at their dollar market value.

At what expense, though, would the two countries be prepared to establish extensive military ties with each other? In the long term, and the new Gulf crisis notwithstanding (unless of course it leads to the emergence of a different sort of regime in Iraq), the Soviet Union cannot afford to alienate its old Gulf ally and profitable arms market too much. Conversely, Iran is in no position to turn its back totally on the old Soviet rival, China, a critical military ally during the war years; nor, indeed, can it integrate itself within the Soviet-supplied orbit and still expect improvements in its diplomatic and economic stature with the West generally and the US in particular.

DEFENCE INVESTMENT AND PROCUREMENT

As far as smaller arms suppliers are concerned, Britain's decision in August 1989 not to sell Iraq the Hawk 100 jet trainer/light fighter may help British military trade prospects with Iran in two ways. First, Tehran is likely to interpret the decision favourably, seeing it as evidence that Britain is willing to transfer sophisticated firepower to Iran when the hostilities eventually cease in the Gulf, even at the expense of losing a lucrative contract with Iran's 'competitor'. Secondly, the isolating of Iraq in the Gulf in this manner could also be interpreted by all concerned as British willingness to support the creation of an axis not unlike the order that existed in the Gulf before the Iranian revolution, thus lending Iran (and of course the GCC states) a prominent profile in the alliance of the moderate forces in the region. The Iraqi invasion of Kuwait may well raise the prospect of general Western support for the emergence of such a 'regional order'. As a major regional actor, Iran has already put out feelers, contending that there is a need for a Gulf-wide security arrangement to emerge from the lessons of the Gulf War and Gulf crisis II, that would involve Iran and the GCC countries as partners in guaranteeing peace and security in this vital waterway. Past experience shows, furthermore, that such a 'respectable' profile is usually accompanied by major arms transfers to the favoured country.

Thus, with diplomatic relations between the two countries restored and with the Rushdie affair apparently buried, Britain could well be showing the carrot to Tehran in the best and most visible way possible.[6] The Iranians are fully aware that Britain could play a key role in the re-building of their armed forces. In addition, the monopolisation of the Iraqi market by France and the Soviet Union on the one hand, and the intense competition amongst the Western defence manufacturers for the GCC markets on the other, make the huge 'untapped' Iranian market an engaging proposition. As relations improve, it is more than likely that Iran will be considering the acquisition of modernised Chieftain and Challenger MBTs for its ground forces. It is also known that, despite its major arms deal with the Soviet Union, Iran has shown considerable interest in the Tornado and BAe Hawk jet trainers and modernised Jaguar fighters for its airforce, and in British-made frigates and mine sweepers for its navy. Additionally, as Iran proceeds to modernise and to improve its weakened national tactical and strategic air defence facilities and to procure advanced missile systems for its air and naval defences, it may well look towards British or other European suppliers (France, Italy and Germany for example) to satisfy these needs.

The 'British connection' can, of course, open the door to other Western suppliers, thus eventually enabling Iran to re-establish ties with the United States, its former main supplier for over a decade before 1979. The problem for the Iranian armed forces continues to be their lack of access to the US—and other Western-manufactured weapons systems that were operated by Iran for over 20 years.[7] Although the denial of arms to Iraq by Britain, one of Iran's former major suppliers, was, from Tehran's point of view, sweet, it has not—as yet—brought Iran any positive gains.

To compensate for the lack of direct access to the advanced weapons producers themselves, Tehran has been trying hard to gain such access through secondary channels such as Brazil, Argentina, Pakistan, Turkey, Israel, South Korea and Taiwan. There are strong indications that from these contacts Tehran has been able to establish military ties (maintenance, servicing and/or manufacturing assistance) with Pakistan, Israel, South Korea, Taiwan and China. Pakistan is to help primarily with providing advanced military training and servicing advice, as well as assisting with aspects of defence production through joint-ventures. Israel and South Korea were approached to help with overhauling equipment and modernisation techniques, as well as with know-how and technology for the ageing US-made weapons in Iran's inventories. Taiwan is said to have been willing to offer advice and assistance in the modernisation of the F-5 Tiger fighter and to provide some missile systems, and China has apparently agreed to establish assembly plants in Iran for the production of modernised J-6 and J-7 fighters, to sell it SSMs, and to transfer to Iran any relevant know-how gained through its contacts with the US arms manufacturers.[8]

In sum, therefore, Iran has been pursuing a three-layered arms procurement strategy involving:

(i) the purchase of (and limited production rights for) sophisticated Soviet-made weapons from the USSR and Eastern European countries, and standard Chinese-made and -improved (Soviet-designed) military hardware from China;

(ii) the search for modernised US-made weapons from America's Third World allies; and

(iii) the gaining of access through direct channels to Western-made advanced weapons (excluding French and Swedish) manufactured in Europe or the United States.

As the above analysis has shown, while the first two objectives may already be fulfilled, it is the third, and probably the most important, layer that remained unsatisfied at the turn of the decade.

DEFENCE INVESTMENT AND PROCUREMENT

IRAQ

Iraq's efforts to maintain its substantial lead over the country which it regarded as its main competitor in the Gulf in the 1980s—*viz.* Iran—continued after active hostilities had ceased in 1988. Some of the Soviet-supplied advanced airpower—MiG-29s and MiG-27s for instance—was in fact transferred to Iraq towards the end of the war, and consequently became fully operational and integrated only towards the end of the decade. At the start of the 1990s, therefore, Iraq already had a healthy lead over Iran's air and ground forces, and could as a result focus more on consolidation and, wherever appropriate, on administering improvements in technique and weapons quality, rather than on the demanding task of rebuilding and developing depleted forces, as Iran was having to do. Nonetheless, as Iraq improved its position in the war, it became quite clear that its front line forces needed modernisation; they relied on obsolete and out-dated Soviet equipment, and much of the new weaponry which had been obtained from China was based on old Soviet designs that in most cases showed little improvement on their 1950s and 1960s Soviet-made counterparts. Therefore Iraq's military lead over Iran could not allow the Iraqis to sit idly by and watch their advantage disappear. This was the case even though such a modernisation process would cost billions of dollars—money which, in view of Iraq's economic situation, could arguably have been better spent in improving the country's economic infrastructure and its money-earning economy.

It was clear to the Iranians, as well as to the Iraqis, that while they had been busy trying to destroy each other's civilian infrastructures and military forces, their weaker Gulf Arab neighbours, with substantial Western assistance, had been acquiring equally significant arsenals and military infrastructures of their own.

Thus, for Iraq at least, the race was on to convert its relative military superiority in the Gulf into an absolute one. For this task they partly relied on France. During the war France had sold substantial quantities of sophisticated military hardware and software to Iraq, which, according to French sources, included an average of 2 billion French francs' worth of arms between 1981 and 1987–8. The more visible components of these sales were attack helicopters, Mirage F-1s, the 'loan' of five Exocet AM-39-armed Super Etendard aircraft, guns, advanced anti-aircraft and anti-ship missiles, and early warning radars. It emerged in 1988, moreover, that Paris and Baghdad had been negotiating for the transfer of more Mirage F-1s to Iraq and for the establishment of local workshops for the repair and maintenance of this aircraft. Based on the success of this project, Paris had also expressed its willingness to sell the advanced Mirage-2000 fighter to Iraq. Britain's refusal to sell the Hawk 100 aircraft to Iraq in 1989 spurred Iraqi efforts to find a substitute. As talks had already been held with France about the purchase of Alpha Jet trainer/light attack aircraft, and as this aircraft was already being produced under license in Egypt (itself one of Iraq's ACC partners), the Iraqis opted for the Alpha Jet provided that local assembly and in due course production rights for this aircraft could be secured.

With Iran substantially weakened in terms of the quality of hardware at its disposal as well as in quantitative terms, Iraq had now to compete with Saudi Arabia and with some of the GCC partners for the all-important qualitative edge. This is illustrated in Table 5.2. With the exception of the navy, the Iraqi armed forces emerged in quantitative and weapons-quality terms, much more powerfully from the war, in a sense prepared, tried and tested for other campaigns. But whether the balance of power between the two belligerents would have remained to Iraq's advantage without the war is a moot point, because all along Iran would have had the advantage—lacked by its competitors in the Gulf—of the unpredictable weapon of revolutionary appeal.

TABLE 5.2 A survey of Iraq's sophisticated airpower, 1978–90

Aircraft	1978	1988	1990
Mirage F-1	—	94	94
MiG-21/J-7	115	150	195
MiG-23/27 Flogger	80	70	90
MiG-25 Foxbat	—	33	32
MiG-29 Fulcrum	—	18	30
Su-24 Fencer	—	—	16
Su-25 Frogfoot	—	30	60
Tu-22 Blinder	12	8	8
Il-76 Adnan (AEW)	—	—	2
An-12 Cub	8	6	10
An-26 Curl	2	2	2
Total	217	411	539

Source: See Table 5.1.

DEFENCE INVESTMENT AND PROCUREMENT

In one sense Iraq could be said to have already achieved the edge over its Gulf Arab neighbours. Its invasion and occupation of weaker Kuwait was one aspect of this process; Saudi Arabia's need to invite foreign military forces on to its soil as the only way of ultimately guaranteeing the security of the lower Gulf was another. With the invasion of Kuwait, Iraq had boldly staked its claim to being the final arbiter in the Gulf. However, to maintain the supreme role it had carved for itself, Iraq would need to digest Kuwait, to succeed in fighting off the forces lined up against it in Saudi Arabia and around the Gulf region, and to maintain its military cohesion without losing the technological edge and its quantitative weapons superiority to the GCC (largely Saudi Arabia) and Iran: an extremely tall order! While Iran's armed forces would probably not be rebuilt sufficiently to pose an immediate or a medium-term threat to Iraq, the promise in the summer of 1990 of more sophisticated weapons for Saudi Arabia, while Iraq's supply lines were cut (because of the UN-imposed embargo) may enable Saudi Arabia to take the lead from Iraq at least for the first half of the 1990s. Much, however, will be contingent upon the nature of the Iraqi regime which emerges out of the Kuwait crisis, and the demands of the post-Cold War order that is still being shaped.

At this point one can only speculate, but if force is to be the final arbiter in resolving this second Gulf crisis, then we envisage that a considerably weakened Iraq, in military and political terms, will emerge.[9] The prolonged isolation of Iraq by its traditional arms suppliers could, moreover, have a direct bearing on the future role of Iraq in the Gulf. Without the comprehensive military embargo that is in place at the time of writing, Baghdad would have been able to compensate for the lost access to certain military equipment needed by its forces by relying upon its newly-found Third World suppliers (including China). However, this stop-gap measure would necessarily have to give way to a much larger drive to acquire sophisticated hardware from the industrialised countries. In view of the initial role played by both France and the Soviet Union in isolating Iraq after its invasion of Kuwait, Iraq would need to develop military relationships with other countries besides those two, as a kind of insurance policy.

Of course, another medium-term option would lie in Iraq's redoubling of its efforts to assimilate diverse military technologies and to expand the country's indigenous arms-making base. Its already considerable research and development efforts in specific military fields could be expanded, but even here Iraq is desperately dependent on expatriate scientific and technical personnel, technology and know-how. Nevertheless, one can safely predict that, regardless of the outcome of the crisis, the 'indigenisation' of arms procurement will be at the top of the military agenda in Iraq for future development. In other words, the ostracising of Iraq will compel it to go the way of Israel, South Africa, Taiwan and Iran, to name but a few.

Prospects for domestic arms industries

IRAN

Modern arms production in Iran began in earnest after the oil price rises in 1973, when various aspects the of assembly and production expertise of US and European (including Israel) defence manufacturers were transferred to Iran. However, the revolution prevented the completion of many of the projects that were under way, and caused the carefully-planned Iranian military-industrial complex to collapse. The Islamic Republic thus inherited a system of defence procurement and production based on the expertise of expatriate labour, technology and military personnel. In this sense the military-industrial complex of the new regime remained a hostage to the pre-1979 arrangements that had been concluded between the Shah and his closest allies in the West. As a result the country's domestic arms production potential was neglected for some time, and received serious attention only after the start of the war with Iraq, and in the course of the rapid depletion of the army's arsenal of Western-made weapons and support systems and the difficulty of obtaining replacements cheaply and easily.

The regime therefore set out to rejuvenate already-established military-industrial processes, and at the same time proceeded to import lower-level technology and expertise for the production of less sophisticated standard weapons systems. The warm relations between Iran and the two Asian Communist powers, China and North Korea, enabled this formula to be applied. The most dramatic example of locally produced lower-level technology weapons is in the field of surface-to-surface missile development and production. Besides the modifications administered to the Soviet-made Scud B and Frog-7 SSMs, the Iranian defence establishment has developed and produced a number of other missile systems which include the Oghab, the Nazeat, the Shahin 1 and 2 missiles, and a new version of the Oghab SSM. Furthermore, the Iranian army may already be self-sufficient in the production of low-calibre ammunition and small arms.

Further up the technology ladder, Iran has taken full advantage of the small aerospace infrastructure created by the Shah to move into production and assembly of Communist-bloc military aircraft. The

DEFENCE INVESTMENT AND PROCUREMENT

assistance here of Pakistan (itself a long-standing user of Chinese-made weaponry) could be invaluable. The defence establishment's experience of carrying out repairs on the US-made F-5s, F-4s, and possibly F-14s, will have made evaluations of projects appreciably more efficient and the decision to move towards local assembly/production quite realistic.

The nerve centre of these efforts is the Defence Industries Organisation (DIO), which supervises the activities of the aircraft (IAI) and helicopter (IHI) maintenance divisions as well as the efforts of the ammunition and other arms production divisions. In addition it controls the impressive activities of the military-industrial efforts of the IRGC. The changes in the formal power structures of the defence establishment—i.e., the creation of the new defence ministry which constitutionally controls the defence industries as well—has inevitably led to rationalisation of the Second Republic's defence industries, and to the setting up of a new division of labour in military-industrial activities. A comprehensive plan of action has enabled a more uniform development in such activities, which will eventually enable those sectors, such as the navy, that are lagging behind to catch up with the others. For instance, the IAI has a new facility in operation for repairing military aircraft and aircraft engines, and the IAI and the IHI work closely together in research and development of engines, air frames and materials. Concentrating the efforts of the IRGC, the Construction Crusade and the regular army into one institution will bring together the various divisions that have produced—on many occasions independently of each other—an impressive array of equipment which include missiles, radar parts, ammunition, artillery pieces, small arms, naval craft, etc., and that have managed to carry out complex repair and maintenance duties on foreign-made aircraft engines, equipment and bodies.

Ultimately, though, if Iran is seeking a modern and self-generating military-industrial capacity, it must look westwards—particularly towards Western Europe. Concomitant with large-scale weapons purchases, Iran will demand the transfer of military technologies and processes to augment and improve its current defence production capabilities. Offset arrangements modelled on the arrangements between BAe and Saudi Arabia (Al-Yamamah I and II), and Boeing and Saudi Arabia are not inconceivable, and given of Iran's current industrial base, would greatly increase the indigenous arms-making potential of the Second Republic.

Iran's lone experiences and limited efforts in the field of arms production may have been costly in many ways as well as economically inefficient, but its achievements will also have enabled the military technocrats to home in on the technologies they have missed, thus somewhat reducing the assimilation time-lag that is involved in complex technological and advanced weapons transfers. In this context, a lasting impression of Soviet-made weaponry is likely to remain, as a testimony to Iran's isolation and to the subtle changes in its diplomatic profile since the revolution, and that will provide the country with a valuable opportunity to cash in on the booming international market for cheap copies and refined versions of older Soviet-designed equipment. Familiarity with Soviet-made equipment of course reduces the dependence of the armed forces on Western (largely US-made) arms, and makes planning and deployment less contingent on external influences. Finally, Iran may, in the coming years, elect to abandon its selective weapons production strategy in favour of the 'global' model—research and development and production of weapons systems and processes for all three forces and under all contingencies. The latter, however, requires a comprehensive infrastructure (in plant, laboratories and labour) as an essential prerequisite, coupled with political stability, continuous capital expenditure and a pool of reliable skilled labour. Of the countries in the region, only Israel has achieved this feat, while Egypt is displaying signs of progress along the same path. Iran therefore has a long way to go before the current strategy of selective arms manufacture can be superseded.

IRAQ

The disbanding of the Military Industries Corps that was created in the 1970s, and its replacement in July 1988 by the newly-created Ministry of Industry and Military Production (MIMP) (which also took over the activities of the General Organisation for Technical Industries), marked a new beginning for Iraq's nascent military industries. The MIC's reorganisation into a ministry was, first of all, an indication of the organic growth and organisational expansion of this sector of the Iraqi industry throughout the 1980s. Secondly, the fact that the new ministry also incorporated the former independent ministries of mineral resources and industries, highlights its strategic significance in relation to Iraq's future plans. The amalgamation of the country's industries with the military sector clearly signals the central government's intention of be able to plan, to invest in and to administer the complex processes of military-industrial development through a fully integrated network—in short, to create a fully-fledged military-industrial complex.

The absorption of the Ministry of Mineral Resources by the new ministry warrants special attention because it indicates government perceptions of future directions: the re-channelling of its financial and physical resources towards the state's military-industrial activities. As another consequence of this merger, the transfer of resources from one economic activity to another would become an internal matter and as such therefore be largely disguised. Procedurally, the new ministry's inheritance of productive units that were either owned or controlled by the former 'civilian' ministries increases its overall control of Iraq's economy, thus making planning and targeting more feasible. If further evidence is required to prove the importance of this new ministry to the Iraqi regime's future plans, we need only note that, like many other similar appointments that have been crucial to the longevity of Saddam Hussein's rule, the first minister appointed to it was none other than General Hussein Kamil Hassan, the President's son-in-law.

The Ministry of Industry and Military Production (MIMP) controls all of Iraq's military-related industries and supervises the activities of the fifteen or so state-owned firms that are dedicated to the aim of making Iraq nearly self-sufficient in requirements for its ground forces. The successes of the 1980s in cloning, improving and developing Soviet-designed Scud B and Frog-7 SSMs on the one hand, and Iraq's ability to design and manufacture its own missile systems on the other, were being capitalised upon at the turn of the decade to make further inroads in the near future in the related fields of aerospace research and industrial materials development. These activities had already borne fruit in late 1989 when Iraq launched its first three-staged space rocket system, weighing 48 tonnes, known as Tammuz-1, from the Anbar space research base near the Syrian border. According to General Hassan, the launching of this rocket marked the successful completion of the first phase of the country's space programme, putting Iraq well ahead of Iran in missile development and rocket technology, and on course to close the gap with Israel.[10] At another site in Kerbala, MIMP supervises the progress of another rocket and missile programme, code-named Project 395. Iraq developed its intermediate-range (2,000 km) ballistic missile, Al-Abid (and apparently the 1,860 km range missile designated Badr-2000), at the same establishment, using foreign technology and personnel (mainly Argentinian, Austrian, British, Brazilian, Chinese, Egyptian, French, North Korean, Spanish and West German).[11] The solid fuel required for these longer-range missiles was produced at another MIMP site, al-Hilla, and some of the engineering activities for these missile projects took place at al-Falluja workshops, near Baghdad. Much of the effort to boost the range of Iraq's Scud B SSMs during the Gulf War also took place at these sites.

Whereas the Islamic Republic's efforts to develop its domestic arms industries in the 1980s were hampered by its international isolation, Iraq took advantage of its 'most favoured' status during the same decade to create a complex network of covert operations throughout Europe and the United States, setting up dummy companies to gain access to the technologies vital to its arms industries and the to foreign loans with which to finance these operations. Some of these efforts have produced results in fields where they were not expected by Western analysts. The Iraqis have, for instance, used French technology to develop their own airborne early-warning and control system (in two models—Baghdad-1 and Adnan-1), and have made the Adnan-1 version operational on Soviet-supplied Il-76 Candid jet transporters.[12] Iraq has also developed an in-flight refuelling capability to enable its four squadrons of MiG-23s to transfer fuel from its Mirage F-1s, has developed the technique to mount Soviet-made laser-guided air-to-air missiles on its Mirage F-1s, and has in fact assisted France to develop the option of converting the French Mirage F-1 reconnaissance aircraft into ground attack and fighter aircraft.[13]

Iraq's efforts to expand its military-industrial base were evident in other directions besides missile production and aircraft modifications. Again with foreign assistance, the Iraqis were able to produce weapons that are used exclusively by their country's ground forces: these include the production (with Yugoslav help) of the 122 mm towed howitzer and its 122 mm ammunition, which is capable of firing 22 kg projectiles some 17 km, as well as up-graded versions of Soviet-made BMP-1 infantry combat vehicles (carrying Iraqi-fitted new armour) and improved versions of Soviet-designed self-propelled 120 mm MT-LB multi-purpose tracked armoured vehicles, in addition to the production of light armoured vehicles based on a Brazilian design, and, with Soviet assistance, extensively improved and upgraded versions of Soviet-designed T-55 MBTs (that replace the gun of the T-55 with T-72's 125 mm gun and automatic loading system).[14]

Besides these initiatives, Iraq also secured the right to produce under licence the 125 mm gun, breech, ammunition and limited electronics and optics parts of the T-72 MBT for its own eventual deployment, and in addition was able by the turn of the decade to mass-produce a large variety of light arms, artillery pieces and mortars, RPG-7s, small calibre ammunition, shells, grenades, mines, four kinds of Iraqi-developed remotely-piloted vehicles, and a range of field communications equipment (under French licence).[15] If we add to these Iraq's chemical and biological weapons capabilities, it is impossible not to be astonished by the rate of growth of the country's military industries and its successes in applying important imported technologies in specific fields and for well-defined objectives. Without doubt the war with Iran served as a push factor, but Iraq's path to local development and assimilation would have been considerably more arduous had it not been for the easy and uninterrupted access over a whole decade to arms manufacturers and military suppliers from the West, the Soviet Union (and Soviet clients) and the Third World.

The future development of Iraq's military-industrial establishment will still rely in part on inputs from the outside world. Without its expatriate technicians and their technologies, Iraq will be hard pushed to repeat, or indeed to sustain, the achievements of the 1980s during the coming decade. Despite the important reorganisation efforts already undertaken, and despite the well-planned military-industrial division of labour, the fate of its military industries wil ultimately depend on how it it is able to retain its international friends and still satisfy its hegemonic regional ambitions. Because of the changes in the international climate, it would appear that, contrary to the situation that prevailed during the 1980s, Iraq may eventually be unable to square this circle.

The regional setting and arms balance

As already discussed in Chapter 4, Iran's regional and international isolation, its military losses during the war and the rapid increases in the quantity and quality of weapons transferred to the other Gulf states, all helped to move the Gulf military balance against it in the 1980s. The disequilibrium in arms transfers can be summarised in the type of military hardware that has been transferred to the other Gulf states over the last decade. The Gulf Arab states deploy a variety of modern tanks, including the US-made M-60 A3, the French-made AMX-40, the Italian OF-40 MK2, the Soviet T-72, and the Brazilian Engesa, as well as a host of sophisticated military aircraft designed for the 1990s. These include the Su-24 Fencer, MiG-29 Fulcrum, the Tornado, the Su-25, the Mirage 2000, the F/A-18 Hornet, the F-15 Eagle and the F-16 Falcon. In addition, the GCC states and Iraq have taken delivery of advanced missile systems for air defence and for their missile boats and frigates.[16] In terms of quality, Saudi Arabia's squadrons of Tornadoes alone are far superior to the entire airforce of the Islamic Republic. Naturally the large numbers of these advanced aircraft in the inventories of the Gulf Arab states pushed Iran into third place in the quantitative race as well.

Elsewhere in the Middle East the arms race seemed to be levelling off at the turn of the decade, the four main players in the Levant—Syria,

TABLE 5.3   SSMs in the Gulf

Country/Missile	Range (km)
Iran	
Oghab	40
Frog-7	70
Shahin 2	110
Iran 130	130
Scud B	280
Iraq	
Ababil	40
Frog-7	70
Laith	90
Nissan	110
Kasir	150
Baraq	250
Scud B	280
Al-Hussein	600
Fahd	500
Al-Abbas	900
Tammuz-1	2000
Al-Abid	ICBM
S. Arabia	
CSS-2	2,200
Kuwait	
Frog-7	70

Sources: *The Military Balance* (various years); JCSS, *The Middle East Military Balance 1988–89*; *SIPRI Yearbook, 1990*; *Middle East Strategic Studies Quarterly*, Vol 1, No 3, 1989.

Jordan, Israel and Egypt—having apparently reached saturation point.[17] But the dip in military expenditures may conceal two important phenomena. First, these countries have in recent years been purchasing some of the most advanced military hardware systems developed by the West and the Soviet Union, and are thus relieved of the need for further supplies until these systems have been absorbed, or newer weapons have been made available. Secondly, the general defence cuts recorded over the last two or three years conceal the increasing domestic component of military expenditures: this is often not recorded as such, either because it is mainly research-oriented, or because 'creative' accounting methods have been adopted to move defence figures out of the national military accounts and into the civilian sector. The real problem with missile proliferation in the region is that it has acquired an indigenous footing so that missile additions do not necessarily mean additional imports of these weapons. Their deployment has been moving ahead at an alarming rate regardless of external influences, and in the Levant and North Africa, Israel, Syria, Egypt and Libya have developed domestic SSM development and production facilities with a minimum amount of fuss.

In the Gulf region, Iran and Iraq are well advanced in the missile development field, posing a danger to each other as well as to other Middle Eastern and non-Middle Eastern countries; Saudi Arabia's purchase of IRBMs from China has brought into range targets as far afield as the Soviet Union, the Mediterranean, North and East Africa and the Indian Ocean. These new trends in the arms race are more destabilising than the conventional race in fighter, tank and naval vessel transfers, for not only are they rooted domestically, beyond the full control of influential external forces, but the SSM forces being developed and deployed by these Middle Eastern countries also endanger countries that are not directly involved in the region's simmering conflicts. These processes could eventually and increasingly lead to foreign interference in the disagreements and confrontations that have characterised the Middle East since the 1940s.

Finally, the decline in military expenditures in other parts of the Middle East raises the premium for access to the rich markets of the Gulf states, and therefore encourages further large arms transfer agreements to this part of the region. Within the Gulf area, Iran's defence market may during the 1990s turn out to be the new bonanza for the international arms manufacturers—in a repeat of the situation that prevailed before the 1979 revolution disturbed the regional balance.

6 DOCUMENTS: FROM THE 1975 ALGIERS ACCORD TO THE 1990 UN SECURITY COUNCIL RESOLUTIONS ON KUWAIT

1	The Algiers Accord, 1975	*page 143*
2	National Charter for the Arab States, 1980	*152*
3	UN Security Council Resolution 598, 20 July 1987	*155*
4	Arab Co-operation Council Foundation Agreement, 16 February 1989	*157*
5	Iraqi-Saudi non-Aggression Pact, 27 March 1989	*165*
6	Iraqi memorandum to the Arab League, 15 July 1990	*166*
7	Kuwaiti memorandum to the Arab League, 19 July 1990	*174*
8	Proclamation of the Republic of Kuwait, 7 August 1990	*178*
9	Kuwaiti Provisional Government call for unity with Iraq, 8 August 1990	*179*
10	Iraqi RCC statement on merger with Kuwait, 8 August 1990	*181*
11	Arab League Foreign Ministers statement, 3 August 1990	*186*
12	Extraordinary Arab Summit Resolution, 10 August 1990	*187*

DOCUMENTS

13 Islamic Conference Organisation Foreign Ministers
    statement, 4 August 1990   *188*
14 King Fahd's statement on US troops' arrival,
    9 August 1990   *189*
15 Joint US-Soviet statement, Moscow, 3 August 1990   *191*
16 US-Soviet Summit statement, Helsinki, 9 September
    1990   *192*
17 EC Statement, 4 August 1990   *194*
18 NATO statement, 10 August 1990   *196*
19 GCC Summit Communiqué, 25 December 1990   *198*
20 UN Security Council Resolutions:
    660, 2 August 1990   *206*
    661, 6 August 1990   *207*
    662, 9 August 1990   *210*
    664, 18 August 1990   *211*
    665, 25 August 1990   *212*
    666, 13 September 1990   *213*
    667, 16 September 1990   *215*
    669, 24 September 1990   *217*
    670, 25 September 1990   *218*
    674, 29 October 1990   *221*
    678, 29 November 1990   *224*

DOCUMENTS

1. *The Algiers Accord, 6 March 1975*

During the convocation of the OPEC Summit Conference in the Algerian capital and upon the initiative of President Houari Boumedienne, the Shah of Iran and Saddam Hussein (Vice-Chairman of the Revolution Command Council) met twice and conducted lengthy talks on the relations between Iraq and Iran. These talks, attended by President Houari Boumedienne, were characterized by complete frankness and a sincere will from both parties to reach a final and permanent solution of all problems existing between the two countries in accordance with the principles of territorial integrity, border inviolability and non-interference in internal affairs.

The two High Contracting Parties have decided to:

First: Carry out a final delineation of their land boundaries in acordance with the Constantinople Protocol of 1913 and the Proceedings of the Border Delimitation Commission of 1914.

Second: Demarcate their river boundaries according to the *thalweg* line.

Third: Accordingly, the two parties shall restore security and mutual confidence along their joint borders. They shall also commit themselves to carry out a strict and effective observation of their joint borders so as to put a final end to all infiltrations of a subversive nature wherever they may come from.

Fourth: The two parties have also agreed to consider the aforesaid arrangements as inseparable elements of a comprehensive solution. Consequently, any infringement of one of its components shall naturally contradict the spirit of the Algiers Accord. The two parties shall remain in constant contact with President Houari Boumedienne who shall provide, when necessary, Algeria's brotherly assistance whenever needed in order to apply these resolutions.

The two parties have decided to restore the traditional ties of good neighbourliness and friendship, in particular by eliminating all negative factors in their relations and through constant exchange of views on issues of mutual interest and promotion of mutual co-operation.

The two parties officially declare that the region ought to be secure from any foreign interference.

The Foreign Ministers of Iraq and Iran shall meet in the presence of Algeria's Foreign Minister on 15 March 1975 in Tehran in order to make working arrangements for the Iraqi-Iranian joint commission which was set up to apply the resolutions taken by mutual agreement as specified above. And in accordance with the desire of the two parties,

Algeria shall be invited to the meetings of the Iraqi-Iranian joint commission. The commission shall determine its agenda and working procedures and hold meetings if necessary. The meetings shall be alternately held in Baghdad and Tehran.

His Majesty the Shah accepted with pleasure the invitation extended to him by His Excellency President Ahmad Hasan al-Bakr to pay a state visit to Iraq. The date of the visit shall be fixed by mutual agreement.

On the other hand, Saddam Hussein agreed to visit Iran officially at a date to be fixed by the two parties.

HM the Shah of Iran and Saddam Hussein expressed their deep gratitude to President Houari Boumedienne, who, motivated by brotherly sentiments and a spirit of disinterestedness, worked for the establishment of a direct contact between the leaders of the two countries and consequently contributed to reviving a new era in the Iraqi-Iranian relations with a view to achieving the higher interest of the future of the region in question.

TREATY CONCERNING THE FRONTIER AND NEIGHBOURLY RELATIONS BETWEEN IRAN AND IRAQ

His Imperial Majesty the Shahinshah of Iran,

His Excellency the President of the Republic of Iraq,

Considering the sincere desire of the two Parties as expressed in the Algiers Agreement of 6 March 1975, to achieve a final and lasting solution to all the problems pending between the two countries,

Considering that the two Parties have carried out the definite redemarcation of their land frontier on the basis of the Constantinople Protocol of 1913 and the minutes of the meetings of the frontier Delimitation Commission of 1914 and have delimited their river frontier along the thalweg,

Considering their desire to restore security and mutual trust throughout the length of their common frontier,

Considering the ties of geographical proximity, history, religion, culture and civilization which bind the peoples of Iran and Iraq,

Desirous of strengthening their bonds of friendship and neighbourliness, expanding their economic and cultural relations and promoting exchange and human relations between their peoples on the basis of the principles of territorial integrity, the inviolability of frontiers and non-interference in internal affairs,

Resolved to work towards the introduction of a new era in friendly relations between Iran and Iraq based on full respect for the national independence and sovereign equality of states,

Convinced that they are helping thereby to implement the principles and achieve the purposes and objectives of the Charter of the United Nations,

Have decided to conclude this Treaty and have appointed as their plenipotentiaries:

His Imperial Majesty the Shahinshah of Iran:
His Excellency Abbas Ali Khalatbary, Minister of Foreign Affairs of Iran.

His Excellency the President of the Republic of Iraq:
His Excellency Saadoun Hamadi, Minister for Foreign Affairs of Iraq.

Who, having exchanged their full powers, found to be in good and due form, have agreed as follows:

Article 1

The High Contracting Parties confirm that the State land frontier between Iraq and Iran shall be that which has been redemarcated on the basis of and in accordance with the provisions of the Protocol concerning the redemarcation of the land frontier, and the annexes thereto, attached to this Treaty.

Article 2

The High Contracting Parties confirm that the State frontier in the Shatt Al Arab shall be that which has been delimited on the basis of and in accordance with the provisions of the Protocol concerning the delimitation of the river frontier, and the annexes thereto, attached to this Treaty.

Article 3

The High Contracting Parties undertake to exercise strict and effective permanent control over the frontier in order to put an end to any infiltration of a subversive nature from any source, on the basis of and in accordance with the provisions of the protocol concerning frontier security, and the annex thereto, attached to this Treaty.

Article 4

The High Contracting Parties confirm that the provisions of the three Protocols, and the annexes thereto, referred to in article 1, 2, and 3 above and attached to this Treaty as an integral part thereof shall be final and permanent. They shall not be infringed under any circumstances and shall constitute the indivisible elements of an over-all settlement. Accordingly, a breach of any of the components of this over-all settlement shall clearly be incompatible with the spirit of the Algiers Agreement.

Article 5

In keeping with the inviolability of the frontiers of the two States and strict respect for their territorial integrity, the High Contracting Parties confirm that the course of their land and river frontiers shall be inviolable, permanent and final.

Article 6

1. In the event of a dispute regarding the interpretation or implementation of this Treaty, the three Protocols or the annexes thereto, any solution to such a dispute shall strictly respect the course of the Iraqi-Iranian frontier referred to in articles 1 and 2 above, and shall take into account the need to maintain security on the Iraqi-Iranian frontier in accordance with article 3 above.

2. Such disputes shall be resolved in the first instance by the High Contracting Parties, by means of direct bilateral negotiations to be held within two months after the date on which one of the Parties so requested.

3. If no agreement is reached, the High Contracting Parties shall have recourse, within a three-month period, to the good offices of a friendly third State.

4. Should one of the two Parties refuse to have recourse to good offices or should the good offices procedure fail, the dispute shall be settled by arbitration within a period of not more than one month after the date of such refusal or failure.

5. Should the High Contracting Parties disagree as to the arbitration procedure, one of the High Contracting Parties may have recourse, within 15 days after such disagreement was recorded, to a court of arbitration.

With a view to establish such a court of arbitration each of the High Contracting Parties shall, in respect of each dispute to be resolved, apoint one of its nationals as arbitrators and the two arbitrators shall choose an umpire. Should the High Contracting Parties fail to appoint their arbitrators within one month after the date on which one of the Parties received a request for arbitration from the other Party, or should the arbitrators fail to reach agreement on the choice of the umpire before that time-limit expires, the High Contracting Party which requested arbitration shall be entitled to request the President of the International Court of Justice to appoint the arbitrators or the umpire, in accordance with the procedures of the Permanent Court of Arbitration.

6. The decision of the court of arbitration shall be binding on and enforceable by the High Contracting Parties.

7. The High Contracting Parties shall each defray half the costs of the arbitration.

Article 7

This Treaty, the three Protocols and the annexes thereto shall be registered in accordance with Article 102 of the Charter of the United Nations.

Article 8

This Treaty, the three Protocols and the annexes thereto shall be ratified by each of the High Contracting Parties in accordance with its domestic law.

This Treaty, the three Protocols and the annexes thereto shall enter into force on the date of the exchange of the instruments of ratification in Teheran.

IN WITNESS WHEREOF the Plenipotentiaries of the High Contracting Parties have signed this Treaty, the three Protocols and the annexes thereto.

DONE at Baghdad, on 13 June 1975.

(*Signed*)	(*Signed*)
Abbas Ali Khalatbary	Saadoun Hamadi
Minister for Foreign	Minister for Foreign
Affairs of Iran	Affairs of Iraq

This Treaty, the three Protocols and the annexes thereto were signed in the presence of His Excellency Abdel-Aziz Bouteflika, Member of the Council of the Revolution and Minister for Foreign Affairs of Algeria.

(*Signed*)

PROTOCOL CONCERNING THE DELIMITATION TO THE RIVER FRONTIER BETWEEN IRAN AND IRAQ

Pursuant to the decisions taken in the Algiers communiqué of 6 March 1975,
The two Contracting Parties have agreed as follows:

DOCUMENTS

Article 1

The two Contracting Parties hereby declare and recognize that the State river frontier between Iran and Iraq in the Shatt Al Arab has been delimited along the thalweg by the Mixed Iraqi-Iranian-Algerian Committee on the basis of the following:

1. The Teheran Protocol of 17 March 1975;
2. The record of the Meeting of Ministers for Foreign Affairs, signed at Baghdad on 20 April 1975, approving, *inter alia*, the record of the Committee to Delimit the River Frontier, signed on 16 April 1975 on board the Iraqi ship *El Thawra* in the Shatt Al Arab;
3. Common hydrographic charts, which have been verified on the spot and corrected and on which the geographical co-ordinates of the 1975 frontier crossing points have been indicated; these charts have been signed by the hydrographic experts of the Mixed Technical Commission and countersigned by the heads of the Iran, Iraq and Algerian delegations to the Committee. The said charts, listed hereinafter, are annexed to this protocol and form an integral part thereof:

Chart No. 1: Entrance to the Shatt Al Arab, No. 3842, published by the British Admiralty:
Chart No. 2: Inner Bar to Kabda Point, No. 3843, published by the British Admiralty:
Chart No. 3: Kabda Point to Abadan, No. 3844, published by the British Admiralty:
Chart No. 4: Abadan to Jazirat Ummat Tuwaylah, No. 3845, published by the British Admiralty.

Article 2

1. The frontier line in the Shatt Al Arab shall follow the thalweg, i.e., the median line of the main navigable channel at the lowest navigable level, starting from the point at which the land frontier between Iran and Iraq enters the Shatt Al Arab and continuing to the sea.

2. The frontier line, as defined in paragraph 1 above, shall vary with changes brought about by natural causes in the main navigable channel. The frontier line shall not be affected by other changes unless the two Contracting Parties conclude a special agreement to that effect.

3. The occurrence of any of the changes referred to in paragraph 2 above shall be attested jointly by the competent technical authorities of the two Contracting Parties.

4. Any change in the bed of the Shatt Al Arab brought about by natural causes which would involve a change in the national character of

the two States' repsective territory or of landed property, constructions, or technical or other installations shall not change the course of the frontier line, which shall continue to follow the thalweg in accordance with the provisions of paragraph 1 above.

5. Unless an agreement is reached between the two Contracting Parties concerning the transfer of the frontier line to the new bed, the water shall be re-directed at the joint expense of both Parties to the bed existing in 1975—as marked on the four common charts listed in article 1, paragraph 3, above—should one of the Parties so require within two years after the date on which the occurrence of the change was attested by either of the two Parties. Until such time, both Parties shall retain their previous rights of navigation and of use over the water of the new bed.

Article 3

1. The river frontier between Iran and Iraq in the Shatt Al Arab, as defined in article 2 above, is represented by the relevant line drawn on the common charts referred to in article 1, paragraph 3, above.

2. The two Contracting Parties have agreed to consider that the river frontier shall end at the straight line connecting the two banks of the Shatt Al Arab, at its mouth, at the astronomical lowest low-water mark. This straight line has been indicated on the common hydrographic charts referred to in article 1, paragraph 3, above.

Article 4

The frontier line as defined in article 1, 2 and 3 of this protocol shall also divide vertically the air space and the subsoil.

Article 5

With a view to eliminating any source of controversy, the two Contracting Powers shall establish a Mixed Iraqi-Iranian Commission to settle, within two months, any questions concerning the status of landed property, constructions, or technical or other installations, the national character of which may be affected by the delimitations of the Iranian-Iraqi river frontier, either through repurchase or compensations or any other suitable arrangement.

Article 6

Since the task of surveying the Shatt Al Arab has been completed and the common hydrographic chart referred to in article 1, paragraph 3, above has been drawn up, the two Contracting Parties have agreed that a new survey of the Shatt Al Arab shall be carried out jointly, once every 10 years, with effect from the date of signature of this Protocol. However, each of the two Parties shall have the right to request new surveys, to be carried out jointly, before the expiry of the 10-year period.

Article 7

1. Merchant vessels, State vessels and warships of the two Contracting Parties shall enjoy freedom of navigation in the Shatt Al Arab and in any part of the navigable channels in the territorial sea which lead to the mouth of the Shatt Al Arab, irrespective of the line delimiting the territorial sea of each of the two countries.

2. Vessels of third countries used for purposes of trade shall enjoy freedom of navigation, on an equal and non-discriminatory basis, in the Shatt Al Arab and in any part of the navigable channels in the territorial sea which lead to the mouth of the Shatt Al Arab, irrespective of the line delimiting the territorial sea of each of the two countries.

3. Either of the two Contracting Parties may authorize foreign warships visiting its ports to enter the Shatt Al Arab, provided such vessels do not belong to a country in a state of belligerency, armed conflict or war with either of the two Contracting Parties and provided the other Party is so notified no less than 72 hours in advance.

4. The two Contracting Parties shall in every case refrain from authorizing the entry to the Shatt Al Arab of merchant vessels belonging to a country in a state of belligerency, armed conflict or war with either of the two Parties.

Article 8

1. Rules governing navigation in the Shatt Al Arab shall be drawn up by a mixed Iranian-Iraqi Commission, in accordance with the principle of equal rights of navigation for both States.

2. The two Contracting Parties shall establish a Commission to draw up rules governing the prevention and control of pollution in the Shatt Al Arab.

3. The two Contracting Parties undertake to conclude subsequent agreements on the questions referred to in paragraphs 1 and 2 of this article.

Article 9

The two Contracting Parties recognize that the Shatt Al Arab is primarily an international waterway, and undertake to refrain from any

DOCUMENTS

operation that might hinder navigation in the Shatt Al Arab or in any part of those navigable channels in the territorial sea of either of the two countries that lead to the mouth of the Shatt Al Arab.

DONE at Baghdad, on 13 June 1975.

(Signed)
Abbas Ali Khalatbary
Minister for Foreign
Affairs of Iran

(Signed)
Saadoun Hamadi
Minister for Foreign
Affairs of Iraq

Signed in the presence of His Excellency Abdel-Aziz Bouteflika, Member of the Council of the Revolution and Minister for Foreign Affairs of Algeria.

(Signed)

DOCUMENTS

2. National Charter for the Arab States, proposed 8 February 1980

In view of the present international situation and its potential future developments, and in the light of the serious possibilities threatening the Arab sovereignty and national security, on the one hand, and world peace and security on the other; and in response to the demands of national responsibility to the Arab nation's land, culture and heritage; and in accordance with the principles of the non-Aligned Movement, Iraq feels called upon to take the initiative by issuing the following declaration, to be taken, first, as a charter regulating the national relations among the Arab countries, and secondly as a pledge by the Arab nation to the neighbouring states which declare their respect and commitment to this charter.

The declaration is based on the following principles:

ONE. The rejection of the presence in the Arab homeland of any foreign armies and military forces, or any foreign forces and military bases, or any facilities in any form, or under any pretext or cover, or for any reason whatsoever. Any Arab regime that fails to abide by this principle should be isolated and boycotted politically and economically, and its policies should be resisted by all means available.

TWO. Prohibiting the use of armed force by any Arab state against any other Arab state. All disputes that may arise between Arab states should be settled by peaceful means and in accordance with the principles of joint national action and the supreme Arab interests.

THREE. The principle mentioned in Article 2 applies to the relations of the Arab nation and countries with the neighbouring nations and states. No armed force should be used to resolve disputes with these states except in defending sovereignty in self-defence, and in cases where the security and fundamental interests of the Arab countries are threatened.

FOUR. Solidarity of all Arab countries in the face of any foreign agression or violation committed by any foreign power against the territorial integrity and sovereignty of any Arab country. In the event of any foreign power declaring war on any Arab country, all Arab countries should jointly resist and thwart that aggression or violation by all means available, including military action and total political and economic embargo, and in all other fields deemed necessary and in the national interest.

FIVE. Confirming the commitment of all Arab countries to the international laws and conventions regarding the use of waterways, air and territory by any state that is not at war with any Arab country.

SIX. Arab countries should keep away from the arenas of international conflicts and wars, and should observe complete neutrality and non-alignment towards any party in conflict or war, except when such party violate the Arab territory, sovereignty or rights of Arab countries guaranteed by international laws and conventions. Arab countries should refrain from military participation—wholly or partially—in wars and military disputes, inside or outside the area, on behalf of any foreign state or party.

SEVEN. Commitment of the Arab countries to establish advanced and constructive inter-Arab economic relations, to provide and solidify the common ground for advanced Arab economic structure and Arab unity. Arab countries should avoid any act that may harm these relations or block their continuity and development, regardless of their different systems of government, or the marginal differences that may arise among them, so long as the parties concerned remain committed to the principles of this Declaration.

Arab countries should abide by the principle of national economic integration. Arab countries economically able should offer all kinds of economic aid to other Arab countries to safeguard against dependence on foreign powers in a manner infringing these countries' independence and national will.

EIGHT. In presenting the principles of this Declaration, Iraq confirms its readiness to abide by it with respect to every Arab country, and every party committed to it. Iraq is also ready to discuss this Declaration with the Arab brethren, and listen to their comments thereon, to enhance the effectiveness of its principles and deepen its implications.

Iraq also confirms that this Declaration is no substitute for the Arab League Charter or the Treaty of Joint Defence and Economic Cooperation concluded by the Arab League members. Rather, Iraq deems it a reinforcement of the Charter and Treaty, and a development thereupon, in line with the developing international conditions, the dangers threatening the Arab nation and its consequent national responsibilities towards the present and future circumstances.

Great people of Iraq!

Masses of the great Arab nation!

In presenting this declaration, Iraq is urged by its national responsibility which supersedes any subjective or regional interest. While we approach the Arab governments with this declaration, as the authority responsible for applying it and abiding by its principles, we deeply believe that these principles cannot be ascertained and become a charter for Arab relations except through the struggle and support of the Arab masses, because the Declaration ensures their basic interests and responds to their national aspirations in liberty and independence, and paves the way for the Arab Unity.

Saddam Hussein
Chairman, R.C.C.,
President of the Republic of Iraq
Baghdad February 8th 1980

DOCUMENTS

3. UN Security Council Resolution 598, 20 July 1987

The Security Council, reaffirming its Resolution 582 (1986),
deeply concerned that, despite its calls for a ceasefire, the conflict between Iran and Iraq continues unabated, with further heavy loss of human life and material destruction,
deploring the initiation and continuation of the conflict,
deploring also the bombing of purely civilian population areas, attacks of neutral shipping or civilian aircraft, the violation of international humanitarian law and other laws of armed conflict and, in particular, the use of chemical weapons contrary to obligations under the 1925 Geneva Protocol,
deeply concerned that further escalation and widening of the conflict may take place,
determined to bring to an end all military actions between Iran and Iraq,
convinced that a comprehensive, just, honourable and durable settlement should be achieved between Iran and Iraq,
recalling the provisions of the United Nations Charter, and, in particular, the obligation of all member states to settle their international disputes by peaceful means in such a manner that international peace and security and justice are not endangered,
determining that there exists a breach of the peace as regards the conflict between Iran and Iraq,
acting under Articles 39 and 40 of the Charter of the United Nations:

1 *Demands* that, as a first step towards a negotiated settlement, Iran and Iraq observe an immediate ceasefire, discontinue all military actions on land, at sea and in the air, and withdraw all forces to the internationally recognized boundaries without delay;

2 *Requests* the Secretary-General to dispatch a team of United Nations observers to verify, confirm and supervise the ceasefire and withdrawal and further requests the Secretary-General to make the necessary arrangements in consultation with the parties and to submit a report thereon to the Security Council;

3 *Urges* that prisoners of war be released and repatriated without delay after the cessation of active hostilities in accordance with the Third Geneva Convention of 12 August, 1949;

4 *Calls upon* Iran and Iraq to co-operate with the Secretary-General in implementing this resolution and in mediation efforts to achieve a

comprehensive, just and honourable settlement, acceptable to both sides, of all outstanding issues, in accordance with the principles contained in the Charter of the United Nations;

5 *Calls upon* all other states to exercise the utmost restraint and to refrain from any act which may lead to further escalation and widening of the conflict, and thus to facilitate the implementation of the present resolution;

6 *Requests* the Secretary-General to explore, in consultation with Iran and Iraq, the question of entrusting an impartial body with enquiring into responsibility for the conflict and to report to the Security Council as soon as possible;

7 *Recognizes* the magnitude of the damage inflicted during the conflict and the need for reconstruction efforts, with appropriate international assistance, once the conflict is ended and, in this regard, requests the Secretary-General to assign a team of experts to study the question of reconstruction and to report to the Security Council;

8 *Further requests* the Secretary-General to examine in consultation with Iran and Iraq and with other states of the region, measures to enhance the security and stability of the region;

9 *Requests* the Secretary-General to keep the Security Council informed on the implementation of this resolution;

10 *Decides* to meet again as necessary to consider further steps to ensure compliance.

DOCUMENTS

4. Agreement on the Establishment of The Arab Co-operation Council

Baghdad on Rajab 1409 Hijrah corresponding to 16 February 1989 A.D.

In the Name of God
the Merciful, the Compassionate

Whereas the Arab Nation,

Guided by its rich and time-honoured cultural heritage and its great role in building the edifice of human civilization, aspires with legitimate determination, to achieve co-operation, solidarity and joint action in all fields; impelled by its deep sense of unity and by its desire to reaffirm its national attributes which have been consolidated through the ages and its distinctive cultural identity, to safeguard its security, to tend its legitimate interests, to continue its efforts for progress and prosperity, and to strengthen its positive and constructive international role in serving the cause of peace, security, progress and equitable and fruitful co-operation amongst the peoples of the world;

Having experienced, in recent times, a number of attempts at joint Arab action, co-operation and solidarity and been able to achieve certain forms of unity and learn some rich lessons from the positive and negative aspects of such attempts;

Recognizing that to the forefront of those lessons has been the co-operation for establishing the infrastructures which would consolidate all forms of spiritual, cultural and practicable ties amongst the citizens of the Arab States, a co-operation which assumes priority in any serious, continual and incessant endeavour for joint Arab action and which creates strong and practical foundations for such an endeavour to reach the high levels and wide prospects leading to the Arab Nation's ultimate goal of unity according to the circumstances prevailing and the practical means available;

Whereas this realistic and constructive approach is consonant with the current international trends towards the establishment of economic groupings which would create such circumstances for the countries affiliated to them as would better protect their interests and ensure their economic development and progress;

Believing that co-operation amongst the Arab States in these fields acquires a special importance in view of the dangers which continue to threaten Arab national security politically, economically, and culturally;

Proceeding from the fact that the establishment of security, peace and stability in the whole region requires the strengthening of Arab awareness of the integral nature of Arab national security and of its requirements and conditions through practical co-operation, co-ordination and solidarity;

Considering that the circumstances which bring together the Hashemite Kingdom of Jordan, the Republic of Iraq, the Arab Republic of Egypt and the Yemen Arab Republic are of a similar nature in many fields;

Proceeding from the belief of these Arab States in the above-stated principles and values;

Expressing their deep desire to find practical and realistic ways of strengthening and developing the co-operation that, for many years now, continued amongst them and yielded significant results within the framework of the circumstances prevailing and the means available in every stage with a view to elevating it to the highest levels of solidarity and joint action;

Guided by the Covenant of the League of Arab States which permits Member States, desirous of achieving closer co-operation and ensuring stronger ties, to conclude such agreements amongst them as may achieve these objectives;

Pursuant to the Agreement reached during the historic meeting held in Baghdad amongst His Majesty King Hussein bin Talal of the Hashemite Kingdom of Jordan, His Excellency President Saddam Hussein of the Republic of Iraq, His Excellency President Mohammed Hosni Mubarak of the Arab Republic of Egypt and His Excellency President Ali Abdallah Salih of the Yemen Arab Republic, during 9–10 Rajab 1409 of Hijrah, corresponding to 15–16 February 1989, it is hereby decided to establish, with God's blessings, the Arab Co-operation Council in accordance with the following:

Article One

The Arab Co-operation Council shall be constituted of the Hashemite Kingdom of Jordan, the Republic of Iraq, the Arab Republic of Egypt and the Yemen Arab Republic, in accordance with the provisions of this Agreement. The Council shall be considered as one of the institutions of the Arab Nation which adheres to the Covenant of the League of Arab States, the Treaty of Common Defence and Economic Co-operation and the institutions and organizations emanating from the League of Arab States and shall establish co-operative relations with Arab and international regional groupings.

Article Two

The Arab Co-operation Council shall aim at:

1. The achievement of the highest levels of co-ordination, co-operation, integration and solidarity amongst the Member-States and the gradual elevation thereof according to the circumstances, capabilities and expertise.

2. The gradual attainment of economic integration by co-ordinating policies at the level of various production sectors, co-ordination of development plans of Member-States taking into consideration the growth rate, the economic situation and the circumstances of Member-States as they pass from one stage to another, and the attainment of the desired integration and co-ordination, particularly in the following fields:

    a. Economy and finance
    b. Industry and agriculture
    c. Transport and communications
    d. Education, culture, and information
    e. Scientific research and technology
    f. Social affairs, health and tourism
    g. Labour, travel and residence arrangements

3. The encouragement of investment, joint ventures and economic co-operation amongst the public, private co-operative and mixed sectors.

4. Pursuing the establishment of a common market amongst Member-States as a step towards the establishment of the Arab common market and Arab economic union.

5. Strengthening the relations and ties between the citizens of Member-States in all fields.

6. The enhancement and development of joint Arab action so as to strengthen Arab ties.

Article Three

For the achievement of its objectives, the Council shall lay down practical plans and measures, including the consideration of the possibility of promulgating, adapting or unifying legislation in the different fields.

DOCUMENTS

Article Four

1. Membership of the Council is open to every Arab State which wishes to join it.

2. Approval of accession to the membership of the Council shall be made by the unanimity of the Member-States.

Article Five

The Council shall consist of the following organs:
 1. The Supreme Body
 2. The Ministerial Body
 3. The General Secretariat

Article Six

The Supreme Body shall be composed of the heads of the Member-States. It shall be the Supreme authority of the Council.

Article Seven

The Supreme Body shall have the following powers:
 1. Drawing up the high policies of the Council.
 2. Adopting the necessary decisions relating to the recommendations placed before it by the Ministerial Body.
 3. Entrusting the Ministerial Body with any question that falls within the competence and the work of the Council.
 4. Approving the rules of procedure of the Council and the amendments thereof.
 5. Appointing the Secretary-General of the Council.
 6. Accepting the accession of new members.
 7. Amending the Agreement on the Establishment of the Council.
 8. Following up progress in implementing agreed-upon procedures for co-ordination, co-operation and integration.
 9. Setting up other organs and permanent commissions when necessary.

Article Eight

1. The Supreme Body shall hold a regular session once every year in one of the Member-States alternately. The Head of the host State shall preside over the Supreme Body for a full annual term.

2. Extraordinary meetings may be convened by an invitation from the President of the Supreme Body or at the request of one Member State supported by at least one other Member State. The Extraordinary

meetings shall be convened in the state whose Head of State presides over the Supreme Body.

3. Special meetings may be held with the agreement of the Heads of the Member-States in any capital or city of Member-States. The convening of such meetings shall not affect the rules relating to the Presidency of the Supreme Body.

4. The convening of the meetings of the Supreme Body shall be considered as valid by the presence of a majority of Member-States.

Article Nine

The Ministerial Body shall be composed of the Heads of Government of the Member-States or those acting as such.

Article Ten

The Ministerial Body shall have the competence to deal with the following:

1. Studying affairs and questions relating to matters falling within the competence of the Council.

2. Placing before the Supreme Body plans, proposals and recommendations relating to the achievement of the objectives of the Council.

3. The adoption of the necessary practical measures for the implementation of the decisions of the Supreme Body.

4. Studying any matter relating to the affairs of co-operation, including the reference thereof to specialized and ad hoc committees, when necessary, in order to examine it and submit appropriate proposals relating thereto.

5. Preparing the rules of procedure of the Council and the placing thereof before the Supreme Body for its approval and proposing amendments thereto when necessary.

6. Approval and amendement of financial and administrative regulations of the general Secretariat.

7. Consideration of the reports of the Secretary-General relating to the work of the Council.

8. Consideration and approval of the budget of the general Secretariat and approval of its final accounts and of the financial and administrative status of the general Secretariat.

9. Setting up temporary committees as required by the work of the Council.

10. Preparation of the draft agenda of the Supreme Body.

Article Eleven

1. The Ministerial Body shall hold a regular meeting every six months in the State holding the Presidency of the Supreme Body. The Ministerial Body shall be presided over by the Head of Government, or whoever acts as such in that State.

2. Extraordinary meetings may be convened at the invitation of the President of the Ministerial Body or upon a proposal by one Member-State supported at least by another. The extraordinary meeting shall be held in the State holding the Presidency.

3. The convening of the meetings of the Ministerial Body shall be considered as valid by the presence of a majority of member-States.

Article Twelve

In adopting decisions in all organs of the Council, Member-States shall seek to achieve unanimity and consensus amongst themselves. In the absence thereof, decisions shall be taken by a majority of Member-States and such decisions shall be binding upon all. As for decisions relating to membership and amendment of the Agreement on the Establishment of the Council, they shall be taken unanimously.

Article Thirteen

1. The Council shall have a general Secretariat with its headquarters in Amman, headed by a Secretary-General and composed of a number of officials as necessary.

2. The Supreme Body shall appoint the Secretary-General from amongst the citizens of the States of the Council on the basis of personal competence and belief in the objectives of the Council. The appointment shall be for a period of two years, renewable twice at the most.

3. The staff of the General Secretariat shall be selected from the citizens of Member-States on the basis of personal competence and belief in the objectives of the Council.

4. The Secretary General and the senior staff of the General Secretariat shall enjoy such privileges, immunities and facilities as would enable them to accomplish their duties in the host State and Member-States.

Article Fourteen

1. The Secretary-General is the Executive Head of the General Secretariat of the Council and shall be directly responsible before the Ministerial Body for all the work of the General Secretariat and the proper conduct of its work.

2. The Secretary-General shall undertake the following duties:
   a. Following up the implementation of decisions of the Supreme Body and the Ministerial Body.
   b. Preparing the necessary reports on the work of the Council in order to present them to the Ministerial Body and the Supreme Body.
   c. Preparing the draft agenda of the Ministerial Body.
   d. Preparing the draft Budget and the Final Accounts of the Council.
   e. Proposing the administrative and financial regulations of the General Secretariat and presenting them to the Ministerial Body.
   f. Appointing the staff of the General Secretariat and terminating their employment.
   g. Any other duties entrusted to him by the Supreme Body or the Ministerial Body.

Article Fifteen

A Headquarters Agreement for the General Secretariat shall be concluded between the host State and the Secretary General on behalf of the Council following the approval of the Agreement by the Ministerial Body.

Article Sixteen

The General Secretariat shall have an annual budget to which Member-States shall contribute equally.

Article Seventeen

1. This Agreement shall enter into force as of the date of its ratification by the signatory States in accordance with the applicable constitutional procedures, and the depositing of the instruments of ratification with the Ministry of Foreign Affairs of the Hashemite Kingdom of Jordan in its capacity as the Headquarters State for the General Secretariat.

2. This Agreement shall come into force for States that accede to the membership of the Council in accordance with the provisions of Article Four as of the date of depositing the instrument of accession with the General Secretariat of the Council.

3. Amendments of this Agreement shall be made by a unanimous decision of the Supreme Body. The amendment shall come into force as of the date of ratification by Member-States in accordance with their applicable constitutional procedures and the depositing of the instruments of ratification with the general Secretariat of the Council.

4. The Headquarters of the General Secretariat shall deposit a copy of this Agreement with the League of Arab States and register it with the Secretariat of the United Nations.

Signed at Baghdad on 10 Rajab, 1409 of Hijrah, corresponding to 16 February, 1989 A.D.

5. Agreement on Non-Interference in Internal Affairs and the Non-Use of Force between the Republic of Iraq and the Kingdom of Saudi Arabia, 27 March 1989

The Republic of Iraq and the Kingdom of Saudi Arabia, realising that the protection of Arab national security against the dangers that threaten the sovereignty and security of the Arab states on the one hand and world peace and security on the other requires that peaceful relations should prevail between the Arab states on the basis of sovereignty, the non-use of force, the settlement of disputes by peaceful means, and non-interference in internal affairs;

Subscribing to the principles of national action which bring together the Arab people, the objectives and principles of the Charter of the League of Arab States, and the Agreements of Common Defence and Economic Co-operation of the Member States of the Arab League, and recalling the goals and principles of the Charter of the United Nations and the principles of international law,

Have decided to sign the following agreement:

Article One

The two brotherly states undertake not to use force in the relations existing between them.

Article Two

The two brotherly states undertake to settle any disputes that may arise between them by peaceful means, as laid down in the Charter of the League of Arab States and in international law.

Article Three

Each of the two brotherly states undertakes not to interfere in the internal affairs of the other.

Article Four

This agreement is subject to ratification in accordance with the procedures in force in the two brotherly states and will come into force as of the date of the exchange of the instruments of ratification.

DOCUMENTS

6. *Iraq's memorandum to the Arab League, 15 July 1990*

His Excellency, Chadli al-Klibi, Secretary General of the League of Arab States.

Brotherly greetings,

At the beginning of this letter we must recall the principles which Iraq believes in and which it has implemented in all honesty and faithfulness in its Arab relations. Iraq believes that the Arabs, wherever they may be, are one nation and that its wealth should be distributed for the benefit of everyone and if anyone should suffer harm or grief then everyone suffers. Iraq looks at the wealth of the nation on the basis of these principles, and it has acted with its wealth in accordance with these principles.

Iraq also believes that in spite of all that the Arab community suffered during the Ottoman period and afterwards, under western imperialism, from all types of division, degradation, persecution and attempts to distort the Arab identity, nevertheless the basis of the unity of the Arab nation remained alive and vibrant; and that the Arab nation, despite its division into states, is one nation and every inch of this nation in this state or another should be considered first of all in the context of nationalist considerations and especially in the context of joint Arab national security. It is also necessary to avoid falling into the abyss of narrow and selfish concerns in dealing with the rights and interests of the Arab states.

The higher interests of the Arab nation and the higher strategic calculations of Arab national security should always be present with us. They should always be the top priority in dealing with all these problems among the Arab states. On the basis of these nationalist principles and of sincere and brotherly relations, Iraq dealt with Kuwait in spite of what is known of past and present facts existing between the two states.

What has led us to write this letter is that, with deep sorrow, we are facing now on the part of the government of Kuwait, a situation which is beyond the bounds of the nationalist terms of reference which we have mentioned, and contradicts them and threatens their very nature. It also contradicts the fundamental basis of relations between the Arab states. The officials in the government of Kuwait, despite our sincere and brotherly stand in dealing with them on all issues, and despite our concern to continue the brotherly dialogue with them at all times, have attempted in a planned, predetermined and continuous process to take advantage of Iraq and to cause it harm with the intention of weakening it after the end of the ruinous war which lasted eight years. All sincere Arabs, leaders, intellectuals and citizens, including the heads of the Gulf states, agreed that in the war Iraq was defending the sovereignty of all the Arab nation, especially the Gulf states and in particular Kuwait. The Government of Kuwait also adopted a policy which atempted to weaken Iraq while it was confronting a vicious imperialist Zionist campaign as a result of its nationalist position in defending Arab rights. Unfortunately, this policy was pursued out of selfish and narrow interests and goals which we cannot any longer but consider as suspicious and dangerous.

We would like to raise two issues here. First, we want to draw attention to the well-known fact that since the days of imperialism and division imposed upon the Arab nation, there has been an unresolved issue of border demarcation between Iraq and Kuwait. The contacts made during the 1960s and 1970s, and up until the beginning of the war between Iraq and Iran, with the aim of reaching a solution between the two parties on this subject, were unsuccessful. During the long years of war, particularly during the time when the brave Iraqi sons were shedding their precious blood on the front defending the Arab land, including the land of Kuwait, and Arab sovereignty and dignity, including the dignity of Kuwait, the Government of Kuwait exploited the fact that Iraq was preoccupied as well as Iraq's belief in its fundamental nationalist principles and its correct relations with brothers and in nationalist issues, so that it could execute a plan to escalate its gradual and predetermined encroachment on the land of Iraq. It erected military installations, border posts, oil installations and farms on Iraqi territory. We remained silent about all of this and thought it sufficient to make signs and indications hoping that this would be enough in the context of brotherly principles which we thought everyone believed in. But these actions continued in predetermined and underhand ways, confirming the fact that they had been planned in advance.

After the liberation of Fao we took the initiative during the summit conference in Algiers in 1988 to convey to the Kuwaiti side our sincere desire to solve this problem in the context of brotherly relations and higher national interests. But we found ourselves facing a very surprising situation since, although the logic of the situation would have led Kuwaiti officials to be pleased at the generous and fraternal initiative on our part and have worked to resolve the issue quickly, we encountered deliberate vacillation and foot-dragging on their part with regard to continuing negotiations and contacts. And they raised unnecessary complications while continuing to encroach and erect petroleum and military installations, border posts and farms on Iraqi territory. We bore this behaviour with patience and forbearance. We would have been perfectly willing to be more patient if matters had not moved to a more dangerous level at which we could no longer remain silent; we will discuss this in the second and more critical point. Iraq retains a full record of this matter supported by documents and data which make clear excesses committed by the Government of Kuwait.

Second, Kuwait began, a few months ago and specifically after Iraq raised its voice loudly in calling for the restoration of the rights of Arabs in Palestine and pointing out the dangers of the American presence in the Gulf, adopting a wrong policy the purpose of which was to harm the Arab nation and particularly Iraq.

Here the Government of the UAE participated with the Government of Kuwait in a planned operation to flood the oil market with excess production which was more than their assigned OPEC quotas, advancing superficial justifications that did not have any logical, just or fair basis and using justifications which were not shared by any of the brotherly producing countries. This planned policy led to the collapse of oil prices to a very dangerous level. After the collapse in prices which took place several years ago from the high levels of $29, $28 and $24/b which it had achieved, the policies of the Governments of Kuwait and the UAE led to the collapse of the level of the minimum and modest price which was agreed upon in OPEC recently—from $18/b to $11–$13/b. A simple mathematical calculation shows the extent of heavy losses inflicted upon the Arab oil-producing states.

1. The average oil production of Arab states is 14 million b/d. The collapse of the prices in the period 1981–1990 led to a loss for the Arab states of approximately $500 billion. Iraq's share of that is $89 billion. If the Arabs had not lost this huge sum and if we had saved half of it for national development and assistance to poorer Arab states we would have achieved a high rate of national development and would have assisted the poor in our society and the state of the nation would have been stronger, more prosperous and more advanced than it is now. If we take the minimum price agreed upon in OPEC in 1987 ($18/b) then the loss to the Arab states during this period, 1987–1990, due to the collapse of prices is around $25 billion.

2. The drop of a single dollar in the oil price leads to a loss for Iraq of $1bn annually. It is known that this year the price has fallen several dollars below that level because of the policies of the Governments of Kuwait and the UAE. This means a loss for Iraq of several billion

dollars in revenue this year at a time when it is suffering from a financial crisis because of the cost of its rightful defence of its own land, security and whatever it holds sacred and the defence of Arab lands, their security and whatever they hold sacred during the fierce eight-year war. These substantial losses arising from the collapse of oil prices have not only affected the oil-producing states but they have also caused harm to the other brotherly states which were receiving assistance from the Arab oil-producing countries. Aid funds decreased and in some cases even ceased and the condition of the joint Arab institutions deteriorated. This situation was used as an excuse to cut or even end subsidies and support for joint Arab activities.

The Government of Kuwait has added to its premeditated offences another offence aimed at harming Iraq in particular. Since 1980, and especially during the war, it erected installations on the southern part of the Iraqi Rumailah field and produced oil from it. It is clear from this that it was flooding the world oil market in part with oil which it had stolen from the Iraqi Rumailah field, thus intentionally dealing a double blow to Iraq: once by weakening its economy at a time when it had a dire need of revenues and a second time by stealing its wealth. The value of the oil which the Kuwaiti Government lifted from the Rumailah field in this way, which goes against brotherly relations, amounts to $2.4 billion at the prevailing prices during 1980–1990. We therefore wish to put on record before the Arab League and before all the Arab states, Iraq's right to regain that part of its wealth which was stolen and its right to demand from those concerned a correction of this transgression and compensation for the damage it suffered.

We explained on many previous occasions the dangers of the policy of the Kuwaiti and UAE Governments to our brothers among the oil-producing Arab states, including Kuwait and the UAE. We drew attention to this many times, we complained and we warned. At the Baghdad summit, President Saddam Hussein addressed this problem in the presence of Kings, Presidents and Princes, and all others concerned, in a frank and brotherly way (a text of the speech on this subject is attached). We were expecting, especially with the brotherly and positive atmosphere achieved at the Baghdad summit, that the Governments of Kuwait and the UAE would abandon this course of action. But the bitter truth is that all the bilateral efforts and contacts we undertook with brotherly states to play a positive role in persuading the governments of Kuwait and the UAE to abandon this course, and despite the speech of President Saddam Hussein at the Baghdad summit, these two governments intentionally continued this policy. Moreover, some of the officials in these two countries issued insolent statements when we hinted at these facts and complained about them. Therefore, we could not but conclude that what the Governments of Kuwait and the UAE did in this context was a predetermined policy with covert aims. We were also aware that this policy which led to the collapse of the oil price would in the end cause damage to the economies of these two countries themselves.

We can only conclude that those who adopted this policy directly and openly and those who supported it and pushed for it were carrying out part of an imperialist Zionist plan against Iraq and the Arab nation, especially at this time when there is a serious threat from Israel and from imperialism against the Arab nation in general and Iraq in particular. How can we confront this serious threat and preserve the balance of power realised at a high cost by Iraq which suffered heavy losses during the war and suffered from the collapse in the value of its basic resource as well as the resource of the other Arab oil-exporting countries, namely Iraq, Saudi Arabia, Qatar, Oman, Yemen, Egypt, Syria, Algeria and Libya? Furthermore, this suspect policy leads to the weakening of the ability of the Arab states to confront their serious economic and social problems, which are of a crucial nature. To what fate do the Governments of Kuwait and the UAE wish to lead the Arab nation in this difficult, dangerous and critical period? To whose policies and objectives do they wish to adhere?

We, after having clarified these matters to all brothers, and after having requested directly these two governments to stop these wrong and destructive policies and having explained to them, before, during and after the Baghdad summit, the serious damage inflicted upon us, and after having sent envoys and letters, we condemn what the Governments of Kuwait and the UAE have done as a direct aggression against Iraq as well as a direct aggression against the Arab nation.

As regards the Kuwaiti Government, its attack on Iraq is a double one. On the one hand Kuwait is attacking Iraq and encroaching on our territory and oilfields and stealing our national wealth. Such action is tantamount to military aggression. On the other hand the Government of Kuwait is determined to cause a collapse of the Iraqi economy during this period when it is confronting the vicious imperialist Zionist threat, which is an aggression no less serious than military aggression.

We present these painful facts to our Arab brothers in the hope that they will raise their voices loudly and put an end to this premeditated aggression and advise the two deviationists to return to the proper behaviour which takes into consideration joint nationalist interests and the needs of joint nationalist security.

DOCUMENTS

3. In discussing higher nationalist interests and the link between Arab wealth and the future of the Arab nation, we would like to propose the following:

If all the Arab oil-producing and non-oil-producing countries were to achieve together political solidarity, and agree to raise the oil price above $25/b and then establish a fund for Arab development and assistance along the lines agreed at the Amman summit, with the fund being financed at the rate of $1 for every barrel of oil sold by the Arab oil-producing countries at a price above $25/b, then a sum of $5 billion a year would be accumulated in this fund. At the same time oil revenues of the oil-producing countries would also increase substantially because the joint Arab solidarity which would be achieved by this fair price would raise their current incomes and would protect them from aggressive attempts aimed at weakening Arab strength by undermining the resource of their oil wealth.

We can imagine how a sum like that would strengthen Arab national security and provide development possibilities for all the Arab countries and enable them to confront the stifling economic crises from which most of our countries suffer. Iraq is submitting its proposal for serious study, and the next Arab summit conference in Cairo could be an occasion to discuss this proposal and approve it.

4. Since we are talking about painful facts we deem it necessary to clarify the misunderstanding which some of our brothers might have had with regard to 'aid' which Kuwait and the UAE accorded to Iraq during the war.

(a) All sincere Arabs in the Arab world were in agreement that the war which Iraq had to wage was not only to defend its sovereignty but also to defend the eastern flank of the Arab homeland, and particularly the Gulf area. This was confirmed by the leaders of the Gulf themselves in the strongest of terms. Thus the war was considered a nationalist battle in which Iraq had undertaken the role of defending nationalist security and the security of the Gulf in particular.

(b) During the war Iraq received various forms of assistance from its brothers in some of the Gulf countries. The principal part of this assistance was provided at the time of the war in the form of interest-free 'loans'. Iraq received such assistance in the early stages of the war, but it was stopped after 1982. Iraq, at the time, did not discuss the form of this assistance with its brothers because it was hoping that the war would not last as long as it did and because it was hoping to return to full economic strength after the war. However, the war dragged on and its cost rose to unprecedented levels. The value of the military hardware alone which Iraq purchased and used in the war amounted to $102 billion in addition to other enormous military and civilian expenditure in a devastating war which lasted eight years along a front which extended 1,200 km.

Despite all the 'assistance' which Iraq had received from its brothers—and this was only a small fraction compared to the massive cost incurred by the Iraqi economy and the Iraqi people who shed rivers of blood in defence of nationalist sovereignty and nationalist dignity—the Iraqi leadership expressed its deep appreciation to all those brothers who provided assistance. President Saddam Hussein expressed it publicly during the visits made by the heads of the Gulf states to Iraq. But the bitter fact which every Arab should know is that the basic part of the assistance which we mentioned is still recorded as 'loans' to Iraq, including that provided by Kuwait and the UAE. We raised the subject with the officials in a brotherly spirit more than a year ago with a view to cancelling this 'debt' but they avoided the subject. In addition a 'debt' was also registered against Iraq for the quantities of crude oil that Kuwait had sold on its behalf from the Khafji area following the closure of the transit pipeline across Syria, despite the fact that this volume was sold outside Kuwait's OPEC quota. In order to understand these facts in full it is important to explain a significant development in the oil market during the period of the war. Iraq was a major producer of crude before the war with an output of around 3.6 million b/d. But at the beginning of the war its production stopped completely for several months and then it started exporting small volumes through Turkey and then through Syria until the pipeline closed down in 1982. Iraq's exports of oil from the south were halted from September 1980 until 1985 when the IPSA-1 pipeline was commissioned. As a result of this massive fall in exports due to the war Iraq lost a huge sum of money estimated at $106 billion. From a practical point of view these funds found their way to the treasuries of the other oil-producing countries in the area, whose exports increased to compensate for the eight-year shortfall in Iraqi exports. Using basic arithmetic it becomes obvious that the Kuwaiti and UAE claims on Iraq were not all provided by the treasuries of these countries but were the result of increased revenues realised after the fall in Iraqi export during the war years.

We ask: considering that Iraq shouldered the responsibility of Arab national defence and Arab sovereignty and dignity and the wealth of the

Gulf states which would have all gone to waste and fallen into the hands of others in the event that Iraq had lost the war, should that assistance be considered a 'loan' to us?

During the Second World War the United States provided huge sums of money, which it collected from American tax-payers, as assistance to the Soviet Union and its western aliles even though they are not part of the same nation. After the Second World War the United States extended massive aid under the Marshall Plan to rebuild Europe. It acted in a comprehensive and strategic way taking into consideration its own security and the security of its allies who participated in the war against a common enemy. So how can these sums still be considered as a claim on Iraq from its brothers in the Arab nation when Iraq sacrificed this debt many times over from its own resources throughout the destructive war and offered rivers of blood from the flower of its youth in defence of the nation's territory and its honour, dignity and wealth? Does not the nationalist logic and security, if we take the American precedent as an example, impel these states to cancel this claim on Iraq and furthermore to organise an Arab plan similar to the Marshall Plan to compensate Iraq for part of what it lost in the war?

Such would be the nationalist logic if there was any conviction in Arabism, in Arab belonging, and in a serious stand towards nationalist security. But instead of pursuing this responsible nationalist path we find two of the Gulf governments, whose wealth Iraq has preserved through the blood of its sons and indeed whose wealth it has increased by the fall in Iraqi production, now trying to destroy the Iraqi economy and reduce its resources, and we find that the premeditated policy of one of them—the Government of Kuwait—is to commit aggression against the territory of Iraq and to steal the wealth of those who protected the land, honour and wealth of Kuwait.

We submit these painful facts to the conscience of all honourable Arabs, foremost among them the brotherly Kuwaiti people, so that they may realise the pain, harm and injury which we have sustained and from which we are still suffering.

We request the Secretary General to distribute this letter to the Arab states.

Greetings

Tariq Aziz
Deputy Prime Minister of the Iraqi Republic, Foreign Minister of the Iraqi Republic,
22 Dhu al-Hijja 1410, 15 July 1990.

7. Kuwait's memorandum to the Arab League, 19 July 1990

His Excellency Chadli al-Klibi
Secretary General of the League of Arab States

19 July

Greetings,

We received with the utmost astonishment and surprise the memorandum of the Iraqi Government addressed to Your Excellency and dated 22 Dhu al-Hijja 1410 AH corresponding to 15 July 1990, which was distributed to the brotherly Arab states in the Arab League. The allegations and accusations included in the memorandum against Kuwait have no basis in fact and the expressions it uses do not correspond with the existing spirit of brotherly relations between Kuwait and Iraq. It also negates the simplest rules by which we all try to govern our Arab relationships. It is surprising that this memorandum comes at an important and crucial period for the Arab nation where all Arab efforts should be directed towards the decisive issues after the region has finished with a bloody and destructive war.

It is a painful matter that the Arab League should hold an extraordinary meeting to discuss Zionist and imperialist threats to the Arab nation, and that this meeting should end with a memorandum like this whose contents include threats to its members.

While Kuwait expresses its indignation at this memorandum it would like to emphasise that it has dealt, and will continue to deal, with its brotherly Arab states on the basis of its commitments to the principles and values stated in the charter of the Arab League, perhaps the most prominent of which is the concern to strengthen brotherly relations and the concern also for good neighbourly relations and non-interference in internal affairs, and the respect for the sovereignty of all states as well as the Arab values and customs which govern relations among brothers. Kuwait also has taken and will continue to take a lead in providing all possible opportunities which will enhance Arab relations and it will avoid anything which could disturb these relations.

Perhaps what adds to Kuwait's surprise is that this memorandum by brotherly Iraq comes at a time when co-ordination of common interests in various fields between the two countries is continuing so that normal relations may develop between the two states. Kuwait had no intention of discussing suspended issues in this heated atmosphere, but rather it left the follow-up of these questions to specialised committees of the two countries in order to focus on fields of co-operation, safeguard them and take them forward so that co-operation could supersede differences.

Moreover, this memorandum comes at a time when Kuwait is making good efforts at all levels to enhance security and stability in the region which is longing for the achievement of a just peace in its midst.

Your Excellency, it is surprising that this memorandum from brotherly Iraq and the harm which it has done to brotherly relations betweent the two states comes at the time when Iraq was among the foremost in calling for the achievement of harmony in Arab relations and the avoidance of anything which could damage them and the achieving of a balance which would serve joint Arab action.

Kuwait, on the basis of its belief in the importance of joint Arab action, has participated with all its efforts to enhance this work and to provide the right opportunities to support the development process in the Arab nation. Perhaps what the various Kuwaiti financial institutions have done and are continuing to do in pursuing an active and effective role since the independence of Kuwait is a good example of Kuwait's concern to push the development process towards new horizons that will achieve the legitimate aspirations and interests of the Arab nation. It is well known that Kuwait is one of those leading states in the world where aid constitutes a very high percentage of national income. The brotherly Arab states receive the major part of this income.

Your Excellency, what causes us pain is that this memorandum alleges that Kuwait tried to weaken Iraq at a time when everyone knows that Kuwait's position was supportive of brotherly Iraq. Kuwait upheld this position from the beginning, in accordance with its nationalist principles and its commitment in respect of its nationalist duties in the framework of the Arab League. Everyone knows how much Kuwait endured and how much it suffered from that nationalist position. Kuwait was exposed to direct attacks aimed at its people, its land, its oil installations, its tankers and commercial interests. Yet, it stood tall during the ruinous war and kept to its principles and goals. It is not in Kuwait's nature to reveal publicly what support it supplied to brotherly Iraq because it believes that it is for Iraq alone to disclose or not to disclose that. The Arab blood that was spilled cannot under any circumstances be compared to any material revenues however high they may have been, and through whatever means they were channelled.

It is sad indeed when objectives are turned around so that reality is distorted and events of a period in which we are still living are falsified. What is surprising here is that these accusations against Kuwait come at a time when we still receive positive reactions to the Kuwaiti position from Iraq through statements by Iraqi officials or through the various Iraqi official channels.

Your Excellency, the allegations in the memorandum concerning the border between Iraq and Kuwait—that Kuwait had escalated its gradual and planned encroachment of Iraqi land by establishing military installations, border posts, oil installations and farms on Iraqi territory is a falsification of the facts and the reverse of the truth since Iraq has a long record of encroachment on Kuwaiti land. This record is supported by facts kept with the responsible authorities.

Kuwait has striven on a continual basis to demarcate the border between the two countries and to end the suspended problems resulting from the lack of demarcation. But Iraq has persistently refused to put an end to the long-standing problem between the two countries while striving during the war to demarcate borders with the other Arab states in a conclusive manner.

As a sign of Kuwait's concern to bring to an end this important problem with Iraq and of its confidence in the justness of its case and in response to the dictates of its nationalist belonging, Kuwait calls upon the nation for a judgement by selecting an Arab committee whose members will be agreed upon so that it will decide on the question of demarcation on the basis of standing agreements and documents between Kuwait and Iran. Will brotherly Iraq accept this judgement in accordance with its principles and in implementation of the spirit of the national charter proposed by His Excellency President Saddam Hussein?

Your Excellency, anyone who follows oil price developments realises clearly that the collapse in prices was due to an international problem which has many facets—producers and consumers and those within OPEC and those outside it. Kuwait has suffered, as has Iraq, from the decrease in production during the same periods—the 1980s—at a time when Kuwait had the capacity to produce at higher levels due to its huge oil reserves. But Kuwait was committed to rationalising production which entailed sacrifice in order to conserve its natural resources and to achieve a higher level of prices.

As to what was stated in the memorandum about Kuwait erecting oil installations since 1980 on the southern part of the Iraqi Rumailah field, the truth here in summary is that Kuwait started exploration and drilling operations inside its territory in 1963. Then it stopped these operations for reasons well known to Iraq. Kuwait then continued drilling operations in 1976 to conclude the work and started production at the end of the 1970s.

As regards the allegations in the Iraqi memorandum that Kuwait drew oil from the southern part of the Iraqi Rumailah field, it should be emphasized here that this part of the field lies within Kuwaiti territory. Hence Kuwait has produced oil from wells within its territory south of the Arab League line and far enough away from the international borders to conform with international standards.

The production operations are taking place within Kuwaiti territory. In contrast to what was stated in the Iraqi memorandum, Iraq has repeatedly tried and continues to try to drill wells within Kuwaiti territory and this is causing severe damage to that part of the reservoir which lies within Kuwaiti territory, despite repeated Kuwaiti complaints. And despite the Iraqi encroachments within Kuwaiti territory, Kuwait did not wish to raise the issue at an Arab level but settled for keeping it at a bilateral level.

Your Excellency, Kuwait expresses its readiness to study the proposal in the Iraqi memorandum concerning the establishment of an Arab development and assistance fund, and it believes in all sincerity that it can be submitted for discussion and study in the context of the Arab League. But the thing which Kuwait does not understand, and does not accept, is that this proposal comes attached to an attempt to malign and harm it while it was in the forefront of countries laying the basis for supporting joint Arab action which would achieve the highest nationalist interests of the Arab nation.

Finally, while Kuwait relies on fact alone in replying to the Iraqi memorandum which constitutes a negative development in the brotherly relations between the two states, it draws attention to the dangers which could result from adopting this style of dealing between brothers which would divert us from involvement in the decisive issues of the Arab nation.

To make our position clear, I request His Excellency the Secretary General to distribute this memorandum to the brotherly Arab states.

Sincere greetings

Sabah al-Ahmad al-Jabir Al-Sabah
Deputy Prime Minister and Minister of Foreign Affairs

8. Proclamation of the Republic of Kuwait, 7 August 1990

In the name of God, the Compassionate, the Merciful: Statement issued by the Provisional Free Kuwait Government. The uprising against the agent, rotten regime was not intended to produce a limited reforming change, but to effect an essential change on the path of the comprehensive national and pan-Arab objectives of the uprising. Based on the objectives and liberation principles of the uprising, the government has decided to abolish the Emirate in Kuwait and declare the Republic. Thus, O brother citizens, the agent, rotten regime that was employed by colonialism will be buried forever, and the shining national and pan-Arab dawn sought by the free men will rise.

DOCUMENTS

9. *Kuwaiti Provisional Government Call for Unity with Iraq, 8 August 1990*

In the name of God, the Compassionate, the Merciful. And say: 'Work righteousness. Soon will God observe your work, and his apostle and the believers.'

Honourable citizens of Kuwait, dear kinfolk in great Iraq, O sons of the glorious Arab nation: When the uprising in Kuwait took place on 11th Muharram, corresponding to 2nd August, the objective of this uprising was not just to remove a regime, although it was a corrupt agent regime, and to replace it with a new national system. The objective from the very beginning was a great and historic goal, a dear pan-Arab goal, through which we would rectify comprehensively, eternally and radically what colonialism had imposed on our country.

Dear brothers, the crystal-clear historical fact is that Kuwait is a part of Iraq, its people are Iraqis, and throughout their history they drank the waters of the Tigris and Euphrates rivers; they grew up on the shores of Shatt al-Arab. The colonialism that partitioned the Arab homeland in order to secure itself a foothold in the land of the Arabs, to exploit their resources and weaken them for ever, is what created an artificial entity called the State of Kuwait. It set up a group of its old servants from the Al-Sabah family to rule it, to be their agents in this dear part of Iraq, to execute their goals and schemes and to collaborate with them over our dear homeland, Iraq, so that it and the Arab nation would remain weak to facilitate collaboration against it and continue implementation of the Zionist settlement scheme in Palestine and the whole Arab land.

Prompted by our deep-seated faith in unity and belief that supreme pan-Arab interests take precedence over all other considerations, and for the sake of beloved Palestine and holy Jerusalem, which will only be returned to its owners when the banners of Arabism and unity are held high and when higher pan-Arab interests take priority over selfishness and parochial interests. In order to advance these lofty objectives for which martyrs have fallen in droves on the land of Arabism, and for which Arab blood has been shed in Palestine, the provisional Free Kuwait Government has decided to appeal to the kinfolk of Iraq—the valiant men of the Qadisiya, the honourable, generous, chivalrous guards of the eastern gateway of the Arab homeland, led by the knight of the Arabs and the leader of their march, the hero leader President Field Marshal Saddam Hussein—to approve the return of the sons to their big family, the return of Kuwait to great Iraq, the motherland, and to achieve the complete full unity merger between Kuwait and Iraq, so that the hero Saddam Hussein will be our leader and the leader of our march in his capacity as the President of the Republic of Iraq, just as he is Chairman of the Revolution Command Council.

Brothers in proud Iraq, this is our appeal and decision—the decision to return to the homeland, the decision and appeal to dissipate darkness and to usher in the era of unity and hope. We look to your decision and your heed to our call so that the festival can be complete and so that jubilation may spread throughout Iraq and the land of Arabism. We have relied on God; let the faithful put their trust in God. Having discharged the duty and delivered the trust, we place ourselves at the disposal of the leader President Field Marshal Saddam Hussein, President of the Republic of Iraq, Chairman of the Revolution Command Council and Commander-in-Chief of the Armed Forces, to serve the new march in whatever capacity he decides.

[signed] Colonel Ala Husayn Ali, Prime Minister, Defence Minister and acting Interior Minister, Lt-Col Walid Sa'ud Muhammad Abdullah, Foreign Minister, Lt-Col Fu'ad Husayn Ahmad, Oil Minister and acting Finance Minister, Maj Fadil Haydar al-Wafiqi, Minister of Information and acting Transport Minister, Maj Mish'al Sa'd al-Hadab, Minister of Public Health and Housing; Lt-Col Husayn Ali Duhayman al-Shammari, Minister of Social Affairs and acting Works and Labour Minister; Maj Nasir Mansur al-Mandil, Minister of Education and acting Minister of Higher Education; Maj Isam Abd al-Majid Husayn, Minister of Justice and Legal Affairs and acting Minister of Islamic Affairs; Maj Ya'qub Muhammad Shallal, Minister of Trade, Electricity and Planning. Kuwait, 17th Muharram 1411 AH, corresponding to 8th August 1990.

DOCUMENTS

10. *Iraqi Revolutionary Command Council Statement on Merger with Kuwait, 8 August 1990*

In the name of God, the Compassionate, the Merciful: O great Iraqi people from the land to the sea; O zealous Arabs everywhere: Scarce are the days when the Arabs are jubilant, when they are joyous because of the meanings these days carry, and when they look forward to the days to come. This was the situation of the Arabs for the long time in which the foreigner reigned, when the national and pan-Arab was absent from the seat of government. This has been their situation after national rule began and spread all over the homeland, because although the foreigner has abandoned the formulas of direct colonialism which he previously adopted, he has not departed from within our ranks through his agents and intrigues.

One of the most ignominious criminal acts of colonialism was its partition of the homeland, which was a single homeland in the days that Baghdad was the capital of all the Arabs. Following the independence which Arab countries won, imperialism started intensifying its malicious actions. Thus it partitioned many countries in line with the calculations of its aims and objectives in order to undermine the capabilities of the countries which have acquired a depth of civilisation and a power to act and look forward towards an effective national role, not only within their defined areas, but also in the entire area of the Arab homeland and the Arab nation in its entirety. Thus the spiteful pencil and scissors of imperialism began to draw up maps designed to ensure that every part of the Arab homeland—if it should live within the entity of an independent state—would remain weak and ineffective towards an Arab awakening and unity as a whole, and that this action should cast negative effects and shadows on relations among Arab countries, so that in-fighting and division would replace solidarity and conciliation.

In all cases, while drawing up boundaries of geography and sovereignty for all states, Western colonialism sought to make all states weak and to ensure that partition, with the passage of time, would prevent these states from closing ranks and demonstrating a unified stance. Thus wherever possible it separated civilisation, with its high, strong state of preparedness thanks to a rich culture and demographic density, from the sources of the new wealth—oil and other minerals—where there is a small population, a lack of cultural depth and a weak state of preparedness due to the absence of the prerequisites for this.

Thus, colonialism achieved its objectives. The strongest evidence of its success is that it turned the Arab homeland into 22 states before the launching of the blessed Yemeni unity in May. By pursuing these methods, colonialism divested the Arabs not only of the components of material capabilities, but also of the components of spiritual progress. Poverty among the majority—poverty is akin to infidelity—was coupled with the inequity created by ready wealth which was not gained graudally by the minority, a minority which was not truly prepared to dispose of the wealth that it acquired in excess of balanced human needs, without any effort or persistence. Thus, it corrupted many individuals in this minority, foremost among them the rulers. Hence, it robbed them of spiritual values and made them forget about their duties to God and man. What had befallen other states in the Arab lands befell Iraq when colonialism divested it of a dear part of it, namely Kuwait, and kept Iraq away from the waters to prevent it from acquiring part of its tactical and strategic capabilities, and thus kept part of its people and part of its wealth away from the origin and the wellspring.

Thanks to the qualities of Iraq's individuals and to the nature of the age-old depth of its civilisation, and because the resources of the new wealth in it cover all parts of its land—from the north, the central regions and the south—Western colonialism has not managed to achieve through partition in Iraq what it managed to achieve in other Arab states. Thus, Iraq has remained, with the exception of well-known periods in its march, close to God and its individuals. Therefore, after the great July 1968 revolution, God became present in minds, hearts and consciences.

From another perspective, people generally gained a distinguished status, whether theoretically or in behaviour, on both the level of the citizens and the leadership, except for those sections which deviated from the course—in Kuwait. And because the gates of heaven open up to the active and goodwill and to the determination of the believers who reject oppression, tyranny and injustice, the gates of heaven opened up to Iraq before the day of the call on 2nd August and to its detached part, Kuwait.

Woe to those for whom the gates of heaven open their brightness and who are late in taking their opportunity. Woe to us from God's torture if we are slow in performing our duties towards Him. Some of our duties towards Him and on His land are struggle and jihad for the sake of a deep pan-Arab awakening which rectifies affairs and retrieves for the Arab individual his status and leading role in the message of God and life. This cannot be achieved before the correct conditions are achieved, starting with the self. The self we refer to here is a group, a national self. So the basis of what is right will not be achieved before the part detached from its origin and source is returned. This is what happened on the day of the call on 2nd August.

The day of the call is a great day. The gates of heaven opened up before Iraq; God's will and wide opportunities opened up before all the Arabs. However, at the same time and on a par with this opportunity and as one of its conditions, new battlefields were opened up for all the believers against all the infidels. No one is more capable than the people of the Qadisiya and its leadership of fulfilling this opportunity after taking it.

Based on all this, in response to the appeal in the communiqué of the Provisional Free Kuwait Government, stemming from the great transformation that took place in the lives of our people after the day of the call; for reasons of principle, values and facts brought forth on that glorious day, the 2nd of this month of August, which was blessed by God as the introduction of the Arabs' victory in their second Qadisiya; in view of how the situation after the Croesus entity was shaken and after the earth under its feet and the feet of its collaborators collapsed; with the objective of weakening the hopes of the traitors and evil-doers inside and outside the Arab homeland; in order to place issues in their proper perspective by bringing the part and branch, Kuwait, to the whole, origin and source, Iraq; and to rectify what time had wronged and cancel the injustice and unfairness that had hit Iraq in the heart of its entity before the day of the call; the RCC has decided to return the part and branch, Kuwait, to the whole and root, Iraq, in a comprehensive, eternal and inseparable merger unity. In this union there will prevail the same concepts and values which prevail in the other parts of Iraq, which will bolster the unity of Iraq—its land, individuals, regional waters and area.

O great Iraqi people. O masses of the Arab nation. O Arab leaders, whenever you support the principles of truth and the interests of the Arabs and whenever you overcome obscurity and selfishness and reject the foreigner's pressure, ways and ploys: This has been our decision. It is a rightful, just and fair decision. It is a decision for the present time and for the future. At the same time, after Iraq acted on 2nd August along with all its sons to carry out this honourable national duty, this decision is being made for the Arab nation as a whole in view of the power, capability, faith and aspirations it implies. It is a decision for all Iraqis, from the land to the sea. At the same time, it is for all good Arabs from the Ocean to the Gulf. Having made this decision, we tell all evil-doers and conspirators that all the fleets, planes and centres of oppressive forces in the world, whether inside or outside the Arab homeland, will not shake the palm fronds in Basra, Qadisiya, Muthanna, Kuwait, Jahra and the city of the call, Ahmadi. We say to them we will fight your criminal force, whether you threaten us with it or use it in a way that deserves every sacrifice by the militants and strugglers of the Arabs and all the righteous Arabs. The blood of our martyrs will burn you—so that Iraq will remain glorious and will establish through its glory and the glory of other countries a lofty glory for all the Arabs.

We tell those who are afraid of what they call the Kuwaiti precedent: You must not be deluded into an incorrect asessment of matters; what exists between Iraq and its southern parts in Jahra, the city of Kuwait and the city of the call is a matter that concerns Iraq. We have no ambitions for territory or for the wealth of anyone. Let those who want to heed lessons do so. We tell those who are trying to assemble the ranks of evil that the many names siding against us will not hide from us the manipulators and the lackeys of hell. The tongues of flame will only further expose their shameless faces. Since the matter is still at the beginning, Iraq is generous and God is forgiving and merciful. So, let them stop their transgressions against Iraq and remove the venom from their tongues. This is because the continuation of the treacherous plan and preparation for and initiation of aggression will make us accurately monitor the role of every evil-doer in this conspiracy. They will not escape, but will be taken into account whenever God wishes. Let the Croesus of Kuwait be a lesson to go by instead of being an additional factor for more misguidance, sins and injustice.

The people of Iraq, as they know, have it in them to make a stand until the victorious end willed by God. Cursed be the lowly. There will be those who will triumph and those who reap ignominy. And the dawn will break and the sun will rise to brighten the paths of darkness and aberration. Iraq is rich in bounties and the generous people around it are many. Those looking for benefits and trade are also many and they make their way to Iraq, even if it looks as though a total blockade has been imposed on it. The aggression will fail and so will the economic blockade, as well as—God willing and thanks to the resolve of the Iraqis and the Arabs—the military aggression.

After seeking God's forgiveness and help, we will demolish blasphemy with faith. A new dawn has broken in the lives of the Arabs, so that they may add it to what few days they have rejoiced in together and so that it can act as a beam to dissipate darkness. The dawn has truly broken and the bats will have to go back to their caves. God is omnipotent and omnipresent; and while the vicious men do not mind leading lives of humiliation and dependence, the men who will heed His commands want nothing more than to die when the only option open to them is to die in the cause of God and give their children and grandchildren decent lives. We would tell the foreigners that their accomplices will pay a heavy price. And if hostilities should break out, this will lead to badges and ranks falling from heads and shoulders, while laurel wreaths will increase, as will the ranks of honour and pride on the heads and shoulders of the chivalrous. And God will curse the accursed and everyone will pay the price of his actions. Say: 'Nothing will happen to us except what God has decreed for us. He is our protector and in God let the believers put their trust.'

God is great, God is great, God is great; let the lowly be cursed and God's peace and mercy be upon you, honourable brothers, wherever you are.

[signed] The Revolution Command Council, 17th Muharram 1411 AH, corresponding to 8th August 1990.

11. Arab League Foreign Ministers Statement, Cairo 3 August 1990

At the request of the government of Kuwait to hold an extraordinary summit to consider the Iraqi aggression against Kuwait;
In accordance with Articles 5 and 6 of the Arab League Charter;
In accordance with Article 2 of the Joint Defence and Economic Co-operation Agreement between Arab League States;
In accordance with Article 2 of the Arab Solidarity Pact agreed upon at the third Arab Summit held in Casablanca;
The Council decided:

1. To condemn the Iraqi aggression against the State of Kuwait, to reject any consequences resulting from this aggression, and not to recognise its results;

2. To denounce the bloodshed and destruction of property;

3. To demand the immediate and unconditional withdrawal of Iraqi troops and the return to the position obtaining on 1 August before the invasion;

4. To call on their majesties, highnesses and excellencies the heads of state of all Arab countries to hold an emergency summit to debate the aggression and to find ways to reach a permanent negotiated solution acceptable to the parties concerned, in line with the Arab nation's heritage and the spirit of brotherhood and solidarity, and with the existing Arab legal system;

5. To confirm the Council's commitment to preserving the sovereignty and territorial integrity of the member states, to reiterate its concern for the principles of the Arab League Charter on not resorting to force to solve disputes arising between the member states, to respect their internal systems and not to undertake any action to change them;

6. To reject any foreign intervention or attempt to intervene in Arab affairs;

7. To entrust the Secretary-General with following up the implementation of this decision and report back to the Council; and

8. To consider the Council's extraordinary meeting as a permanent session.

12. Extraordinary Arab Summit Resolution, Cairo, 10 August 1990

In the light of the Arab Council Declaration on 2nd and 3rd August 1990;
In the light of the Islamic Countries Foreign Ministers 19th Conference Declaration issued on 4 August;
According to the Statute of the Arab League Charter and the Joint Defence and Economic pact between Arab League States;
According to the UN Charter, in particular Paragraph 4 of the article 25 and 51;
Conscious of the great historic responsibility dictated by the present situation arising from the annexation of Kuwait and its consequences on the Arab Nation;

The summit decided:

1. To reaffirm the decision of the Arab League Council taken on August 3rd and the Declaration of the Islamic Conference Organisation issued on 4 August.

2. To reaffirm the obligation to the decision of the UN Security Council resolutions No. 660 of 2 August 1990 and No. 662 of 9 August 1990 as an expression of International Law.

3. To condemn Iraqi aggression against the brotherly state of Kuwait and not to recognise Iraqi decision to annex Kuwait or any consequences arising from the invasion of Iraqi troops of Kuwait territory.

4. To call upon the immediate and unconditional withdrawal of the Iraqi troops from Kuwait and the return to the state it was in before 1st August.

5. To reaffirm Kuwait sovereignty, its independence and regional security, being a member state in the Arab League and the UN. It stands by the restoration of the lawful government of Kuwait which was present before the invasion. It supports the measures taken to free its land and fulfil its sovereignty.

6. To respond to Saudi Arabia's and other Gulf Arab States' request to transfer Arab forces to support their armed forces to defend their territories and regional security against any outside invasion.

7. The emergency summit has commissioned the Arab League Secretary General to follow up the implementation of the decision and report back to the council within 15 days.

13. Islamic Conference Organisation Resolution, 4 August 1990

The conference received with deep regret the news of the tragic events which occurred between Iraq and Kuwait, two ICO members. These events coincided with the convening of this conference and took place at a time when hopes were pinned on the imminent success of direct contacts which sincere brotherly Arab good offices have made to contain the crisis between two fraternal countries and achieve a peaceful settlement to resolve their difficulties.

The conference expresses its support for the statement which His Excellency the ICO Secretary-General issued in this regard on 11th Muharram 1411, corresponding to 2nd August 1990.

The conference condemns the Iraqi aggression against Kuwait, rejects all its effects and does not recognise its consequences. The conference calls for the immediate withdrawal of Iraqi forces from Kuwaiti territory and the return of these forces to the positions they occupied before 10th Muharram 1411, corresponding to 1st August 1990. It also calls for abidance by the principles of the ICO Charter, particularly its provision regarding the need to settle conflicts between member states by peaceful means and non-interference in the internal affairs of any state. It also calls on the two countries to take into consideration the requirements of good-neighbourliness; not to try to change the internal regime in either of them by force; to respect the sovereignty, independence and territorial integrity of each state; and to refrain from the use or threat of force against the territorial integrity and political independence of either of them.

The conference, while taking note of the Iraqi government's announcement regarding its intention to withdraw its armed forces from Kuwait, will follow up the implementation of this assurance without any condition on the part of Iraq. The conference supports the legitimate regime in Kuwait under the leadership of His Highness Shaikh Jabir al-Ahmad al-Jabir Al-Sabah, the Emir of the State of Kuwait and chairman of the fifth Islamic summit. It also affirms its total solidarity with the Emir, government and people of Kuwait.

DOCUMENTS

14. King Fahd's address to the Nation, 9 August 1990

In the name of God, the Merciful, the Compassionate. Thanks be to God, master of the universe, and prayers and peace be on the last of the prophets and the messengers, our Lord Muhammad, and on all his kinfolk and companions.

Dear brother citizens, peace, God's mercy and blessings be upon you. No doubt you realise through following the course of the regrettable events in the Arab Gulf region during the last few days, the gravity of the situation facing the Arab nation, under the current circumstances. And you undoubtedly know that the government of the Kingdom of Saudi Arabia did everything it could in efforts and attempts with the governments of the Republic of Iraq and the State of Kuwait, for the sake of containing the dispute that has risen between the two countries.

In this context, I had many telephone calls and fraternal talks with the brothers. And as a result of this a meeting was held between the delegations of Iraq and Kuwait in Saudi Arabia, in a continuing attempt to heal the crack and narrow the views and avoid an escalation of matters. Some Arab fraternal Kings and Presidents of Arab states have contributed big efforts for which they are thanked, out of the belief of all in the unity of the Arab nation and the consolidation of its solidarity and co-operation in all that brings success in the service of its fateful causes.

However, with great regret, matters developed in the opposite direction to that we were striving for; in fact, opposite to the aspirations of the peoples of the Islamic and Arab nations, and all the peace-loving countries of the world. Painful and regrettable events have been taking place since the dawn of last Thursday, 11th Muharram 1411 AH, corresponding to 2nd August 1990 AD, in a way that took the whole world by surprise, when the Iraqi forces stormed the brotherly state of Kuwait in the most vile aggression known to the Arab nation in its modern history, which made the brotherly people of Kuwait homeless and caused them great suffering.

While expressing its profound displeasure at the aggression against the state of Kuwait, a sisterly neighbour, the Kingdom of Saudi Arabia declares its categorical rejection of all the measures and declarations that followed that aggression, which were rejected by all the statements issued by Arab leaderships, the Arab League, the Islamic Conference Organisation and the Gulf Co-operation Council, as well as all Arab and international bodies and organisations.

DOCUMENTS

The Kingdom of Saudi Arabia reaffirms its demand that the situation must be returned to what it was before the Iraqi storming, and the return of the ruling family led by HH Shaikh Jabir al-Ahmad Al-Sabah, the Emir of the State of Kuwait, and his government. We hope that the emergency Arab summit which was called by HE President Muhammad Husni Mubarak of the sisterly Arab Republic of Egypt will lead to results that will realise the Arab nation's hopes and bolster its march towards solidarity and unity of word.

O brothers, that regrettable event was followed by Iraq's massing of huge forces on the borders of the Kingdom of Saudi Arabia. Faced with these bitter realities and out of the eagerness of the Kingdom for the safety of its territory and the protection of its vital and economic constituents, our wish to strengthen its defence potential and increase the level of training of its armed forces and out of the eagerness of the government of the Kingdom of Saudi Arabia to side with peace and non-recourse to force to solve disputes, the Kingdom of Saudi Arabia expressed its wish for the participation of fraternal Arab forces and other friendly forces; thus the government of the USA and the British government took the initiative, on the basis of the relations of friendship which link the Kingdom of Saudi Arabia and these states, to send air and land forces in order to back the Saudi armed forces in performing their duty to defend the homeland and citizens against any aggression, with the complete emphasis that this measure is not directed against anybody but is only for a purely defensive aim imposed by the current circumstances faced by the Kingdom of Saudi Arabia.

It is worth mentioning here that the forces which will participate in the joint training between them and the Saudi armed forces will be present temporarily in the Kingdom's territory and will leave it immediately when the Kingdom of Saudi Arabia wishes so. We pray God to guide our steps towards everything in which lie the good of our religion and the safety of our homelands and to guide us on the right path. God's peace and blessings be upon you.

15. Joint US-Soviet Statement (Baker-Shevardnadze), Moscow, 3 August 1990

The Soviet Union and the United States, as members of the UN Security Council, consider it important that the Council promptly and decisively condemned the brutal and illegal invasion of Kuwait by Iraqi military forces.

The United States and the Soviet Union believe that now it is essential that the Council resolution be fully and immediately implemented. By its action, Iraq has shown its contempt for the most fundamental principles for the United Nations Charter and international law.

In response to the blatant transgression of the basic norms of civilized conduct, the United States and the Soviet Union have each taken a number of actions, including the Soviet suspension of arms deliveries and the American freezing of assets.

The Soviet Union and the United States reiterate our call for unconditional Iraqi withdrawal from Kuwait; the sovereignty, national independence, legitimate authorities and territorial integrity of the state of Kuwait must be completely restored and safeguarded.

The United States and the Soviet Union believe the international community must not only condemn this action, but also take practical steps in response to it.

We take the unusual step of jointly calling upon the rest of the international community to join with us in an international cut-off of all arms supplies to Iraq. The Soviet Union and the United States call on all regional organizations, especially the League of Arab States, all Arab governments, as well as the non-aligned movement and the Islamic Conference, to take all possible steps to ensure that the United Nations Security Council resolution is carried out.

Governments that engage in blatant aggression must know that the international community cannot, and will not, acquiesce in, nor facilitate, aggression.

16. Joint US-Soviet Summit Statement, Helsinki, 9 September 1990

With regard to Iraq's invasion and continued military occupation of Kuwait, President Bush and President Gorbachev issue the following joint statement.

We are united in the belief that Iraq's aggression must not be tolerated. No peaceful international order is possible if larger states can devour their smaller neighbours.

We reaffirm the joint statement of our Foreign Ministers of 3 August 1990, and our support for UN Security Council resolutions 660, 661, 662, 664 and 665.

Today, we once again call upon the government of Iraq to withdraw unconditionally from Kuwait, to allow the restoration of Kuwait's legitimate government, and to free all hostages now held in Iraq and Kuwait.

Nothing short of the complete implementation of the UN Security Council resolutions is acceptable.

Nothing short of a return to the pre-August 2 status of Kuwait can end Iraq's isolation.

We call upon the entire world community to adhere to the sanctions mandated by the UN, and we pledge to work, individually and in concert, to ensure full compliance with the sanctions.

At the same time, the US and the Soviet Union recognise that UN Security Council resolution 661 permits, in humanitarian circumstances, the importation into Iraq and Kuwait of food. The Sanctions Committee will make recommendations to the Security Council on what would constitute humanitarian circumstances.

The US and the Soviet Union further agree that any such imports must be strictly monitored by the appropriate international agencies to ensure that food reaches only those for whom it is intended, with special priority being given to meeting the needs of children.

Our preference is to resolve the crisis peacefully, and we will be united against Iraq's aggression as long as the crisis exists.

However, we are determined to see this aggression end, and if the current steps fail to end it, we are prepared to consider additional ones consistent with the UN charter. We must demonstrate beyond any doubt that aggression cannot and will not pay.

As soon as the objectives mandated by the UN Security Council resolutions mentioned above have been achieved, and we have demonstrated that aggression does not pay, the Presidents direct their foreign minister to work with countries in the region and outside it to develop regional security structures and measures to promote peace and stability.

It is essential to work actively to resolve all remaining conflicts in the Middle East and Persian Gulf. Both sides will continue to consult each other and initiate measures to pursue these broader objectives at the proper time.

DOCUMENTS

17. *European Community Statement on the Kuwait Crisis, 4 August 1990*

The Community and its member states reiterate their unreserved condemnation of the brutal Iraqi invasion of Kuwait and their demand for an immediate and unconditional withdrawal of Iraqi forces from the territory of Kuwait, already expressed in their statement of 2 August.

They consider groundless and unacceptable the reasons provided by the Iraqi Government to justify the military aggression against Kuwait, and they will refrain from any act which may be considered as implicit recognition of authorities imposed on Kuwait by the invaders.

In order to safeguard the interests of the legitimate Government of Kuwait they have decided to take steps to protect all assets belonging directly or indirectly to the state of Kuwait.

The Community and its member states confirm their full support for UN Security Council Resolution Number 660 and call on Iraq to comply with the provisions of that resolution. If the Iraqis fail so to comply, the Community and its member states will work for, support and implement a Security Council Resolution to introduce mandatory and comprehensive sanctions.

As of now, they have decided to adopt the following:

—An embargo on oil imports from Kuwait and Iraq.

—Appropriate measures aimed at freezing Iraqi assets in the territory of member states.

—An embargo on sales of arms and other military equipment to Iraq.

—The suspension of any co-operation in the military sphere with Iraq.

—The suspension of technical and scientific co-operation with Iraq.

—The suspension of the application to Iraq of the system of generalized preferences.

The Community and its member states reiterate their firm conviction that disputes within states should be settled by peaceful means, and are prepared to participate in any effort to defuse the tension in the area.

They are in close contact with the governments of several Arab countries and follow with the utmost attention the discussion within the Arab League and the Gulf Co-operation Council. They hope that Arab initiatives will contribute to the restoration of international legality and of the legislative Government of Kuwait. The Community and its member states are ready to lend their full support to such initiatives and to efforts to resolve by negotiations the differences between the states concerned.

The Community and its member states are carefully monitoring the situation of EC nationals in Iraq and Kuwait—they maintain strict co-ordination in order to guarantee their safety.

DOCUMENTS

18. NATO Secretay-General Wörner's Statement on the Kuwait Crisis, 10 August 1990

NATO Foreign Ministers met today to discuss the Gulf crisis. Iraqi aggression threatens international security and the collective security of the Alies. The NATO Alliance is vitally concerned. The territory of one of its member countries, Turkey, borders that of the aggressor. The economic consequences for the world at large are obvious and serious. The brutal use of force in a world environment which we have worked so hard to make more co-operative and peaceful sets a dangerous new precedent. This is a time when the Alliance must consult, harmonize the policies of its members and demonstrate solidarity for those who are threatened and those who are taking action in response to the threat. That is exactly what happened this morning, and I am very glad to be able to record full consensus by all member countries.

Allies considered that Iraqi aggression calls into question the fundamental principles of international law and thus requires action of the entire international community. They affirmed their full support for the UN Security Council's condemnation of the Iraqi invasion of Kuwait, the imposition of a comprehensive embargo against Iraq, and the rejection of Kuwait's annexation. Allies expressed their resolve to contribute to implementation of the Security Council's Resolutions and to support any action the UN may consider appropriate. It is in the light of those UN resolutions that measures are being taken by individual Allies.

The Allies expressed their support for the current efforts within the community of Arab states to find a political solution for the crisis.

The Alliance endorsed actions which may be taken by member states to enforce the sanctions put in place by the UN Security Council, and agreed on the need to maintain the effectiveness of those sanctions. The goals of this international action are clear:

—Kuwait's full sovereignty and independence must be re-established;

—Iraqi forces in Kuwait must be withdrawn;

—The sovereignty and territorial integrity of the Kingdom of Saudi Arabia and of all other states in the region must be respected.

The Council calls on Iraq to allow all citizens of foreign countries to leave Iraq and Kuwait immediately.

Ministers supported President Bush's decision to assist Saudi Arabia and the dispatch of military forces of the United States, the United

Kingdom, and France in response to requests by the Saudi Government. They agreed that the members of this Alliance will contribute, each in its own way, to stopping further Iraqi military aggression.

The Allies expressed full solidarity with Turkey, which borders immediately on the crisis area, and affirmed that they are ready to stand by our collective defence obligations involving all member states.

Finally, they agreed that NATO is a key forum for consultation and co-operation to meet a common crisis, and it will be essential to maintain the closest possible consultation. They are willing, as before, to consult and co-ordinate actions with others who are implementing the UN resolutions on Iraq and taking steps to resist Iraqi aggression.

DOCUMENTS

19. GCC Summit Communiqué, 25 December 1990

In the name of God, the Merciful and Compassionate. The final communiqué of the 11th session of the GCC Supreme Council, held in Doha in the State of Qatar from 5th to 8th Jumada al-Akhira 1411 AH, corresponding to 22nd–25th December 1990:

In response to an invitation from His Highness Shaikh Khalifa Bin Hamad Al-Thani, the Emir of Qatar, and with God's help and providence, the 11th session of the GCC Supreme Council was held in the city of Doha from 5th to 8th Jumada al-Akhira 1411 AH, corresponding to 22nd–25th December 1990. The session was attended by Their Majesties and Highnesses Shaikh Zayid Bin Sultan Al-Nuhayyan, President of the United Arab Emirates; Shaikh Khalifa Bin Salman Al-Khalifa, the Bahraini Prime Minister; King Fahd Bin Abd al-Aziz, the King of Saudi Arabia and Servant of the Two Holy Places; Sultan Qaboos Bin Sa'id of Oman; Shaikh Khalifa Bin Hamad Al-Thani of Qatar; and Shaikh Jabir al-Ahmad Al-Sabah of Kuwait.

THE IRAQI REGIME'S AGGRESSION AGAINST KUWAIT

The Supreme Council reviewed the serious situation created in the region as a result of the Iraqi regime's occupation of the sovereign state of Kuwait, which has posed a threat to the security and safety of the GCC member-states and resulted in the shedding of the blood of the innocent Kuwaiti people, the displacement of the Kuwaiti people and others residing in Kuwait, arrests and torture, looting of properties and the violation of sanctities in an attempt to obliterate the Kuwaiti identity and entity.

The Supreme Council also discussed the serious repercussions of this aggression on security and stability in the Gulf region and the Arab world, as well as on world peace and security.

The Supreme Council reiterates its strong condemnation of the Iraqi regime for its arbitrary and oppressive aggression against the State of Kuwait and its continued refusal to comply with the principles of the Arab League Charter, Arab summit Resolution 195, the UN Charter and the UN Security Council resolutions concerning the aggression against Kuwait. As it repeats its condemnation of these acts, the council reiterates that the GCC governments and peoples stand beside the State of Kuwait in its ordeal and extend their full support for and solidarity with the struggle of the Kuwaiti government and people until full liberation is achieved.

The Supreme Council commends the Kuwaiti people's steadfast rejection of the occupation and their adherence to their legitimate government under the leadership of His Highness Shaikh Jabir al-Ahmad Al-Sabah. The council also pays tribute to the sacrifices made by the Kuwaiti people in confronting terrorism, oppression, torture and indiscriminate executions and it honours their continued resistance and determination to defeat the forces of evil and aggression. The council expresses pride in the cohesion of the one Kuwaiti family, as demonstrated during the Kuwaiti popular conference in the city of Jiddah.

As it recalls the individual and collective efforts to avert the tragedy made by the GCC members before and after the tyrannical Iraqi aggression against Kuwait on 2nd August and their sincere and serious endeavours to find a peaceful solution, the council expresses gratitude for the good efforts of the leaders of sisterly and friendly states to persuade the Iraqi regime to comply with the principles of legitimacy and respect the resolutions of the Arab League summit and the UN Security Council.

The council reiterates the GCC countries' firm stand in the face of the Iraqi aggression and their determination to resist it and nullify its negative consequences, proceeding from the premise that aggression against any member state is aggression against all GCC member states and that the security of the GCC member states is indivisible.

Therefore, the council reiterates its demand that the Iraqi leadership respect international norms and charters as well as the agreements it concluded with the State of Kuwait and calls on it to choose peace to preserve the Iraqi people's achievements and prevent the squandering of their resources, potential and blood in a confrontation which will only result in losses and destruction. The council calls on the Iraqi regime to begin withdrawing its troops from all Kuwaiti territory immediately and unconditionally so that the legitimate authority can be restored to Kuwait before 15th January 1991. By doing so, the brotherly Iraqi people and the people of the region and the entire world will be spared the horrors of a destructive war.

The council calls on the Iraqi regime to respect civilians and safeguard their lives and property and to protect public and private properties and establishments in accordance with the provisions of Islamic shari'a, the fourth Geneva Convention on the protection of civilians in time of war and international charters and agreements.

The Supreme Council holds Iraq responsible for paying compensation to Kuwait for the damage inflicted on Kuwaiti government establishments, banks and public and private institutions and for the seizure and transfer of their holdings, funds and deposits outside

Kuwait. The council also reiterates the lawful right of Kuwaiti and other nationals to obtain just compensation for damages and losses they suffered as a result of the oppressive Iraqi aggression.

Within the framework of the political and diplomatic efforts to consolidate the Arab and international consensus rejecting the aggression and to guarantee the implementation of the resolutions of international legitimacy, the GCC has decided to entrust a committee comprised of the Foreign Ministers of its member states with the task of visiting the permanent members of the Security Council, certain Arab countries and other important countries.

Recalling the principles outlined in the Muscat declaration released at the GCC's 10th session, principles which emphasise the basic rules and legitimacy to which the GCC member states are committed in their international relations, the GCC expresses its hope that the Iraqi regime will respond to the demands of Arab and international legitimacy. The principles enshrined in the Muscat declaration call for good-neighbourly relations, mutual respect for national sovereignty, non-interference in the domestic affairs of all countries, respect for the sovereignty, independence and territorial integrity of all countries, refraining from the use of force or threat to use force and resorting to dialogue and negotiations as an effective means to settle disputes. The GCC, at the same time, underlines its member states' right and determination to secure the restoration of sovereignty and legitimacy to Kuwait.

The GCC expresses its appreciation and gratitude to all the Arab, Islamic and friendly countries that stood on the side of right and legitimacy, condemned the aggression and sought to end it, responding to the resolutions of Arab and international legitimacy and to the GCC countries' request that they deploy their forces beside the Gulf forces to support the latter in their defensive tasks. The GCC asserts, at the same time, that the Arab, Islamic and friendly forces that came to the region at the request of the GCC member states will return to their countries when the GCC member states request them to do so after the circumstances that required their presence—the Iraqi occupation of Kuwait and the threat to the GCC countries—are removed. The GCC asserts that these honourable stands will have positive effects on relations in all fields between the GCC countries and these Arab, Islamic and friendly countries.

THE GCC MARCH

The GCC Supreme Council reviewed the stages of the march of joint action in the political, security, military, economic and social fields. It discussed ways to promote co-operation and integration among the member states in accordance with the principles and goals outlined in the GCC's statute, while taking into account the security developments in the region in the light of the treacherous Iraqi invasion of Kuwait, the developments and transformations affecting the essence of the order in the Arab world and the current world developments that are transforming the international order.

The GCC stresses its concern to expedite steps and to make a qualitative leap in collective action among the member states in the forthcoming stage in order to achieve further co-ordination, integration and cohesion out of its absolute conviction that its members share the same fate and goals. The GCC notes with satisfaction the development of security and military co-operation among the member states at this critical time in the region caused by Iraq's contempt for values and international charters and its defiance of the international will. The GCC takes pride in the unity of the GCC member states in the face of the Iraqi aggression and their determination to resist it. Out of their conviction of the importance of achieving further security and military co-operation among the member states, especially in view of the Iraqi occupation of Kuwait and the threat this poses to the security of the other member states, the GCC has endorsed the Defence Ministers' recommendations on strengthening the intrinsic defensive capabilities of its member states.

The GCC Supreme Council also reviewed the march of economic action and expressed satisfaction with the achievements of joint action in this field. It stressed its determination to continue working to fulfil the ambitions and aspirations of the GCC peoples in completing the steps towards economic integration. To achieve this goal, the GCC Supreme Council assigned the financial and economic co-operation committee the task of adopting the necessary measures to develop new concepts for joint economic integration and to draw up a programme to complete the establishment of a common Gulf market, agree on a unified trade policy, evaluate economic co-operation and examine the texts of the Unified Economic Agreement and methods of implementing it with the aim of securing new privileges that will enable the citizens of the GCC countries to enjoy new benefits in the march towards prosperity and development.

THE SECURITY SITUATION IN THE REGION

The Supreme Council notes with deep regret the deterioration of security conditions in the region as a result of the Iraqi invasion of the State of Kuwait's territory. It also notes that although the entire region is on the verge of a destructive war, the Iraqi authorities have shown total disregard for the consequences of such a war for the fraternal Iraqi people, the Arab nation and the entire world.

Believing that establishing and safeguarding security in this vital part of the world serves the interests of the region's states, the Arab nation and the entire world, the council reiterates its desire to adopt all measures necessary to protect the region's security and stability. It declares its determination to enhance the effectiveness of co-operation among the GCC members to strengthen their individual and joint defensive capabilities to serve the interests of the region and its security and prosperity and to support world peace.

It this context, the council particularly appreciates the role being played by Arab states in support of Arab legitimacy. It looks forward to co-ordinating efforts with these states to find a way out of the tragedy triggered by the oppressive Iraqi aggression. It is also eager to work alongside these states to heal the rift, unite Arab stands and establish a stronger and more cohesive Arab system.

In the meantime and in view of international detente and the clear movement towards a new world order, the GCC countries will work with the region's countries and the Arab and world family to take the necessary measures to avoid the recurrence of such aggression and to lay the bases for stabilising security in the region and serving the interests of world peace and security.

THE CURRENT ARAB SITUATION

The Supreme Council studied the current deterioration in Arab relations as a result of the Iraqi regime's disregard for Arab norms and charters, the schism created in Arab ranks by the Iraqi aggression, the collapse of Arab solidarity and the lack of trust among members of the Arab family. The council also noted that Arab energies are being wasted in fields far removed from Arab development and interests as a result of the oppressive aggression.

In this context, the council emphasises the importance of working to reverse the current destructive trend in the Arab home and to heal the rift on the basis of a clear commitment in words and deeds to the principles of respect for Arab neighbours, non-interference in internal affairs and refraining from the use of force or political threats and extortion. In this way, all human and material resources can be devoted to Arab and Muslim issues and a better future can be guaranteed for the Arab citizen in all corners of the Arab world.

The GCC states have made effective contributions to Arab development efforts at the bilateral, regional and international levels. The council members desire to draw up new Arab development plans and believe in the importance of a joint Gulf development policy based on a new concept, which takes into account the contributions these efforts will make to political stability and regional security amid the economic difficulties resulting from the Iraqi aggression against the Arab world. Therefore, the council has decided to set up a programme to subsidise development efforts in Arab and Muslim states. This programme aims primarily at encouraging economic openness and market economies, improving Arab economic performances and attracting world support for the Arab development process through encouraging international financing institutions and national development aid agencies to contribute to national development plans in Arab states.

The GCC countries express their determination to provide the necessary financing for such a programme. Accordingly, the GCC Foreign Ministers will meet next week to work out the details and determine the funds required for the programme from members' contributions and each country's share according to its resources.

The Supreme Council reviewed development in the Palestinian issue and voiced concern over the consequences of the Iraqi aggression against Kuwait and its negative repercussions on the Palestinian cause. The council recalls its previous resolutions and statements on the issue. It reiterates its commendation of the heroic struggle of the Palestinian people and their daring intifada in the face of the oppressive Israeli occupation and its suppressive and arbitrary practices.

While reiterating its members' full and absolute support for the historic Palestinian intifada, the council appeals to the international community to provide the necessary support for the intifada and for the sons of the occupied territories in their ordeal. It also appeals to the international community to work to expose the Israeli terrorist methods, put an end to the occupation troops' arbitrary and oppressive measures and stop the deportation of the Palestinian people from and the demolition of their homes, as such practices violate human rights and international laws and charters.

The council welcomes UN Security Council Resolution 681 on providing international protection to Palestinians in the occupied territories. It also welcomes the UN Security Council's call for holding an international peace conference on the Palestinian issue. In this regard, the council reaffirms its support for the convening of an international peace conference in which all parties concerned, including the state of Palestine, will participate. It also calls for taking all measures necessary to hold the conference.

Regarding the situation in Lebanon, the GCC Supreme Council notes with deep satisfaction the recent positive developments and the legitimate Lebanese government's achievements in extending its authority over Greater Beirut and other areas. The GCC Supreme Council expresses its desire that Lebanon achieve its full unity and territorial integrity. In this respect, the GCC Supreme Council expresses its appreciation for the efforts exerted by the Servant of the Two Holy Places, HM King Hasan II and HE President Chadli Bendjdid and for the constructive role played by HE President Hafiz al-Asad in assisting the legitimate Lebanese government. The GCC Supreme Council exhorts the international community to continue to support the Ta'if accord. The GCC Supreme Council reasserts its support for HE President Ilyas al-Hirawi and its desire for the restoration of security and stability throughout Lebanon. Recalling Resolution No. 185 of the emergency Arab summit conference, which provides for the establishment of an international fund for reconstruction and development in Lebanon, the GCC Supreme Council emphasises its support for this fund to enable Lebanon to begin reconstruction and exercise its cultural role in the Arab and international arenas.

RELATIONS WITH IRAN

The GCC Supreme Council welcomes the desire of the Islamic Republic of Iran to improve and promote its relations with all GCC countries. The GCC Supreme Council underlines the importance of serious and realistic action to settle the outstanding differences between Iran and the GCC member states so that the countries of the region can proceed to achieve their cherished goals and exploit their resources for comprehensive economic development. The GCC Supreme Council stresses its desire to establish distinguished relations with Iran on the basis of good-neighbourliness, non-interference in domestic affairs and respect for sovereignty, independence and peaceful co-existence deriving from the bonds of religion and heritage that link the countries of the region.

INTERNATIONAL DEVELOPMENTS

The GCC Supreme Council examined the report prepared by the tripartite ministerial committee which was given the task of studying international developments and evaluating their effects on the GCC countries. Out of its conviction of the importance of dealing with the requirements of international developments in a way that will safeguard the interests of the GCC member states and peoples, the GCC Supreme

Council endorsed the recommendations submitted to it. The GCC Supreme Council welcomes the new spirit of concord between East and West. It expresses its satisfaction with the political and economic openness being witnessed in Eastern Europe in view of its effective role and the contribution this makes to enhancing peace and allowing human resources to be used for development instead of squandering funds in an exhausting and futile arms race. It praises the rational spirit prevailing in international relations based on mutual respect for sovereignty, balance of interests and rejection of aggression, treachery and occupation. The GCC Supreme Council welcomes unified Germany as a factor for stability and as an effective member of the international community in support of development and international progress in a world permeated with the spirit of peace, understanding, reason, wisdom and prosperity.

The GCC Supreme Council wishes to express its solidarity with developing countries and its continued support for them in their efforts to achieve economic growth and improve the standard of living of their peoples. It asserts that its preoccupation with the repercussions of the sinful Iraqi aggression will not divert the attention of its member states from continuing their co-operation and solidarity with the developing countries in their efforts to establish a more equitable international economic order. The GCC Supreme Council decided to ask GCC Secretary General Abdullah Ya'qub Bisharah to remain in his post. It expresses its utmost appreciation and gratitude to HH Shaikh Khalifa Bin Hamad Al-Thani and to his government and people for the hospitality and reception extended to the GCC leaders and members of their delegations. It lauds the excellent preparations and accurate arrangements for the convenience of the delegations and the success of the summit. The GCC Supreme Council looks forward to its 12th session in Kuwait next December, God willing, in response to the invitation of the Emir of Kuwait, HH Shaikh Jabir al-Ahmad al-Jabir Al-Sabah.

Issued in Doha on 8th Jumada al-Akhira, 1411 AH, corresponding to 25th December 1990.

20. UN Security Council Resolutions on the Kuwait Crisis

RESOLUTION 660 (1990) 2 AUGUST 1990

The Security Council,

Alarmed by the invasion of Kuwait on 2 August 1990 by the military forces of Iraq,

Determining that there exists a breach of international peace and security as regards the Iraqi invasion of Kuwait,

Acting under Articles 39 and 40 of the Charter of the United Nations,

1. *Condemns* the Iraqi invasion of Kuwait;

2. *Demands* that Iraq withdraw immediately and unconditionally all its forces to the positions in which they were located on 1 August 1990;

3. *Calls upon* Iraq and Kuwait to begin immediately intensive negotiations for the resolution of their differences and supports all efforts in this regard, and especially those of the League of Arab States;

4. *Decides* to meet again as necessary to consider further steps to ensure compliance with the present resolution.

RESOLUTION 661 (1990) 6 AUGUST 1990

The Security Council,

Reaffirming its resolution 660 (1990) of 2 August 190,

Deeply concerned that that resolution has not been implemented and that the invasion by Iraq of Kuwait continues with further loss of human life and material destruction,

Determined to bring the invasion and occupation of Kuwait by Iraq to an end and to restore the sovereignty, independence and territorial integrity of Kuwait,

Noting that the legitimate Government of Kuwait has expressed its readiness to comply with resolution 660 (1990),

Mindful of its responsibilities under the Charter of the United Nations for the maintenance of international peace and security,

Affirming the inherent right of individual or collective self-defence, in response to the armed attack by Iraq against Kuwait, in accordance with Article 52 of the Charter,

Acting under Chapter VII of the Charter of the United Nations,

1. *Determines* that Iraq so far has failed to comply with paragraph 2 of resolution 660 (1990) and has usurped the authority of the legitimate Government of Kuwait;

2. *Decides*, as a consequence, to take the following measures to secure compliance of Iraq with paragraph 2 of resolution 660 (1990) and to restore the authority of the legitimate Government of Kuwait;

3. *Decides* that all States shall prevent:

(a) The import into their territories of all commodities and products originating in Iraq or Kuwait exported therefrom after the date of the present resolution;

(b) Any activities by their nationals or in their territories which would promote or are calculated to promote the export or trans-shipment of any commodities or products from Iraq or Kuwait; and any dealings by their nationals or their flag vessels or in their territories in any commodities or products originating in Iraq or Kuwait and exported therefrom after the date of the present resolution, including in particular any transfer of funds to Iraq or Kuwait for the purposes of such activities or dealings;

(c) The sale or supply by their nationals or from their territories or using their flag vessels of any commodities or products, including weapons or any other military equipment, whether or not originating in their territories but not including supplies intended strictly for medical purposes, and, in humanitarian circumstances, foodstuffs, to any person or body in Iraq or Kuwait or to any person or body for the purposes of any business carried on in or operated from Iraq or Kuwait, and any activities by their nationals or in their territories which promote or are calculated to promote such sale or supply of such commodities or products;

4. *Decides* that all States shall not make available to the Government of Iraq or to any commercial, indutrial or public utility undertaking in Iraq or Kuwait, any funds or any other financial or economic resources and shall prevent their nationals and any persons within their territories from removing from their territories or otherwise making available to that Government or to any such undertaking any funds or resources and from remitting any other funds to persons or bodies within Iraq or Kuwait, except payments exclusively for strictly medical or humanitarian purposes and, in humanitarian circumstances, foodstuffs;

5. *Calls upon* all States, including States non-members of the United nations, to act strictly in accordance with the provisions of the present resolution notwithstanding any contract entered into or licence granted before the date of the present resolution;

6. *Decides* to establish, in accordance with rule 28 of the provisional rules of procedure of the Security Council, a Committee of the Security Council consisting of all the members of the Council, to undertake the following tasks and to report on its work to the Council with its observations and recomendations:

(a) To examine the reports on the progress of the implementation of the presentresolution which will be submitted to the Secretary-General;

(b) To seek from all States further information regarding the action taken by them concerning the effective implementation of the provisions laid down in the present resolution;

7. *Calls upon* all States to co-operate fully with the Committee in the fulfilment of its task, including supplying such information as may be sought by the Committee in pursuance of the present resolution;

8. *Requests* the Secretary-General to provide all necessary assistance to the Committee and to make the necessary arrangements in the Secretariat for the purpose;

9. *Decides* that, notwithstanding paragraphs 4 through 8 above, nothing in the present resolution shall prohibit assistance to the legitimate Government of Kuwait, and *calls upon* all States:

(a) To take appropriate measures to protect assets of the legitimate Government of Kuwait and its agencies;

(b) Not to recognize any régime set up by the occupying Power;

10. *Requests* the Secretary-General to report to the Council on the progress of the implementation of the present resolution, the first report to be submitted within thirty days;

11. *Decides* to keep this item on its agenda and to continue its efforts to put an early end to the invasion by Iraq.

DOCUMENTS

RESOLUTION 662 (1990) 9 AUGUST 1990

The Security Council,

Recalling its resolutions 660 (1990) and 661 (1990),

Gravely alarmed by the declaration by Iraq of a 'comprehensive and eternal merger' with Kuwait,

Demanding, once again, that Iraq withdraw immediately and unconditionally all its forces to the positions in which they were located on 1 August 1990,

Determined to bring the occupation of Kuwait by Iraq to an end and to restore the sovereignty, independence and territorial integrity of Kuwait,

Determined also to restore the authority of the legitimate Government of Kuwait,

1. *Decides* that annexation of Kuwait by Iraq under any form and whatever pretext has no legal validity, and is considered null and void;

2. *Calls upon* all States, international organizations and specialized agencies not to recognize that annexation, and to refrain from any action or dealing that might be interpreted as an indirect recognition of the annexation;

3. *Further demands* that Iraq rescind its actions purporting to annex Kuwait;

4. *Decides* to keep this item on its agenda and to continue its efforts to put an early end to the occupation.

DOCUMENTS

RESOLUTION 664 (1990) 19 AUGUST 1990

The Security Council,

Recalling the Iraqi invasion and purported annexation of Kuwait and resolutions 660, 661 and 662,

Deeply concerned for the safety and well being of third state nationals in Iraq and Kuwait,

Recalling the obligations of Iraq in this regard under international law,

Welcoming the efforts of the Secretary-General to pursue urgent consultations with the Government of Iraq following the concern and anxiety expressed by the members of the Council on 17 August 1990,

Acting under Chapter VII of the United Nations Charter:

1. *Demands* that Iraq permit and facilitate the immediate departure from Kuwait and Iraq of the nationals of third countries and grant immediate and continuing access of consular officials to such nationals;

2. *Further demands* that Iraq take no action to jeopardize the safety, security or health of such nationals;

3. *Reaffirms* its decision in resolution 662 (1990) that annexation of Kuwait by Iraq is null and void, and therefore demands that the government of Iraq rescind its orders for the closure of diplomatic and consular missions in Kuwait and the withdrawal of the immunity of their personnel, and refrain from any such actions in the future;

4. *Requests* the Secretary-General to report to the Council on compliance with this resolution at the earliest possible time.

RESOLUTION 665 (1990) 25 AUGUST 1990

The Security Council,

Recalling its resolutions 660 (1990), 661 (1990), 662 (1990) and 664 (1990) and demanding their full and immediate implementation,

Having decided in resolution 661 (1990) to impose economic sanctions under Chapter VII of the Charter of the United Nations,

Determined to bring an end to the occupation of Kuwait by Iraq which imperils the existence of a Member State and to restore the legitimate authority, and the sovereignty, independence and territorial integrity of Kuwait which requires the speedy implementation of the above resolutions,

Deploring the loss of innocent life stemming from the Iraqi invasion of Kuwait and determined to prevent further such losses,

Gravely alarmed that Iraq continues to refuse to comply with resolutions 660 (1990), 661 (1990), 662 (1990) and 664 (1990) and in particular at the conduct of the Government of Iraq in using Iraqi flag vessels to export oil,

1. *Calls upon* those Member States co-operating with the Government of Kuwait which are deploying maritime forces to the area to use such measures commensurate to the specific circumstances as may be necessary under the authority of the Security Council to halt all inward and outward maritime shipping in order to inspect and verify their cargoes and destinations and to ensure strict implementation of the provisions related to such shipping laid down in resolution 661 (1990);

2. *Invites* Member States accordingly to co-operate as may be necessary to ensure compliance with the provisions of resolution 661 (1990) with maximum use of political and diplomatic measures, in accordance with paragraph 1 above;

3. *Requests* all States to provide in accordance with the Charter such assistance as may be required by the States referred to in paragraph 1 of this resolution;

4. *Further requests* the States concerned to co-ordinate their actions in pursuit of the above paragraphs of this resolution using as appropriate mechanisms of the Military Staff Committee and after consultation with the Secretary-General to submit reports to the Security Council and its Committee established under resolution 661 (1990) to facilitate the monitoring of the implementation of this resolution;

5. *Decides* to remain actively seized of the matter.

DOCUMENTS

RESOLUTION 666 (1990) 13 SEPTEMBER 1990

The Security Council,

Recalling its resolution 661 (1990), paragraphs 3 (c) and 4 of which apply, except in humanitarian circumstances, to foodstuffs,

Recognizing that circumstances may arise in which it will be necessary for foodstuffs to be supplied to the civilian population in Iraq or Kuwait in order to relieve human suffering,

Noting that in this respect the Committee established under paragraph 6 of that resolution has received communications from several Member States,

Emphasizing that it is for the Security Council, alone or acting through the Committee, to determine whether humanitarian circumstances have arisen,

Deeply concerned that Iraq has failed to comply with its obligations under Security Council resolution 664 (1990) in respect of the safety and well-being of third State nationals, and reaffirming that Iraq retains full responsibility in this regard under international humanitarian law including, where applicable, the Fourth Geneva Convention,

Acting under Chapter VII of the Charter of the United Nations,

1. *Decides* that in order to make the necessary determination whether or not for the purpose of paragraph 3 (c) and paragraph 4 of resolution 661 (1990) humanitarian circumstances have arisen, the Committee shall keep the situation regarding foodstuffs in Iraq and Kuwait under constant review;

2. *Expects* Iraq to comply with its obligations under Security Council resolution 664 (1990) in respect of third State nationals and reaffirms that Iraq remains fully responsible for their safety and well-being in accordance with international humanitarian law including, where applicable, the Fouth Geneva Convention;

3. *Requests*, for the purposes of paragraphs 1 and 2 of this resolution, that the Secretary-General seek urgently, and on a continuing basis, information from the relevant United Nations and other appropriate humanitarian agencies and all other sources on the availability of food in Iraq and Kuwait, such information to be communicated by the Secretary-General to the Committee regularly;

4. *Requests further* that in seeking and supplying such information particular attention will be paid to such categories of persons who might suffer specially, such as children under 15 years of age, expectant mothers, maternity cases, the sick and the elderly;

5. *Decides* that if the Committee, after receiving the reports from the Secretary-General, determines that circumstances have arisen in which there is an unrgent humanitarian need to supply foodstuffs to Iraq or Kuwait in order to relieve human suffering, it will report promptly to the Council its decision as to how such need should be met;

6. *Directs* the Committee that in formulating its decisions it should bear in mind that foodstuffs should be provided through the United Nations in co-operation with the International Committee of the Red Cross or other appropriate humanitarian agencies and distributed by them or under their supervision in order to ensure that they reach the intended beneficiaries;

7. *Requests* the Secretary-General to use his good offices to facilitate the delivery and distribution of foodstuffs to Kuwait and Iraq in accordance with the provisions of this and other relevant resolutions;

8. *Recalls* that resolution 661 (1990) does not apply to supplies intended strictly for medical purposes, but in this connection recommends that medical supplies should be exported under the strict supervision of the Government of the exporting State or by appropriate humanitarian agencies.

DOCUMENTS

RESOLUTION 667 (1990) 16 SEPTEMBER 1990

The Security Council,

Reaffirming its resolutions 660 (1990), 661 (1990), 662 (1990), 664 (1990), 665 (1990) and 666 (1990),

Recalling the Vienna Conventions of 18 April 1961 on diplomatic relations and of 24 April 1963 on consular relations, to both of which Iraq is a party,

Considering that the decision of Iraq to order the closure of diplomatic and consular missions in Kuwait and to withdraw the immunity and privileges of these missions and their personnel is contrary to the decisions of the Security Council, the international Conventions mentioned above and international law,

Deeply concerned that Iraq, notwithstanding the decisions of the Security Council and the provisions of the Conventions mentioned above, has committed acts of violence against diplomatic missions and their personnel in Kuwait,

Outraged at recent violations by Iraq of diplomatic premises in Kuwait and at the abduction of personnel enjoying diplomatic immunity and foreign nationals who were present in those premises,

Considering that the above actions by Iraq constitute aggressive acts and a flagrant violation of its international obligations which strike at the root of the conduct of international relations in accordance with the Charter of the United Nations,

Recalling that Iraq is fully responsible for any use of violence against foreign nationals or against any diplomatic or consular mission in Kuwait or its personnel,

Determined to ensure respect for its decisions and for Article 25 of the Charter of the United Nations,

Further considering that the grave nature of Iraq's actions, which constitute a new escalation of its violations of international law, obliges the Council not only to express its immediate reaction but also to consult urgently to take further concrete measures to ensure Iraq's compliance with the Council's resolutions,

Acting under Chapter VII of the Charter of the United Nations,

1. *Strongly condemns* aggressive acts perpetrated by Iraq against diplomatic premises and personnel in Kuwait, including the abduction of foreign nationals who were present in those premises;

2. *Demands* the immediate release of those foreign nationals as well as all nationals mentioned in resolution 664 (1990);

3. *Further demands* that Iraq immediately and fully comply with its international obligations under resolutions 660 (1990), 662 (1990) and 664 (1990) of the Security Council, the Vienna Conventions on diplomatic and consular relations and international law;

4. *Further demands* that Iraq immediately protect the safety and well-being of diplomatic and consular personnel and premises in Kuwait and in Iraq and take no action to hinder the diplomatic and consular missions in the performance of their functions, including access to their nationals and the protection of their person and interests;

5. *Reminds* all States that they are obliged to observe strictly resolutions 661 (1990), 662 (1990), 664 (1990), 665 (1990) and 666 (1990);

6. *Decides* to consult urgently to take further concrete measures as soon as possible, under Chapter VII of the Charter, in response to Iraq's continued violation of the Charter, of resolutions of the Council and of international law.

RESOLUTION 669 (1990) 24 SEPTEMBER 1990

The Security Council,

Recalling its resolution 661 (1990) of 6 August 1990,

Recalling also Article 50 of the Charter of the United Nations,

Conscious of the fact that an increasing number of requests for assistance have been received under the provisions of Article 50 of the Charter of the United Nations,

Entrusts the Committee established under resolution 661 (1990) concerning the situation between Iraq and Kuwait with the task of examining requests for assistance under the provisions of Article 50 of the Charter of the United Nations and making recommendations to the President of the Security Council for appropriate action.

DOCUMENTS

RESOLUTION 670 (1990) 25 SEPTEMBER 1990

The Security Council,

Reaffirming its resolutions 660 (1990), 661 (1990), 662 (1990), 664 (1990), 665 (1990), 666 (1990) and 667 (1990),

Condemning Iraq's continued occupation of Kuwait, its failure to rescind its actions and end its purported annexation and its holding of third State nationals against their will, in flagrant violation of resolutions 660 (1990), 662 (1990), 664 (1990) and 667 (1990) and of international humanitarian law,

Condemning further the treatment by Iraqi forces of Kuwaiti nationals, including measures to force them to leave their own country and mistreatment of persons and property in Kuwait in violation of international law,

Noting with grave concern the persistent attempts to evade the measures laid down in resolution 661 (1990),

Further noting that a number of States have limited the number of Iraqi diplomatic and consular officials in their countries and that others are planning to do so,

Determined to ensure by all necessary means the strict and complete application of the measures laid down in resolution 661 (1990),

Determined to ensure respect for its decisions and the provisions of Articles 25 and 48 of the Charter of the United Nations,

Affirming that any acts of the Government of Iraq which are contrary to the above-mentioned resolutions or to Articles 25 or 48 of the Charter of the United Nations, such as Decree No. 377 of the Revolution Command Council of Iraq of 16 September 1990, are null and void,

Reaffirming its determination to ensure compliance with Security Council resolutions by maximum use of political and diplomatic means,

Welcoming the Secretary-General's use of his good offices to advance a peaceful solution based on the relevant Security Council resolutions and noting with appreciation his continuing efforts to this end,

Underlining to the Government of Iraq that its continued failure to comply with the terms of resolutions 660 (1990), 661 (1990), 662 (1990), 664 (1990), 666 (1990) and 667 (1990) could lead to further serious action by the Council under the Charter of the United Nations, including under Chapter VII,

Recalling the provisions of Article 103 of the Charter of the United Nations,

Acting under Chapter VII of the Charter of the United Nations,

1. *Calls upon* all States to carry out their obligations to ensure strict and complete compliance with resolution 661 (1990) and in particular paragraphs 3, 4 and 5 thereof;

2. *Confirms* that resolution 661 (1990) applies to all means of transport, including aircraft;

3. *Decides* that all States, notwithstanding the existence of any rights or obligations conferred or imposed by any international agreement or any contract entered into or any licence or permit granted before the date of the present resolution, shall deny permission to any aircraft to take off from their territory if the aircraft would carry any cargo to or from Iraq or Kuwait other than food in humanitarian circumstances, subject to authorization by the Council or the Committee established by resolution 661 (1990) and in accordance with resolution 666 (1990), or supplies intended strictly for medical purposes or solely for UNIIMOG;

4. *Decides further* that all States shall deny permission to any aircraft destined to land in Iraq or Kuwait, whatever its State of reigistration, to overfly its territory unless:

(a) The aircraft lands at an airfield designated by that State outside Iraq or Kuwait in order to permit its inspection to ensure that there is no cargo on board in violation of resolution 661 (1990) or the present resolution, and for like purpose the aircraft may be detained for as long as necessary; or

(b) The particular flight has been approved by the Committee established by resolution 661 (1990); or

(c) The flight is certified by the United Nations as solely for the purposes of UNIIMOG;

5. *Decides* that each State shall take all necessary measures to ensure that any aircraft registered in its territory or operated by an operator who has his principal place of business or permanent residence in its territory complies with the provisions of resolution 661 (1990) and the present resolution;

6. *Decides further* that all States shall notify in a timely fashion the Committee established by resolution 661 (1990) of any flight between its territory and Iraq or Kuwait to which the requirement to land in paragraph 4 above does not apply, and the purpose for such a flight;

7. *Calls upon* all States to co-operate in taking such measures as may be necessary, consistent with international law, including the Chicago Convention, to ensure the effective implementation of the provisions of resolution 661 (1990) or the present resolution;

8. *Calls upon* all States to detain any ships of Iraqi registry which enter their ports and which are being or have been used in violation of resolution 661 (1990), or to deny such ships entrance to their ports except in circumstances recognized under international law as necessary to safeguard human life;

9. *Reminds* all States of their obligations under resolution 611 (1990) with regard to the freezing of Iraqi assets, and the protection of the assets of the legitimate Government of Kuwait and its agencies, located within their territory and to report to the Committee established under resolution 661 (1990) regarding those assets;

10. *Calls upon* all States to provide to the Committee established by resolution 661 (1990) information regarding the action taken by them to implement the provisions laid down in the present resolution;

11. *Affirms* that the United Nations Organization, the specialized agencies and other international agencies in the United Nations system are required to take such measures as may be necessary to give effect to the terms of resolution 661 (1990) and this resolution;

12. *Decides* to consider, in the event of evasion of the provisions of resolution 661 (1990) or of the present resolution by a State or its nationals or through its territory, measures directed at the State in question to prevent such evasion;

13. *Reaffirms* that the Fourth Geneva Convention applies to Kuwait and that as a High Contracting Party to the Convention Iraq is bound to comply fully with all its terms and in particular is liable under the Convention in respect of the grave breaches committed by it, as are individuals who commit or order the commission of grave breaches.

DOCUMENTS

RESOLUTION 674 (1990) 29 OCTOBER 1990

The Security Council,

Recalling its resolutions 660 (1990), 661 (1990), 662 (1990), 664 (1990), 665 (1990), 666 (1990), 667 (1990) and 670 (1990),

Stressing the urgent need for the immediate and unconditional withdrawal of all Iraqi forces from Kuwait, for the restoration of Kuwait's legitimate sovereignty, independence and territorial integrity and of the authority of its legitimate government,

Condemning the actions by the Iraqi authorities and occupying forces to take third-State nationals hostage and to mistreat and oppress Kuwaiti and third-State nationals, and the other actions reported to the Security Council, such as the destruction of Kuwaiti demographic records, the forced departure of Kuwaitis, the relocation of population in Kuwait and the unlawful destruction and seizure of public and private property in Kuwait, including hospital supplies and equipment, in violation of the decisions of the Council, the Charter of the United Nations, the Fourth Geneva Convention, the Vienna Conventions on Diplomatic and Consular Relations and international law,

Expressing grave alarm over the situation of nationals of third States in Kuwait and Iraq, including the personnel of the diplomatic and consular missions of such States,

Reaffirming that the Fourth Geneva Convention applies to Kuwait and that as a High Contracting Party to the Convention Iraq is bound to comply fully with all its terms and in particular is liable under the Convention in respect of the grave breaches committed by it, as are individuals who commit or order the commission of grave breaches,

Recalling the efforts of the Secretary-General concerning the safety and well-being of third-State nationals in Iraq and Kuwait,

Deeply concerned at the economic cost and the loss and suffering caused to individuals in Kuwait and Iraq as a result of the invasion and occupation of Kuwait by Iraq,

Acting under Chapter VII of the Charter of the United Nations,

★ ★ ★

Reaffirming the goal of the international community of maintaining international peace and security by seeking to resolve international disputes and conflicts through peaceful means,

Recalling the important role that the United Nations and its Secretary-General have played in the peaceful solution of disputes and conflicts in conformity with the provisions of the Charter,

DOCUMENTS

Alarmed by the dangers of the present crisis caused by the Iraqi invasion and occupation of Kuwait, which directly threaten international peace and security, and seeking to avoid any further worsening of the situation,

Calling upon Iraq to comply with the relevant resolutions of the Security Council, in particular its resolutions 660 (1990), 662 (1990) and 664 (1990),

Reaffirming its determination to ensure compliance by Iraq with the Security Council resolutions by maximum use of political and diplomatic means,

A

1. *Demands* that the Iraqi authorities and occupying forces immediately cease and desist from taking third-State nationals hostage, mistreating and oppressing Kuwaiti and third-State nationals and any other actions, such as those reported to the Security Council and described above, that violate the decisions of this Council, the Charter of the United Nations, the Fourth Geneva Convention, the Vienna Conventions on Diplomatic and Consular Relations and international law;

2. *Invites* States to collate substantiated information in their possession or submitted to them on the grave breaches by Iraq as per paragraph 1 above and to make this information available to the Security Council;

3. *Reaffirms* its demand that Iraq immediately fulfil its obligations to third-State nationals in Kuwait and Iraq, including the personnel of diplomatic and consular missions, under the Charter, the Fourth Geneva Convention, the Vienna Conventions on Diplomatic and Consular Relations, general principles of international law and the relevant resolutions of the Council;

4. *Also reaffirms* its demand that Iraq permit and facilitate the immediate departure from Kuwait and Iraq of those third-State nationals, including diplomatic and consular personnel, who wish to leave;

5. *Demands* that Iraq ensure the immediate access to food, water and basic services necessary to the protection and well-being of Kuwaiti nationals and of nationals of third States in Kuwait and Iraq, including the personnel of diplomatic and consular missions in Kuwait;

6. *Reaffirms* its demand that Iraq immediately protect the safety and wel-being of diplomatic and consular personnel and premises in

Kuwait and in Iraq, take no action to hinder these diplomatic and consular missions in the performance of their functions, including access to their nationals and the protection of their person and interests and rescind its orders for the closure of diplomatic and consular missions in Kuwait and the withdrawal of the immunity of their personnel;

7. *Requests* the Secretary-General, in the context of the continued exercise of his good offices concerning the safety and well-being of third-State nationals in Iraq and Kuwait, to seek to achieve the objectives of paragraphs 4, 5 and 6 above and in particular the provision of food, water and basic services to Kuwaiti nationals and to the diplomatic and consular missions in Kuwait and the evacuation of third-State nationals;

8. *Reminds* Iraq that under international law it is liable for any loss, damage or injury arising in regard to Kuwait and third States, and their nationals and corporations, as a result of the invasion and illegal occupation of Kuwait by Iraq;

9. *Invites* States to collect relevant information regarding their claims, and those of their nationals and corporations, for restitution or financial compensation by Iraq with a view to such arrangements as may be established in accordance with international law;

10. *Requires* that Iraq comply with the provisions of the present resolution and its previous resolutions, failing which the Security Council will need to take further measures under the Charter;

11. *Decides* to remain actively and permanently seized of the matter until Kuwait has regained its independence and peace has been restored in conformity with the relevant resolutions of the Security Council.

B

12. *Reposes* its trust in the Secretary-General to make available his good offices and, as he considers appropriate, to pursue them and to undertake diplomatic efforts in order to reach a peaceful solution to the crisis caused by the Iraqi invasion and occupation of Kuwait on the basis of Security Council resolutions 660 (1990), 662 (1990) and 664 (1990), and calls upon all States, both those in the region and others, to pursue on this basis their efforts to this end, in conformity with the Charter, in order to improve the situation and restore peace, security and stability;

13. *Requests* the Secretary-General to report to the Security Council on the results of his good offices and diplomatic efforts.

DOCUMENTS

RESOLUTION 678 (1990) 29 NOVEMBER 1990

The Security Council,

Recalling and reaffirming its resolutions 660 (1990), 661 (1990), 662 (1990), 664 (1990), 665 (1990), 666 (1990), 667 (1990), 669 (1990), 670 (1990), 674 (1990) and 677 (1990),

Noting that, despite all efforts by the United Nations, Iraq refuses to comply with its obligation to implement resolution 660 (1990) and the above subsequent resolutions, in flagrant contempt of the Council,

Mindful of its duties and responsibilities under the Charter of the United Nations for the maintenance and preservation of international peace and security,

Determined to secure full compliance with its decisions,

Acting under Chapter VII of the Charter of the United Nations,

1. Demands that Iraq comply fully with resolution 660 (1990) and all subsequent relevant resolutions and decides, while maintaining all its decisions, to allow Iraq one final opportunity, as a pause of goodwill, to do so;

2. Authorizes Member States co-operating with the Government of Kuwait, unless Iraq on or before 15 january 1991 fully implements, as set forth in paragraph 1 above, the foregoing resolutions, to use all necessary means to uphold and implement Security Council resolution 660 (1990) and all subsequent relevant resolutions and to restore international peace and security in the area;

3. Requests all States to provide appropriate support for the actions undertaken in pursuance of paragraph 2 of this resolution;

4. Requests the States concerned to keep the Council regularly informed on the progress of actions undertaken pursuant to paragraphs 2 and 3 of this resolution;

5. Decides to remain seized of the matter.

Vote: 12 in favour, Cuba and Yemen against, China abstained.

7 CHRONOLOGY OF GULF EVENTS, 1980–1991

1980

In the course of the year, limited military clashes and intensifying verbal attacks between Iraq and Iran occur with increasing frequency.

JANUARY

26 Abol Hassan Bani-Sadr is elected President of the Islamic Republic of Iran.

MARCH

14 The first round of the elections for the Iranian parliament or *Majlis*.

APRIL

1 An assassination attempt on Tariq Aziz, Iraq's Deputy Prime Minister, fails. Iran is accused of inspiring it.

8 The Iraqi Ayatollah Muhammad Baqir al-Sadr, a prominent religious leader of Iraq's Shi'is, is executed by the Ba'th regime.

MAY

9 The second round of the elections for Iran's Majlis.

JUNE

20 Elections (strictly controlled) for the first National assembly in Iraq.

AUGUST

5 Saddam Hussein visits Saudi Arabia, most likely discussing the possibility of attack on Iran.

SEPTEMBER

4 The date subsequently claimed by Iraq as the start of the Gulf War, as Iran on that day shelled the border towns of Mandali and Khanaqin.

CHRONOLOGY

17   Saddam Hussein abrogates the 1975 Algiers Agreement with Iran, claiming full sovereignty over the Shatt al-Arab.

22   Iraq invades Iran; fast advance until early October.

UN Security Resolution 479 calls for cease-fire.

OCTOBER

Slow Iraqi advance, culminating in the capture of Khorramshahr on 24 October.

Meanwhile, however, Iran destroys Iraq's oil export facilities in the Gulf.

NOVEMBER–DECEMBER

Stalemate sets in.

1981

JANUARY–FEBRUARY

Continued stalemate, with Iraqi initiative.

MARCH

19–20   Iraq tries to take Susangerd but fails: the end of any Iraqi preponderance.

APRIL

4   Iran destroys 46 Iraqi airplanes at Al-Walid airbase.

MAY

25   Gulf Cooperation Council (GCC) is formed.

JUNE

7   Israeli planes bomb Iraqi Osirak nuclear reactor facility.

21   Iranian President Bani Sadr is dismissed by Khomeini.

30   New Iranian President Rajai is killed by Mojahedin bomb.

JULY–AUGUST

Continued stalemate, with a number of small Iranian attacks.

SEPTEMBER

28   The Iranians start recovering ground, when the siege of Abadan is broken.

CHRONOLOGY

OCTOBER

5 Khamenei is elected President of Iran.

DECEMBER

7 Iranians recover Bustan.

1982

MARCH

Major Iranian offensive starts (to June).

22 Iranian attack expels the Iraqis from Dezful-Shush region.

APRIL

8 Syria closes the border with Iraq.
10 Closure of pipeline carrying Iraqi oil across Syrian territory.
11 Iraq announces start of economic austerity measures.
30 New Iranian offensive drives Iraqis back to the border in the area between Husseiniya and Khorramshahr.

MAY

24 Iranians recapture Khorramshahr.

JUNE

Iranian advances continue, large numbers of prisoners are taken.
Iraq launches air raids against the Kharg oil terminal.

12 Start of 'Ramadhan' offensive against Basra: Iran carries the war into Iraq.
20 Saddam announces that Iraqi troops will be withdrawn to the international border by 30 June.
27 End of the Ninth Regional Ba'th Party Congress, at which Saddam's supreme position of power is made part of the new credo.

JULY

A stalemate begins to re-emerge, as the morale of Iraqi troops improves with the defence of their own territory, and as Soviet arms supplies resume.

AUGUST

12 Iraq declares an exclusion zone in the northern Gulf, including Kharg.

CHRONOLOGY

1983

FEBRUARY–MARCH

Major Iranian offensive efforts continue, without significant successes. In preparation for the internationalisation of the conflict, Iraq steps up attacks on Iranian tankers and oil export terminals.

MAY

Iraqi Foreign Minister Tariq Aziz meets US Secretary of State Shultz in Paris, as part of the internationalisation effort and with the aim of obtaining effective support against Iran.

OCTOBER

France delivers to Iraq, on loan, five Super Etendard aircraft capable of firing Exocet missiles.

1984

FEBRUARY

Iran launches offensives to cut off road to Basra, and into the Huwaiza marshes. The former fails.

27   Iraq declares the start of the siege of Kharg.

MARCH

Iran conquers the oil-rich Majnoon islands in the Huwaiza marshes.

27   Iraq fires Exocets in attacks on tankers.

APRIL

18   With an Iraqi attack on a Panamanian tanker, the tanker war begins in earnest.

MAY

13   Iran retaliates by attacking shipping carrying non-Iraqi Arab oil and other cargo in the lower Gulf.

17   Conclusion of the elections for the second Majlis in Iran.

JUNE

1   UN Security Council Resolution 552 condemns attacks on neutral (Kuwaiti and Saudi) shipping, and urges the upholding of free navigation.

CHRONOLOGY

5   Saudi F-15s shoot down one, possibly two Iranian Phantom fighters.

OCTOBER

20 Elections for the second National Assembly in Iraq.

DECEMBER

3   Kuwaiti airliner is highjacked to Tehran.

1985

MARCH

5   A War of the Cities breaks out, lasting some three months.

APRIL

25 Car bomb attack on the Emir of Kuwait, who escapes.

JULY

11 Bomb attacks on two Kuwaiti cafés: 11 dead, 89 injured.

AUGUST

14–onwards: attacks on Kharg become more damaging, seriously hampering Iranian oil exports. Iran starts inspecting/seizing ships with Iraq-bound cargo.

17 Khamenei is re-elected President of Iran.

SEPTEMBER

13 Iran receives 508 TOW missiles from the US in a secret deal.

NOVEMBER

22 Council of Experts appoints Montazeri as Khomeini's successor.

DECEMBER

Oil prices slide to $26/barrel.

1986

JANUARY

17 US President Reagan approves CIA sale of 4000 TOW missiles to Iran.

CHRONOLOGY

FEBRUARY

9   Iran advances into southern Iraq and captures Fao.

25   Iran attacks on the northern front, capturing some territory in the Sulaimania region within a month.

1000 US TOW missiles are delivered to Iran.

MARCH

24   UN report on the use of chemical weapons by Iraq is followed by UN Security Council Resolution condemning Iraq on this count while also criticising the prolongation of the conflict.

APRIL

Oil price drops below $10/barrel.

MAY

17   Iraq captures Mehran. Iran rejects offer to exchange it for Fao.

25   Failed mission to Iran by Robert McFarlane, US envoy.

JUNE

In early June, Khomeini calls for total mobilisation.

JULY

Tanker war and Iraqi strikes on economic targets escalate.

Further US arms are delivered to Iran via Spain and Yugoslavia.

3   Kuwaiti Assembly is dissolved, without prospect of reinstatement.

4   Saddam Hussein's power position is further consolidated by an extraordinary Ba'th Party congress, and a reshuffle of the RCC, the Ba'th Party Regional Command, and the cabinet.

9   Iran retakes Mehran.

AUGUST

Iranian-Saudi understanding restores oil price to around $15/barrel.

12   Iraqi long-range strike on Sirri Island oil terminal.

Air war is stepped up.

SEPTEMBER

Iranian offensives in Kurdistan and around Fao.

CHRONOLOGY

OCTOBER

8   UN Security Council urges implementation of Resolution 582, and mediation by the Secretary-General is intensified.

NOVEMBER

3   Secret US arms sales to Iran are revealed in Beirut newspaper *Al Shiraa*, starting off the 'Irangate' scandal.

Kuwait asks the UN for protection of its tankers.

25   Furthest Iraqi air raid yet, hitting targets near Larak.

DECEMBER

In late December, the poorly prepared Iranian Kerbala IV offensive against Basra results in heavy Iranian casualties.

Kuwait approaches both the US and USSR for reflagging and escorting its tankers.

1987

JANUARY

Kerbala V begins, bringing Basra under siege. A bloody stalemate develops after the Iraqis are forced back from the southern border to the main defensive lines around the city.

Iran starts firing Sea Killer missiles at Kuwaiti ships.

MARCH

In the Kerbala VII to X offensives (to April), Iran continues to make minor advances, especially in the north.

APRIL

14   Soviet Union agrees to charter 3 tankers to Kuwait and to escort them.

MAY

16   Soviet tanker chartered to Kuwait strikes a mine.

17   USS *Stark* is hit by an Iraqi missile, apparently by mistake.

19   US agrees in principle to reflag 11 Kuwaiti tankers.

JUNE

2   Khomeini dissolves the Islamic Republican Party.

CHRONOLOGY

JULY

20   UN Security Council adopts Resolution 598 (see document in appendix); Iraq accepts three days later, Iran prevaricates and plays for time, insisting on prior condemnation of Iraq as the aggressor. The initial official reply reads: 'Resolution 598 (1987) has been formulated without seeking consultation from the Islamic Republic of Iran. As it reflects the Iraqi formulae for the resolution of the conflict, it cannot therefore be considered a balanced, impartial, comprehensive and practical resolution.'

24   In the first escort operation of US-flagged Kuwaiti tankers, the *Bridgeton* hits a mine. Rafsanjani announces that Iran will retaliate at sea against Iraq's allies.

30   Hundreds of Iranian and other pilgrims die in Mecca during the Hajj, in the chaos and violence ensuing from political demonstrations by Iranians.

AUGUST

9   Second reflagged convoy gets underway, with mine-detecting helicopters.

18   Eight minesweeping helicopters are brought into the Gulf on the USS *Guadalcanal*.

21   USSR says it is ready to join the minesweeping effort if warships are withdrawn.

SEPTEMBER

French and British minesweepers join the US, independently.

21   US ships seize an Iranian vessel, *Iran Ajr*, found laying mines.

OCTOBER

2   Iran and Iraq close down their diplomatic missions in each other's capitals.

16   US-flagged Kuwaiti tanker is hit by missile in Kuwaiti waters.

19   US strikes Iranian oil platform Rostam, used as a base for Pasdaran, and sinks patrol boats.

22   Kuwait's Sea Island oil terminal is hit by Iranian missile.

NOVEMBER

8   Arab summit in Amman (with the exception of Libya) condemns Iran.

CHRONOLOGY

20   Four Belgian and Dutch minesweepers enter the Gulf.

1988

FEBRUARY

6   Khomeini appoints Council for the Determination of Expediency (or 'what is best').

27   Iraq restarts War of the Cities.

MARCH

15   Iran captures Halabja with Kurdish help.

16   Iraqi forces use chemical weapons in attack on Halabja, killing an estimated 5000 people.

APRIL

5   Kuwaiti airliner is hijacked to Mashad.

14   US frigate strikes mine off Bahrain.

16–18 Iraq retakes Fao; the use of chemical weapons is reported.

18   US naval forces blow up two Iranian oil platforms, put two Iranian frigates out of action, and sink an Iranian missile boat.

20   End of War of the Cities.

26   Saudi Arabia cuts diplomatic relations with Iran.

MAY

13   Conclusion of Iranian elections for the third Majlis.

25   Iraq recaptures Salamcheh.

JUNE

2   Rafsanjani is appointed acting Commander-in-Chief of the Iranian armed forces.

26   Iraq retakes Majnoon.

JULY

3   USS *Vincennes* shoots down an Iranian airliner over the Gulf, killing all 290 passengers and crew.

During the first half of July, further Iraqi offensives and successes result in penetration of Iranian territory.

17   Saddam Hussein renews his peace offer on the 20th anniversary of the Ba'th Party's assumption of power, including a cease-fire,

return to the international border, a peace treaty, and pacts of non-aggression and non-interference.

18 Iran accepts SCR 598. In his letter to the UN Secretary-General, President Khamenei states: 'We have decided to officially declare that the Islamic Republic of Iran—because of the importance its attaches to saving the lives of human beings and the establishment of justice and regional and international peace and security—accepts Security Council Resolution 598.'

20 Iraq insists on direct negotiations; this is rejected.

22–29 Further Iraqi offensives and by the Iranian National Liberation Army.

AUGUST

1 UN report concludes that Iraq has intensified the use of chemical weapons since the spring.

6 Saddam Hussein accepts that the cease-fire can come into place without direct talks.

20 Cease-fire takes effect. The 350-strong UNIIMOG force (drawn from 25 countries and commanded by General Slavko Jovic) observing the cease-fire is in place.

After the Cease-Fire

AUGUST

25 Start of peace talks in Geneva, chaired by UN Secretary-General.

SEPTEMBER

1 Saudi Arabia sends Prince Bandar as special envoy to Geneva to help break diplomatic deadlock, but no breakthrough is achieved.

4 France and Italy announce plans to reduce their naval presence in the Gulf.

15 Iran announces that it will begin clearing mines from its side of the Gulf.

26 US announces that it is lowering its profile in escorting US-flagged ships in the Gulf.

29 Kuwait sends two diplomats to re-open its embassy in Iran.

CHRONOLOGY

OCTOBER

14   Bahrain and Iran agree to upgrade diplomatic representation.

23   Iranian government announces that it will allow political parties to operate freely provided they 'do not conspire' against the country's political system.

31   The last British merchant vessel to be escorted in the Gulf by the Royal Navy is shepherded out through the Strait of Hormuz.

NOVEMBER

8   Iranian Deputy Foreign Minister says Iran is working on a plan to guarantee the security of the regional states, and describes relations with Kuwait as 'very good'.

24   First exchange of POWs takes place, but both sides accuse the other of holding back on agreed numbers.

27   Iran announces the suspension of its agreement with Iraq to repatriate sick and wounded POWs.

DECEMBER

2   Ayatollah Meshkini, head of the Assembly of Experts, calls for a reappraisal of the country's constitution, in view of the end to hostilities and the need for economic reconstruction.

4   British embassy opens in Tehran, after eight years of closure. Following the execution of a number of his supporters, 117 members of parliament call on Ayatollah Montazeri to continue giving guidance on national affairs.

1989

JANUARY

Iraq releases small batches of POWs.

9   Soviet Foreign Minister Shevardnadze describes Khomeini's message to Gorbachev as a 'turning point' in bilateral relations.

16   Saddam Hussein stresses the importance of permitting the formation of political parties in the coming phase of the country's existence.

31   Rafsanjani reveals that Iran is holding talks with Saudi Arabia on resuming diplomatic relations.

CHRONOLOGY

FEBRUARY

6   Kuwait's Crown Prince begins a visit to Iraq to resolve border and other issues. The visit proves a failure.

8   Iraq pulls back 100 units of the Iraqi Popular Army from the Iranian front.

10   Iranian and Iraqi Foreign Ministers hold their first face-to-face meeting in New York in the presence of the UN Secretary-General.

14   Khomeini passes the death sentence on Salman Rushdie, the British author of *The Satanic Verses*.

16   The Arab Cooperation Council (ACC) between Iraq, Egypt, Jordan and North Yemen is created.

21   In retaliation to the EC decision to withdraw its ambassadors from Tehran over the Rushdie affair, Iran announces that it will recall its ambassadors from Europe.

24   Soviet Foreign Minister visits both Iran and Iraq, being received by Khomeini on 26 February; this signals a turning point in Soviet-Iranian relations.

MARCH

EC (except British) ambassadors trickle back to Iran

7   Iran says it will block the Shatt al-Arab until all Iraqi troops are withdrawn from Iranian territory.

Iran officially cuts off diplomatic relations with Britain.

27   Ayatollah Montazeri resigns as Khomeini's heir-designate.

Iraq and Saudi Arabia sign non-aggression pact.

APRIL

1   Elections for the Iraqi National Assembly take place; vetted non-Ba'th party members are allowed to stand.

18   Bahrain and China establish diplomatic relations.

25   Khomeini appoints a committee to revise Iran's constitution.

MAY

6   Iraqi war hero and Defence Minister Adnan Khairallah dies in suspicious helicopter crash. He was the President's cousin and married to his estranged wife.

CHRONOLOGY

JUNE

3   Ayatollah Khomeini dies. President Khamenei is named his successor and made Ayatollah.

8   Official Kuwaiti sources confirm that Kuwait will break the OPEC production agreement.

12   Rafsanjani is re-elected as Speaker of the Majlis.

20   Rafsanjani arrives in Moscow at the head of a large delegation in an effort to improve Iran's economic, political and military links with the USSR.

JULY

29   Rafsanjani is proclaimed Iran's new executive President.

AUGUST

One year after the implementation of the cease-fire, Iran and Iraq appear no nearer to formal peace.

16   Mehdi Karrubi is elected as the new Speaker of the Iranian Majlis.

18   President Rafsanjani announces his new cabinet.

29   Rafsanjani's cabinet receives approval from the Majlis.

SEPTEMBER

21   Saudi Arabia executes 16 Kuwaiti Shi'is arrested for causing explosions in Mecca during the Hajj in July.

NOVEMBER

Reports concerning the maltreatment of thousands of Egyptian workers and their wholesale departure from Iraq as a result, sour relations between the two countries.

In Kuwait, the dialogue on the restoration of democracy re-emerges more forcefully.

1990

FEBRUARY

Kuwait, Saudi Arabia and the UAE are together producing 1.6 million b/d of oil above their designated OPEC quota.

CHRONOLOGY

APRIL

War of words between the Arab states and the West over Iraq's increasingly defiant posture continues. Iraqi threats towards Israel raise anxiety in the West over the expansion of Iraq's military capabilities. Reports surface of Iraqi attempts to acquire a 'supergun' with private sector Western assistance.

MAY

3 OPEC summit agreement for three-month production cutback. Saudi Arabia switches to production discipline.

22 North and South Yemen unite, forming the Yemeni Republic.

30 At an Arab Summit session behind closed doors in Baghdad, Saddam Hussein implicitly threatens the overproducers, accusing them of economic warfare.

JUNE

10 Voting in Kuwait, limited to males of over 21 years of age, begins for the new and controversial National Council. The 75-seat National Council (50 of which are elected and 25 selected by the Emir), is given a temporary four-year mandate and is to meet behind closed doors.

22 Iraqi Oil Minister for the first time attacks the UAE by name.

JULY

11 Jeddah agreement among Gulf oil producers implies Kuwait and the UAE returning to a 1.5 million b/d quota.

15 Iraq submits memorandum to the Arab League equating Kuwaiti and UAE oil policy with military aggression, and accusing Kuwait of taking Iraqi oil and territory.

18 Rafsanjani states that Iran and Iraq have narrowed their differences over a border settlement—one of the main causes of the Gulf War. He reportedly tells senior clerics that 'the Iraqis' attitude towards peace has become more positive . . . The two countries' viewpoints have come closer within the framework of the Algiers Agreement'.

19 Kuwait rejects Iraqi accusations in memorandum to the Arab League.

20 Egyptian President Mubarak calls for brotherly dialogue between Iraq and Kuwait.

22	Saudi Arabia establishes diplomatic relations with China.
24	Iraq moves 30,000 troops to Kuwaiti border.
25	US Ambassador April Glaspie has an interview with Saddam Hussein, which is subsequently interpreted as not having been used to deliver a stern enough warning against military adventurism.
27	OPEC agrees to a new oil price target of $21/b, and cut-backs in production along lines of Jeddah agreement.
	Iraq warns Kuwait that, at the planned high-level talks, it must honour Baghdad's 'legitimate rights'. Iraqi troop concentrations on the Kuwaiti border approach 100,000.

AUGUST

1	Senior Kuwaiti and Iraqi officials have a two-hour meeting in Jeddah.

Iraq Invades Kuwait

2	Iraqi tanks and troops move into Kuwait at 2 am. By the end of the day the country is under Iraqi occupation. The US, the UK, Italy and France freeze Kuwaiti and Iraqi assets; the USSR suspends weapons shipments. UN Security Council Resolution 660 condemns the invasion.
3	Joint US-USSR statement condemns the invasion and calls for withdrawal. GCC Foreign Ministers condemn the invasion. Arab League Foreign Ministers do likewise, with 14 members voting in favour.
4	The 'Free Provisional Kuwaiti Government' is named. The Islamic Conference Organisation condemns the invasion. EC condemns the invasion and imposes trade sanctions and a freeze on Iraqi and Kuwaiti assets.
6	UN Security Council Resolution 661 imposes sanctions (13–0).
7	US orders American forces to Saudi Arabia in response to Saudi request. Kuwaiti Republic is declared.
8	Iraq annexes Kuwait.
9	King Fahd's speech to the nation issues harsh condemnation of Iraq.
10	Arab Summit in Cairo decides with 12 votes in favour to send troops in defense of Saudi Arabia and calls for Iraqi withdrawal.

CHRONOLOGY

	EC and NATO express full solidarity with the UN and the US respectively.
12	Saddam Hussein suggests linking the Kuwait issue with the withdrawal of all foreign troops—including those of Israel—from the occupied territories.
15	**Iraq offers to accept Iran's terms for peace, two years after the cease-fire.**
17	Iraq announces officially that nationals of 'aggressive' nations will be held in the country.
18	UN Security Council calls for the release of all foreigners in Iraq.
19	All GCC states have now promised co-operation with the international military effort. Iran's Foreign Minister confirms Iran's backing for the UN sanctions against Iraq. Iran and Iraq agree to raise POW exchanges from 1000/day each, to 8000/day each.
20	Iraq orders embassies in Kuwait closed by 24 August.
21	Iraq announces the completion of troop withdrawal from the Iranian front. Western European Union (WEU) agrees to step up and coordinate military operations in the Gulf.
22	US calls up military reserves.
24	A number of prominent Western embassies in Kuwait are surrounded. Iran's President Rafsanjani implicitly condones the possible use of force to remove Iraqi troops from Kuwait.
25	UN Security Council Resolution 665 authorises the enforcement of the trade embargo.
28	Iraq declares Kuwait its 19th province.
29	OPEC agrees to boost output to make up for Iraqi-Kuwaiti shortfall.
30	Saddam reiterates refusal to withdraw from Kuwait.
31	UN Secretary-General de Cuellar meets the Iraqi Foreign Minister in Amman; talks are a failure.

Saudi oil production during August is raised to 5.8 mn b/d.

SEPTEMBER

| 3 | Soviet spokesman supports US deployment in the Gulf. Arab League Secretary-General resigns. |

CHRONOLOGY

4   US forces seize first Iraqi ship for inspection. US Secretary of Defence Cheney says Saudi Arabia will be consulted before any offensive operations against Iraq.

5   Saddam Hussein appeals to the people of the states opposing him to rebel against their rulers.

9   Presidents Bush and Gorbachev meet in Helsinki and issue a joint statement on the Gulf crisis. Iraqi and Iranian Foreign Ministers meet in Tehran.

10   US Secretary of State Baker announces that Saudi Arabia, the UAE and Kuwait have promised $12 billion to aid the international campaign.

Twelve members of the Arab League decide to proceed with plans to move the headquarters back to Cairo. Iran and Iraq agree to re-establish diplomatic relations.

14   Iraqi assault on the French Ambassador's residence in Kuwait, and actions against Dutch, Belgian and Canadian embassies. Britain decides to send 6,000 troops and 120 Challenger tanks.

15   France follows the UK in deciding to send ground forces. US Secretary of State's fund raising tour is announced to have resulted in a total of $24.8 billion.

16   UN Security Council Resolution 667 unanimously condemns Iraqi moves against embassies in Kuwait. Egypt follows Syria in committing extra ground troops to the Gulf. The total number of troops on the ground in Saudi Arabia approaches 200,000; over 500 allied fighters and bombers are already deployed in and around the Gulf.

Saudi Arabia re-establishes diplomatic relations with the USSR.

18   Iraqi troops in and near Kuwait have increased to 360,000, with 2,800 tanks.

23   Saddam Hussein threatens to attack Israel and Gulf oil fields if Iraq feels strangled by sanctions.

25   UN Security Council approves (14–1) Resolution 670, barring flights to and from Iraq and Kuwait.

29   GCC Foreign Ministers meet their Iranian counterpart in New York—the first ever such meeting—to discuss the Gulf crisis.

By the end of September, oil prices have risen to $40/barrel.

CHRONOLOGY

OCTOBER

7   Sheikh Rashid, Ruler of Dubai and Vice-President of the UAE, dies.

8   Rafsanjani states that Iran would use any means at its disposal to prevent the hand-over of any Kuwaiti territory to Iraq in a peace deal.

Elections are held in Iran for the Council of Experts.

13   At a Kuwaiti people's congress held in Jeddah, the ruling family pledges to restore fully the 1962 constitution upholding democratic rights.

NOVEMBER

In the course of November, several allies, including Britain, commit further troops to the Gulf. On the 8th, the US announces that its 210,000 troops in place will be complemented with a further 200,000.

14   Iranian Foreign Minister arrives in Baghdad.

18   Iraq announces it will release all foreign hostages from Christmas Day onwards 'unless something disrupts the climate of peace'.

29   UN Security Council Resolution 678 authorises member states 'to use all necessary means' to make Iraq withdraw from Kuwait if it has not done so by 15 January 1991 (12 vote in favour, China abstains and Cuba and Yemen vote against).

30   President Bush invites Tariq Aziz to Washington and offers to send Secretary of State Baker to Baghdad for talks with the Iraqi President.

DECEMBER

1   Saddam Hussein does not reject the US offer of talks but insists that the Palestinian question be high on the agenda.

3   US Defence Secretary Cheney tells the Senate Arms Services Committee; 'I don't see any evidence that Iraq has any intention of leaving Kuwait . . . it would be far better for us to deal with him now . . . [than to] deal with him five or ten years down the road' and says that waiting for sanctions to work could hurt the coalition more than Iraq.

5   Secretary Baker announces that if the use of force proves necessary 'it will be used suddenly, massively and decisively'.

CHRONOLOGY

6 Iraqi President orders the unconditional release of all hostages held in Iraq and Kuwait.

9 The US rejects Iraq's suggested 12 January date for Saddam-Baker talks as too close to the UN deadline.

15 Tariq Aziz's visit to Washington is called off following the failure to agree on a date for the Baghdad talks.

24 Saddam Hussein says that Israel will be Iraq's first target when war breaks out.

25 GCC Supreme Council in Doha announces the grouping will seek improved relations with Tehran.

26 Iran says it is ready to discuss Gulf security arrangements with the GCC states to avoid great power interference.

1991

JANUARY

3 President Bush proposes talks between Aziz and Baker in Geneva on 9 January.

4 Iraq accepts the proposed talks.

9 Iraq and US delegations meet in Geneva. After more than six hours of discussion, the talks fail.

12 Following Capitol Hill's debate on the Gulf crisis, the US president narrowly wins the right to use American forces in the Gulf to enforce the UN resolutions.

13 UN Secretary-General Perez de Cuellar's efforts in Baghdad to find a peaceful solution to the crisis end in failure.

14 Yemen sends a high-level delegation to Baghdad to discuss a six-point plan to avert war in the Gulf. The plan envisages direct linkage between Iraqi withdrawal from Kuwait to a UN commitment to speed up an international Middle East peace conference.

15 Diplomatic efforts to end the crisis peacefully continue. France offers a multipoint proposal for talks on the Gulf crisis. It implies a de facto linkage with the Palestinian issue through an international conference. Iraq spurns this and other last minute initiatives to avert war in the Gulf.

After a ten-year break Iran and Jordan resume diplomatic relations.

16 **11:00 PM GMT: Operation Desert Storm begins.**

POSTSCRIPT

Exactly a month after the UN deadline had passed and the subsequent allied military assault on Iraq's war machine had begun, Iraq's Revolutionary Command Council announced on 15 February 1991 that Baghdad 'was ready to deal with UN Security Resolution 660', while linking this with a large number of conditions that were unacceptable to the coalition. Importantly, the word 'withdrawal' from Kuwait was mentioned for the first time, although Iraq's insistence on appending a wide range of political, diplomatic and economic conditions rather diluted the statement's significance. The previous day, the allied military command had confidently declared that the continuous air bombardment and naval action had reduced Iraq's military capacity by up to 50 per cent in some sectors, including 30 per cent of its tank and artillery arsenal in the Kuwait theatre of operations. If correct, such allied success could hardly have been a major surprise, given the range of high-technology firepower ranged against Iraq. Many observers, military spokesmen and government officials in countries of the coalition had, if anything, forecast a quicker Iraqi defeat.

Although in broad terms the operation was looked upon positively and was supported by the countries lined up against Saddam Hussein's forces, it should perhaps have received a more cautious welcome from anyone with an interest in the future stability of the Middle East. The demise of Iraq's military might would not necessarily mean that peace had been won. While it soon became clear that the allies would not lose the war, the price of winning it was less apparent. In the heat of the battle this price was largely calculated in terms of allied casualties. A longer-term perspective, however, would have to count equally the political, socio-economic and diplomatic cost. When such variables are included, it is clear that military bullishness alone could not be a sufficient reason for confidence in the outcome of Operation Desert Storm.

The underlying question of the moral permissibility of the military option, as realised in the form of Desert Storm, must also be addressed. Perhaps the most fruitful way to approach this question is to ask three subsidiary questions—the first being whether the initial choice of the military option was acceptable. Assuming that one agrees that the UN Security Council resolutions had to be enforced, it is clear that the only instruments available for this purpose were those of sanctions and military force: negotiations on the existing disputes between Iraq and Kuwait could not be a prior condition for withdrawal. We must then ask whether or not the established network of sanctions against Iraq ought to have been given more time to prove its effect. There can be no doubt that even another six months of sanctions would have seriously affected Iraq; while it is true that they *might* not have forced Saddam Hussein to decide to pull his troops out of Kuwait, there was, nevertheless, a considerable chance that they would have. More importantly, perhaps, sanctions would have increased the likelihood of internal agitation against his rule without turning him into a hero; and certainly the strength of the Iraqi military machine would have been seriously eroded in several sectors. Finally, of course, if war between the allies and Iraq could be avoided, then so would the casualties that would inevitably result from any major armed conflict, as well as the bitterness against the West that would certainly ensue in much of the Islamic world.

Against this, however, there would have been a number of equally weighty negative considerations. First, to give sanctions another six months to a year to take effect would imply the continued destruction of Kuwait and its population for that same length of time. Secondly, it would allow for the possibility of Iraq's strengthening its defences in and around Kuwait and building up its military stocks in the area—thus potentially necessitating much larger sacrifices in allied lives if the use of armed force did in the end prove the only way out. In addition, there was the pragmatic consideration of the possibility that the coalition's strength and unity of purpose could dissipate over time. The main decision-makers, primarily the governments in Washington and London, are likely to have based their decision against an extension of sanctions on a close examination of the latter two points—one military, one political. If the available evidence, particularly on the military question, constituted a sound case against a major delay, then it would follow that a decision to use force sooner would be justified. The kind of military intelligence that allows such an assessment to be made is, by its very nature, not available to outsiders—nor was it in this case. An absolute judgement of the resultant decisions must therefore remain beyond the reach of the authors of the present volume as well. What is clear, however, is that once the decision was taken not to give sanctions any significantly longer time, considerations of tactical surprise and weather dictated that military action should be launched at the first possible opportunity—in effect, on the night of 16 January 1991.

The second subsidiary question concerns the modalities of such military action, once started. The intensity of the conflict was to be determined not only by the military task at hand—the engagement of the Iraqi war machine—but also by political considerations such as the minimalisation of civilian casualties in Iraq and Kuwait. These considerations were, however, matched by pertinent questions regarding the form and substance of the war itself. Most countries as well as substantial quarters in the home bases of the allies remained in agreement with the broad scheme of implementing the eviction orders against Iraq; but not all were convinced that the enforcement of the UN Security Council resolutions necessarily included—or indeed required—large-scale and debilitating attacks on Baghdad and other Iraqi towns and cities, or the bombardment of economic and industrial targets throughout the country. Did the UN resolutions permit attacks on such targets in Iraq or not? The allies argued that the only way to implement SCR 678 was through attacks on Iraq's military machine and its potential to wage war. The liberation of Kuwait, it soon emerged, had to start in Baghdad. Even the isolation of the Iraqi forces in Kuwait would, at the very least, require the crippling of the supply routes up and down Iraq. The implementation of the same strategy also required that the potential for replenishment of Iraq's arsenal in the Kuwaiti theatre of operations had to be curtailed. In short: it was plausibly argued that in order to stop the flow the fountain itself had to be capped.

Objections to the allies' military strategy were manifested not so much in the debates on the various interpretations of the UN resolutions as in the context of an apparent widening of allied war aims to include the removal of Saddam Hussein from office. With the UN itself taking a back seat, it was suggested that the outcome of the crisis lay in the hands of Washington and its closest allies; by sanctioning the use of force, the UN Security Council had in effect marginalised the organisation from the minute the military move actually began. From then on, the end to hostilities would lie in the Gulf itself and not in the UN's corridors of diplomacy.

As promised by Secretaries Baker and Cheney, the bombings against Iraqi targets were massive. Much of the military campaign was conducted from the air. The allies deployed over twenty varieties of aircraft, whose bomb load on the first night alone amounted to some 18,000 tonnes of munitions. The extensive use of advanced missile systems and other airborne guided weapons served two purposes: the destruction of Iraq's military-industrial infrastructure and the minimising of casualties on the allies' side. Naval units deployed in the conflict participated initially in the war effort by providing additional aircraft as well as sea-launched missiles; from the third week of the war, it became apparent that US battle ships in the Gulf would also take part in the bombardment of targets in the Kuwaiti theatre of operations and in keeping open the option of rapid amphibious landings of combat units along the Kuwaiti shore. The land troops that made up the largest part of the US-led forces in fact saw very little action in the first four weeks of fighting. As the largest numbers of casualties were expected to occur on land, it is not surprising that the allies preferred not to engage their ground troops in large-scale battle before Iraq's ability to inflict unacceptable casualties had been substantially reduced. The strategy appears on the whole to have been effective. The era of 'Star Wars' seemed upon us, with 'collateral' damage apparently controllable. The strategy of 'selective targeting' gained a new meaning in this war. Even though inevitably the human cost on the Iraqi side (also in terms of civilian casualties) was considerable, without the advanced weapons systems used and the strategy adopted by the allies, the end result might well have been even more tragic.

Our third and final subsidiary question is in two parts: should the Iraqis be (or have been) given an opportunity to reconsider, in the form of a cease-fire? And, more generally, which should be the conditions for an end to Operation Desert Storm? Many peace activists throughout the world, including in the Arab states of Yemen and Algeria, advocated a cease-fire either to allow Iraq the option of withdrawing gracefully, or at least to restart negotiations. While this would allow Iraq to regroup, to resupply and to repair transport and communications facilities, such a course of action would be counter-productive as long as no solid commitment to withdraw was evident; during the first month of the fighting there was no credible indication in that direction. It could also be argued that the declaration of a cease-fire should originate from the UN Security Council itself, as part of the process of implementing the relevant resolutions; otherwise the integrity of the whole UN system could be undermined. With the key principle being the imposition of the will of the international community, all actions by members of the coalition were necessarily bound by the conditions of the UN Security Council resolutions. If implementation by Iraq of these resolutions was seen to be under way, there could be no further justification for military action.

Even if the military action which was undertaken could perhaps be considered a necessary evil (even allowing for doubts about timing and misgivings about specific operations), intense concern with the contextual issues and with the future of the region are all the more crucial. History has shown that war, in itself, does not generally solve anything. In so far as it represents a breakdown in the functioning of the international system, it cannot be expected to bring about international tranquility and normalcy. In order to repair the ruptures and remove the catalysts for war, much effort is needed at the diplomatic level, with equal amounts of foresight, courage and generosity. By definition also, war creates human tragedy, and so tests the tolerance and the capacity to forgive of societies and of individuals. The outcome of this process greatly depends, of course, on the level and nature of the violence unleashed. Here the examples of Nicaragua, of Vietnam and of the Iran-Iraq War teach us that if the will is present among the political elites of the conflicting states, then relatively rapid healing is indeed possible.

In the instance of the Kuwait war and its aftermath, we would suggest that a further agent of such healing could be found in the United Nations. From 2 August 1990, the United Nations Organisation has demonstrated that it is able and willing, in the new international context, to use its authority to repulse aggression by a state member. Following the end of hostilities it will be of the utmost importance for the UN to illustrate that it can use the same authority in the search for a peace acceptable to all parties, in the monitoring and safeguarding of cease-fire or other non-aggression pacts, and in the wider effort to find just solutions to the remaining problems between regional actors.

For many ordinary Arabs and Muslims throughout the world, the extent of the action against Iraq recalled the previous experience of their nations with the 'imperialism' of the West. For a number of governments too, popular pressures and a genuine perception that the United States in particular might want to turn the exercise into one of humbling both Iraq and the Arab and Muslim World, produced a stance highly critical of the West. It was clear throughout that the destruction of Iraq would result in dire consequences for the West's standing and interests in the Arab and Muslim world, as well as in Iraq itself—*unless* that danger was recognised and a concerted effort made to counter it. If post-war policy was to have any chance of success, a number of elements needed to be observed, related to the situation in Iraq itself, to the maintenance of the peace between Iraq and Kuwait, to the wider regional context, and to the issue of Western involvement in the region.

In a post-war, and presumably post-Saddam Iraq, there would be no place for any intrusive Western political management. Any government put in place as a result of such intervention would be unlikely to survive for very long. Nevertheless, the lack of any well-established democratic tradition, and the disruption wrought by the conflict itself, would leave a possible role in Iraq for the United Nations. Ideally, a coalition of all opposition parties, with a number of prominent representatives from various sections of Iraqi society, could, together with UN administrators, prepare the country for free elections for a new government and a constituent assembly. The UN could then play a supervisory role in the elections themselves. After this transitional period, which would need to be kept short, any further non-Iraqi involvement should be excluded. All of this, of course, rests on the premise that opposition groups and initiatives should be taken seriously. An alternative strongman is not the answer. As illustrated in Chapters 2 and 3, it was, after all, the wholly undemocratic and extreme concentration of power in Iraq which was in large measure responsible for the Kuwait crisis. Moreover, if long-term instability is to be avoided, the rights of Iraq's various ethnic (e.g. Kurdish) and religious (e.g. Shi'i) groups must be safeguarded.

In addition, both the economic and the political effects of the destruction caused in the process of the military campaign should be alleviated with a massive aid programme, preferably including major debt relief arrangements. Although costly, such a 'Marshall Plan' for Iraq would amply pay for itself in political terms—while at the same time involving businesses in the donor country. To avoid alienating Tehran, it would be prudent to address the issue of war reparations as raised in SCR 598 and to arrange for easy credit to speed up the task of Iran's economic reconstruction.

In Iraqi-Kuwaiti relations, the first role for the UN would of course be that of monitoring any cease-fire, followed by the sending of peace-keeping troops. Such troops should as quickly as possible replace those of the United States and Britain in particular: the bulk of Western troops should in any case be withdrawn from the Gulf region as a whole (though this would not exclude a return to the kind of presence obtaining before the Kuwait crisis). Only thus could the backlash of further popular anger be contained. Fortunately, one of the most hopeful instances of the use of UN contingents for this purpose already exists in the area, in the shape of UN Iran-Iraq Military Observer Group (UNIIMOG) which was deployed with the cease-fire in the previous Gulf War, and whose mandate was smoothly extended for a further month on 31 January 1991, in the midst of Operation Desert Storm.

POSTSCRIPT

The crisis, as well as the way regional perceptions and reactions to it have evolved, has also highlighted the need to look beyond the immediate environment of the Gulf states and this particular conflict. The conditions that are needed for the dream of a more peaceful future Middle East to become a reality, after the trauma of the present crisis, and for Western interests in the region to be safeguarded more than superficially, lie mainly in four areas.

Firstly, there is the painfully obvious need for the international community, ideally represented by the United Nations, to tackle the other festering problems of the Middle East. The Arab-Israeli dispute in particular illustrates how these issues continue to cause increasing bitterness while simultaneously enabling a variety of potentates to legitimise their claims or to rouse the masses (whether out of genuine concern or sheer opportunism). It is of supreme importance—for peace and stability within the region as well as for the long-term benefit of the outside world—that a solution be found which comprehensively addresses the concerns both of Israel and the Arabs—Palestinians and others.

To achieve a satisfactory solution of this kind seems impossible unless a second concern is addressed—namely that of the Middle Eastern arms race and the absence of a regional security structure, where the latter continually reinforces the former, and the former throughout heightens the propensity for, and the level of, violence. Here again, the United Nations can play a role.

In the search for viable solutions to the endemic instabilities and the cycle of violence that have been so dramatically displayed in the Gulf in recent years, one will have inevitably to take stock of the international reactions to the crisis—some of them perhaps disturbing, others rather promising. The UN's positive role—current and projected—in the Kuwait situation is by no means the first instance of UN action in dealing with 'regional problems'. In the course of the 1980s, Afghanistan, southern Africa, Cambodia, Central America and the Iran-Iraq War all came under the close scrutiny of the UN and its specialist agencies. In all these instances the UN played a decisive and constructive role. Of course the thaw between East and West greatly facilitated such developments; the fact that neither superpower chose, for instance, to interpret the Iraqi invasion of Kuwait as an opportunity for competition, was a key factor that enabled the UN to perform its role effectively. At the same time, there appears to have been a growing awareness both in the East and the West that the uncontrolled transfer of military technology and large arsenals of sophisticated weapons systems to regional buyers has added to the existing tensions and risks.

POSTSCRIPT

In the context of the Gulf at least, this fact seems also to have started sinking in at governmental level. The discussion of a viable arms control regime to be put in place in the Gulf, even as an exercise in self-preservation, was gaining increasing currency in many Western capitals with every passing day of the new Gulf crisis.

With regard to arms control and confidence-building measures, one may hope that lessons will have been learnt from the example of Europe. The latter's evolution, indeed, demonstrates that not only is arms control possible—it is a natural progression of 'civilised' discourse even in a divided and highly militarised environment. Admittedly, political reforms within states would have a very important role in boosting this process, but even here the UN can make a major contribution, if only by insisting that its members faithfully and diligently adhere to the letter and spirit of the charter of human values to which each has put its signature: the Universal Declaration of Human Rights. Iraq's domestic scene is only one, albeit an acute, example of the need for this.

Even without such reforms much initial progress can be made in arms control talks as well as in establishing the principle of co-ordinated regional disarmament. The European example illustrates that in the interest of collective security, even enemies can learn not only to tolerate each other but successfully to live side by side with an ever-diminishing threat of attack. Events in the Gulf region itself put a silver lining on the cloud of war and destruction so prevalent in recent times: Iraq's full acceptance of Iran's conditions for peace, after eight years of bloodletting and two further years of threats and distrust, shows that under certain conditions the instinct for regime survival propels the actors toward compromise. Witness also UNIIMOG's extended mandate referred to above. This is not to suggest that it takes a string of crises to solve the region's outstanding security problems; yet a combination of pressures, inducements and suggestion may well bring the right responses from regional actors.

If one accepts, in addition, that self-control in arms transfers to the region would greatly limit the capacity of the 'hegemonic' or expansionist regional actors to wage war or to issue threats, it would appear that there is indeed a viable road towards security in this part of the world. The first step would be an international decision to stop supplying offensive weapons systems to Middle Eastern states. The strengthening of the Missile Technology Control Regime coupled with agreements to impose costs on those states that attempted to transfer missile technology and other processes for developing and manufacturing offensive weapons systems, could allow a fairly water-tight system of international controls to emerge.

It is important that any regional security structure should not be imposed by outside powers or based to any significant extent on the participation of outside military might, since this would lose it local legitimacy and would simply be a recipe for future friction and failure.

It must be stressed that viable security structures for the Gulf cannot exclude the Middle East's two non-Arab Muslim states, Iran and Turkey, which have legitimate security concerns of their own. The structures may be new, but these 'old' actors will necessarily need to be consulted and involved at every stage of planning and execution. Of the two, Turkey's role is unlikely to be in dispute. However, because of its track record since the late 1970s, Iran poses a challenge: can the other states accept it as an element for stability rather than as a revolutionary challenger? Apart from the fact that, given the country's size, location and history it would clearly be futile to attempt to move ahead without it, the evidence we have presented in earlier chapters also indicates that the Islamic Republic under its new leadership has been taking on a new international persona: thus its new-found readiness to embrace the norms of the community of nations could be further encouraged by the suggested process of consultation and involvement.

Clearly, much of this would face virtually insurmountable obstacles unless the question of Israel's armed might is taken into account; this, in turn, would not be feasible without progress towards a settlement of the Arab-Israeli question. The actual, if not legal, linkages between each of these problem areas—Palestine, arms control, regional security structure—are there for all to see.

The fourth area of concern is one which has received all too little attention in the past, but which has been sharply highlighted by the Kuwait crisis: *viz.* the Middle East's unequal distribution of wealth. Immense riches in sparsely-inhabited countries are contrasted with the lack of resources, the often abject poverty and inexorably growing debts found in those other states of the region that accommodate the vast majority of the Arab world's population. The need for a genuine mechanism of redistribution is not only economic, but also intensely political.

Attitudes in evidence among the members of the anti-Iraq coalition at the time of writing gave some cause for hope. At the United Nations, following Iraq's mid-February 'offer', Secretary-General Perez de Cuellar stressed that the organisation would be ready to perform its role without delay: initial monitoring delegations could be dispatched immediately, with peacekeeping troops following within a few days. As to individual members of the coalition, the most hopeful signs were coming from Europe. In keeping with tradition, France insisted on the need to address the Palestine question seriously and, equally importantly, President Mitterrand stressed that 'it is up to the UN Security Council to organise the peace. No other authority can serve as a substitute'. Perhaps the most significant indication, however, came in a number of statements from the United Kingdom, America's key Western partner in the allied operation, and most explicitly in the address on 4 February 1991 by the Foreign Secretary Douglas Hurd to the European Foreign Ministers' Forum. He called for special attention to be given to four areas in the aftermath of the war: (1) an *indigenous* regional security structure, including some Western assistance but at the invitation of the regional states; (2) the control of arms capable of causing mass destruction; (3) a settlement of the Palestine question that would be acceptable to all parties including the Palestinians; and (4) a more equitable distribution of wealth. Mr Hurd also stated that the option to retain any significant numbers of British troops 'East of Suez' was 'not realistic'.

The signals from the United States were less clear, but nevertheless left some light shining through. There were repeated commitments that the outstanding issues in the Middle East would be tackled—even though no date or form for this was put forward—and President Bush confirmed that America would not maintain ground troops in the area after the war ended. Clearly some elements in the US Administration were strongly tempted to retain a more active presence and role in the area than were the Europeans. The Adminstration was also unwilling to be drawn on the issue of a Middle East Peace Conference, as urged by its European partners and others. A key question concerned the American attitude towards the United Nations in the post-war period. Fears that Washington might want to revert to its earlier dismissiveness and suspicion of the organisation were not wholly unfounded. Nevertheless, there was perhaps reason to hope that the authority acquired by the United Nations during the Kuwait crisis, with such prominent American involvement, would permit sufficient international pressure to be brought to bear for the US not to oppose an increased status and authority for the organisation in other such situations in the future.

Meanwhile, another cause for cautious optimism was the recognition in Europe and in the US that a major effort would be needed in the rebuilding of Iraq as well as of Kuwait. While this general concern was reflected in official comments from several European governments, a more specific suggestion was made by the US Secretary of State James Baker, on 7 February 1991. In a testimony to the Senate Foreign

POSTSCRIPT

Relations Committee, he proposed that a Middle East bank for reconstruction and development be established, arguing that the entire region, including Iraq, 'warrants the same spirit of multilateral commitment to reconstruction and development' as developed nations had shown in other areas. No details were provided of the bank proposal. Yet the idea opened up the interesting possibility of using such an institution not just for the reconstruction of Iraq and Kuwait, but as part of a mechanism for achieving a more equitable distribution of wealth in the whole of the region. However tragic the events from August 1990 into 1991 may have been, and however traumatic their consequences may yet be, not all is lost for the Gulf or, for that matter, for the Middle East region at large.

(February 1991)

NOTES

Notes to Chapter 1

1. An earlier version of the material in this chapter appears in the March 1991 issue of *Political Studies*, entitled 'After Khomeini: the structure of power in the Iranian Second Republic'.
2. Ayatollah Khomeini issued a controversial religious ruling in February 1989, condemning Rushdie to death for the publication of *The Satanic Verses*, considered blasphemous.
3. *BBC Summary of World Broadcasts* (henceforth *SWB*), ME, 13 October 1989.
4. *SWB*, ME, 31 August 1989. Judging by the harsh treatment by the Majlis of the previous cabinets under Rafsanjani himself, and also by its resoluteness in undermining President Bani Sadr's authority in 1981, this threat was not a hollow one.
5. For some of the local political commentaries on President Rafsanjani's cabinet see *Abrar*, 30 August 1989; *Jomhuri Eslami*, 30 August 1989, and *Ettala'at*, 30 August 1989 and 1 September 1989.
6. Hojjatoleslam Mohammadi Eraqi replaced Nouri: *SWB*, ME, 28 June 1990.
7. Ayatollah Khamenei's second representative in the NSC was Hassan Rouhani, a cleric member of the Majlis's Defence Committe.
8. As is shown by the run-up to and the eventual outcome of the October elections (8 October 1990) for the 83-member theologically based Assembly of Experts (*Majlis-e-Khebregan*), the body which, among other things, is empowered to choose the supreme leader of the republic and if necessary dismiss him, the Leader-President alliance managed to sweep the rug from under the feet of the radical clergy opposed to the Rafsanjani government's domestic economic and foreign policies, in order to gain control of this important institution. Ayatollah Khamenei supervised the implementation of changes to the assembly's election procedures that were proposed by the Leader-President alliance over the summer, and as a consequence of the vetting of the 169 candidates under the new rules, the 12-man Council of Constitutional Guardians (six of whose theologians are appointed by the supreme leader himself) rejected the credentials of 60 hopeful candidates. Notable absentees from this assembly (many of whom refused to take the theological test proposed by Ayatollah Khamenei) include the following: Ayatollah Moussavi Arde-

NOTES

billi, Hojjatoleslam Mohtashemi, Hojjatoleslam Karrubi, Hojjatoleslam Khalkhali, Hojjatoleslam Moussavi and Hojjatoleslam Khoini'a (who refused to participate in the elections in solidarity with the rejected candidates even though his own credentials had been accepted by the Guardians' Council). This successful coup of the leadership alliance has been interpreted by local commentators as a decisive victory over the radicals in the Second Republic. Furthermore, the eight-year term virtually ensures the position of Ayatollah Khamenei as the Supreme Leader, for as of October 1990 most of the members of the assembly belonged to either his or President Rafsanjani's faction. *Keyhan*, 21 July 1990; *Nimrooz* (London), 14 October 1990; *Tehran Times*, 10 October 1990.

9 Karrubi's re-election as the Speaker on 12 June 1990, with 155 votes out of 229 cast, consolidated the radical alliance's presence in the Majlis. In addition, Hojjatoleslam Mohtashemi was elected Secretary-General of the high-profile inter-parliamentary group for two years, on 4 July *SWB*, ME, 13 June and 6 July 1990.

Notes to Chapter 2

1 Sabah Salman, *Saddam Husayn—Qa'id wa-Ta'rikh* [Saddam Hussein— A Leader and History], (Baghdad, 1986).
2 In 1973, the then head of the Security Service, Nadhim Kazzar was responsible for a bloody, but unsuccessful coup attempt. In 1983, the then head of the same service, Saddam Hussein's half-brother, Barzan al-Takriti, was removed from office and placed under virtual house arrest for a while—together with fellow clan members—in circumstances the details of which remain obscure. The primary reason, however, was almost certainly Sadam Hussein's belief that they constituted something of a liability, if not a direct menace to his own position and authority.
3 This message is simultaneous with the repeated theme which Saddam Hussein stresses—namely, the existence of the Iraqi nation, rooted in 5,000 years of civilization. The key to this apparent paradox is Saddam Hussein's claim to have awakened Iraqis to their national identity, as well as to possess the strength to prevent them lapsing back into their old ways whilst they discover the joys of nationhood.
4 I. Al-Khafaji, 'State Incubation of Iraqi Capitalism', *MERIP Report* 142, September/October 1986, p. 4.
5 Saddam Hussein's address to the mayors of Najaf, Misan and Karbala provinces, *SWB*, ME, 16 July 1987.
6 Arab Ba'th Socialist Party Iraq, *The Central Report of the Ninth Regional Congress June 1982* (Baghdad, January 1983), p. 39.
7 *The Independent*, 17 January 1989.
8 S. Chubin and C. Tripp, *Iran and Iraq at War* (London: I.B Tauris, 1988), pp. 114–120.

NOTES

9   It has been observed that the Shi'i officers thus favoured tend to come from the Shi'i tribes of the south. These tribesmen have generally tended to place their tribal identity higher than their formal Shi'i identity and are thus very unlikely to have much sympathy with the collective expression of specifically Shi'i demands.

10 This led to the 'accidental death' of one of the senior northern army commanders and the appointment by Saddam Hussein of one of his kinsmen, Ali Hassan al-Majid (also Head of the Security Services) as overall commander of the Northern Region during 1988. Charles Tripp, 'The Consequences of the Iran-Iraq War for Iraqi Politics', in E. Karsh (ed), *The Iran-Iraq War: impact and implications* (London, Macmillan in association with the Jaffee Center for Strategic Studies, Tel-Aviv University, 1989), pp. 75–77.

11 Israel, Iran and even the Kurds may be seen as 'fair game' to some extent, but Sunni Arab Kuwait cannot be easily so portrayed—as a previous Iraqi President, Abd al-Karim Qasim, found to his cost in the early 1960s.

12 *The Observer*, 10 February 1989.
13 *International Herald Tribune*, 9 February 1989 and 10 February 1989.
14 *Financial Times*, 8 May 1989.
15 *The Times*, 12 July 1990.

Notes to Chapter 3

1   The sections treating pre-1986 developments, are largely based on G. Nonneman, *Iraq, the Gulf states & the War: A Changing Relationship, 1980–1986 and beyond* (London: Ithaca Press, 1986).

2   *The 1968 Revolution in Iraq. Experience and Progress. The Political Report of the Eighth Congress of the Arab Baath Socialist Party in Iraq, January 1974* (London: Ithaca Press, 1979) p. 135.

3   *Waqa'i' al-mu'tamar al-suhufi li-l-ra'is Saddam Husain ma'a-l-suhufiyin al-masriyin fi 20-7-85* [Documents of the press conference of president Saddam Hussein with the Egyptian press on 20 July 1985] (London: Iraqi Embassy, 1985) pp. 17–18.

4   See the Iraqi Ba'th Party's *Al-Taqrir al-Markazi li-l-mu'tamar al-Qutri al-tasi'—haziran 1982* [The Central Report of the Ninth Regional Conference, Haziran 1982], (henceforth Al-Taqrir), Baghdad: Tab' al-Dar al-'Arabiya, 1983: pp. 357–358; and Hussein, *On Social and Foreign Affairs in Iraq* (London: Croom Helm, 1979) pp. 73–87.

5   M. Farouk-Sluglett & P. Sluglett, *Iraq since 1958* (London: KPI, 1988) p. 204.

6   *Al-Taqrir*, pp. 355–358.

7   A. Y. Ahmad, 'The Dialectics of Domestic Environment and Role Performance: The Foreign Policy of Iraq', in B. Korany and A. Dessouki

NOTES

(eds.), *The Foreign Policies of Arab States* (Boulder: Westview Press, 1984), p. 159.

8 R. Springborg, 'Infitah, Agrarian Transformation, and Elite Consolidation in Contemporary Iraq', in *Middle East Journal*, Winter 1986, pp. 38–51.

9 I. al-Khafaji, *Al-Dawla wa-l-tatawwur al-ra'smali fi-l-'iraq* (Cairo: Dar al-Mustaqbal al-'Arabi, 1983). Also: id., 'State incubation of Iraqi Capitalism', in *MERIP Report*, No. 142, September 1986, pp. 8–9.

10 T. Niblock, 'Iraqi Policies towards the Arab States of the Gulf', in Niblock (ed.), *Iraq, the Contemporary State*, (London: Croom Helm, 1982) p. 144; see also pp. 139–144.

11 Nonneman, *Iraq*, p. 14; *SWB* ME, 8 February 1980; *SWB* ME, 12 May 1980.

12 *Emirates News*, 3-6-1980; *Middle East Economic Digest* (henceforth *MEED*), 4 July 1980.

13 Middle East Economic Survey (henceforth *MEES*), 11 and 18 August 1980.

14 *Baghdad Observer*, 28 May 1980; *Arab Report & MEMO*, 2 June 1980.

15 R. K. Ramazani, *The Gulf Co-operation Council: Record and Analysis* (Charlottesville: Univ. of Virginia Press, 1986), p. 5.

16 W. Quandt, *Saudi Arabia in the 1980s* (Washington: The Brookings Institution, 1981), pp. 12, 80–83.

17 N. Safran, *Saudi Arabia. The Ceaseless Quest for Security* (Cambridge, Mass.: the Belknap Press of Harvard University Press, 1985), pp. 353–354; and Quandt, *Saudi Arabia*, pp. 36–40.

18 See N. Sakr, 'Economic Relations between Iraq and other Arab Gulf States', in Niblock, *Iraq*, pp. 150–167.

19 For instance statements by Khomeini (*Foreign Broadcast Information Service*—henceforth *FBIS*—NES-80, 24 March 1980), and Bani Sadr (*Al-Ra'y al-'Amm* (Kuwait), 15 March 1980).

20 See Nonneman, *Iraq*, Appendix III.

21 *Al-Siyasa* (Kuwait), 27 May 1980; *SWB* ME, 28 May 1980; *Baghdad Observer*, 28 May 1980; *Al-Khalij* (Sharjah), 31 May 1980.

22 See Nonneman, *Iraq*, pp. 21–22.

23 *ibid.*, pp. 22–23.

24 See Hussein, *On Social and Foreign Affairs*, pp. 74–75.

25 See *MEES*, 7 and 28 January 1980 (Special Supplement); 26 May 1980.

26 See Nonneman, *Iraq*, Chapter 2; and A. Cordesman, *The Gulf and the Search for Strategic Stability* (Boulder: Westview, 1984), pp. 417, 419.

27 Nonneman, *Iraq*, pp. 39, 96.

28 *ibid.*, pp. 49, 95.

29 See *ibid.*, Chapter 5 and p. 103; *MEES*, 13-2-1989.

30 See *SWB* ME, 10–12 December 1985; *MEED*, 14 December 1985.

31 *Le Monde*, 20 August 1987.

32 *The Arab Gulf Journal*, November 1985, pp. 89–90.

NOTES

33 Ehteshami, 'Iran's Foreign Policy and Attitudes towards the Arab World', paper presented to the conference on *Islamic Republic of Iran: Ten Years of the Revolution*, CIRA/Middle East Institute, Columbia University, 7-9 April 1989; and Nonneman, *Iraq*, pp. 74-76.
34 Nonneman, *Iraq*, pp. 101-102.
35 A. Cordesman, The *Iran-Iraq War and Western Security* (London: Jane's, 1987), p. 109; MEED, 13 September 1986; F. Axelgard, *A New Iraq? The Gulf War and its Implications for US Policy* (New York: Praeger, 1988), p. 75.
36 MEED, 29 November 1986 and 21 March 1987; *The Guardian*, 18 December 1986; *Financial Times*, 12 March 1987; Cordesman, *The Iran-Iraq War*, p. 125.
37 *The Times*, 14 April 1987; *De Standaard* (Belgium), 21 April 1987.
38 *MidEast Mirror*, 20 July 1987.
39 *MidEast Mirror*, 11 May and 1 June 1987; *MEES*, 25 May 1987.
40 *MidEast Mirror*, 18 May 1987; Economist Intelligence Unit, *Country Report: Bahrain, Qatar Oman and the Yemens* (henceforth: EIU *Country Report: Bahrain*...) No. 3—1987, p. 20.
41 See *MidEast Mirror*, 3 August 1987.
42 *Financial Times*, 3 and 28 August 1987; *Sunday Times*, 30 August 1987; *MidEast Mirror*, 29 July and 21 August 1987; IRNA and KUNA dispatches, 10 August 1987; *Al-Thawra* (Baghdad), 19 August 1987.
43 *MidEast Mirror*, 24 and 25 August 1987; *Financial Times*, 26 and 28 August 1987; EIU *Country Report: Bahrain*..., No. 4—1987, p. 19.
44 *MidEast Mirror*, 7 September 1987; EIU *Country Report: Bahrain*..., No. 4—1987, p. 11; *MEES*, 28 September 1987; G. Joffé & K. McLachlan, *Iran and Iraq. Building on the stalemate* (EIU Special Report No. 1164; London: EIU, November 1988), pp. 24, 28-29; D. Hiro, *The Longest War* (London: Grafton, 1989), p. 225.
45 *MidEast Mirror*, 15 October 1987; *Kuwait Times*, 3 October 1987; EIU *Country Report: Bahrain*..., No. 4—1987, p. 19.
46 *Al-Siyasa*, 12 October 1987.
47 *Middle East Report*, January 1989: p. 24.
48 EIU *Country Report: Bahrain*..., No. 1—1988, p. 18.
49 *MEES*, 21 December 1987.
50 EIU *Country Report: Bahrain*..., No. 1—1988, pp. 12, 18; *MidEast Mirror*, 29 December 1987. See also G. Joffé & K. McLachlan, *Iran and Iraq. Building on the Stalemate* (= EIU Special Report No. 1164; London, 1988), p. 15.
51 *Mideast Mirror*, 7, 15 and 18 January 1988; and EIU *Country Report: Bahrain*..., No. 2—1988, p. 10.
52 *Al-Jumhuriya* (Baghdad), 19 January 1988; *Baghdad Observer*, 29 January 1988.
53 T. McNaugher, 'Walking Tightropes in the Gulf', in E. Karsh (ed.), *The Iran-Iraq War* (London: Macmillan, 1989, pp. 171-199), p. 185.

NOTES

54 For instance in a speech in February, recorded in *MidEast Mirror*, 9 February 1988.
55 See *MidEast Mirror*, 3 and 16 March 1988; *Al-Sharq al-Awsat*, 8 March 1988; *Al-Musawwar* (Cairo), 10 March 1988.
56 EIU *Country Report: Bahrain . . .*, No. 2—1988, p. 18.
57 *MidEast Mirror*, 11 April 1988; Riyadh Daily, 13 April 1988.
58 *MidEast Mirror*, 13 April 1988.
59 *MidEast Mirror*, 18–20 April 1988.
60 *MidEast Mirror*, 21 April 1988; *Financial Times*, 28 April 1988; SPA dispatches and the Saudi Press on 16 May 1988.
61 *MidEast Mirror*, 29 April and 3 and 23 May 1988; *Khaleej Times* (UAE), 23 May 1988.
62 EIU *Country Report: Bahrain . . .*, No. 3—1988, p. 10; *MidEast Mirror*, 21 and 24 June 1988.
63 *Financial Times*, 22 December 1988.
64 *MidEast Mirror* 5 July 1988; *Al-Sharq al-Awsat*, 5–6 July 1988.
65 See *MidEast Mirror*, 19–20 July 1988.
66 *Al-Qabas*, 26 July 1988; *Al-Ra'y al-'Amm*, 26 July 1988; *Kuwait Times*, 26 July 1988; *Al-Sharq al-Awsat*, 27 July 1988; *MidEast Mirror*, 1–3 August 1988.
67 *MidEast Mirror*, 4 and 8 August 1988; *Observer*, 7 August 1988.
68 More detail about this may be found in Nonneman, *Iraq*, Chapter 8.
69 *MEES*, 21 November 1988.
70 The instances of opening up and privatisation, even in agriculture and latterly tourism, are sufficiently well documented. See for instance *MEED*, 25 November 1988; *MEES*, 22 February 1988; *MidEast Mirror*, 15 August and 5 September 1988.
71 EIU *Country Report: Bahrain . . .*, No. 4—1988, pp. 22–24; *SWB* ME, 7 September 1988; *Al-Siyasa*, 17 December 1988.
72 *Financial Times*, 17 March 1989.
73 *MidEast Mirror*, 21 September 1988; EIU *Country Report: Bahrain . . .*, No. 4—1988, p. 11; *Iran Focus*, November 1988, p. 3.
74 See *MidEast Mirror*, 5, 17 and 20 October; 3 and 9 November 1988; *Arab News*, 12 October 1988; *Kuwait Times*, 9 November 1988; *Al-Siyasa*, 15 November 1988; *Kayhan International*, 25 November 1988; *Iran Focus*, January 1989; *SWB* ME, 22 December 1988; *FBIS*-NES-88-251, 30 December 1988.
75 *The Middle East*, May 1989, p. 22; *The Independent*, 18 March 1989; *Sunday Times*, 19 March 1989.
76 *SWB* ME, 7 April 1989; *FBIS*-NES-89-085, 4 May 1989; see also 89-087, 8 May 1989.
77 *Financial Times*, 14 June 1989.
78 *The Middle East*, May 1989, p. 23.
79 *Washington Post*, 22 August 1988.
80 *FBIS*-NES-88-173, 7 September 1988.

NOTES

81 *SWB* ME, 16 September 1988; *MidEast Mirror*, 12–15 September 1988.
82 *MidEast Mirror*, 21 and 28 September 1988; *FBIS*-NES-88-186, 26 September 1988; 88–188, 28 September 1988; *The Middle East*, May 1989, p. 23.
83 Voice of America, 21 September 1988; *FBIS*-NES-89-088, 14 May 1989.
84 *MidEast Mirror*, 9–10 August 1988.
85 *MidEast Mirror*, 10 and 22 August and 15 September 1988; *APS Diplomat*, No. 8, 22 August 1988 (Oil Market Trends, p. 2).
86 *FBIS*-NES-88-234, 6 December 1988; *MidEast Mirror*, 7 December 1988; *MEES*, 6 February 1989.
87 *Al-Thawra*, 10 January and 27 February 1989; *Foreign Report*, February 1989; *SWB* ME, 6 February 1989, 8 February 1989, 2 March 1989; *FBIS*-NES-89-025, 8 February 1989; NES-89-027, 10 February 1989; NES-89-028, 13 February 1989; NES-89-031, 16 February 1989; *Al-Sharq al-Awsat*, 30 January and 9 February 1989; *Baghdad Observer*, 8 February 1989; Arab Times, 13 February 1989.
88 *MidEast Mirror*, 6 and 12 September 1989. *Al-Sharq al-Awsat*, 15 September 1989.
89 *Arab Times*, 15 February 1989.
90 *Actualités Arabes*, No. 184/185, September 1988.
91 *MidEast Mirror*, 14 September 1988; *MEES*, 10 October 1988; *FBIS*-NES-88-219, 14 November 1988; NES-88-233, 5 December 1988.
92 An article in the Saudi-funded *Al-Sharq al-Awsat* on 17 January 1989, praised Iraq for 'shedding the mantle of socialism', indicating a belief that the country had well and truly left its past behind.
93 *FBIS*-NES-89-038, 28 February 1989; *SWB* ME, 10 March 1989.
94 EIU *Country Report: Bahrain . . .*, No. 2—1989, p. 31.
95 *The Middle East*, July 1989, p. 9; *MEES*, 23 October 1989.
96 For details see *Financial Times*, 28 March 1989; *MEES*, 3 April 1989; *FBIS*-NES-89-057, 27 March 1989; *SWB* ME, 29 March 1989.
97 See Nonneman, *Iraq*, pp. 95–102; Joffé & McLachlan, *Iran and Iraq*; and *MEED*, 13 September 1986.
98 *MEES* 9 January, 6 February, 27 March and 3 April 1989; and *MidEast Mirror*, 17 January 1989.
99 *The Middle East*, April 1989, pp. 28–30.
100 *MidEast Mirror*, 23 October 1987 and 1 March 1989; *MEES*, 21 November 1988 and 20 March 1989; Nonneman, *Iraq*, p. 109; *SWB* ME/W0096 21 March 1989.
101 *FBIS*-NES-89-088, 9 May 1989.
102 *SWB* ME/W0066, 28 February 1989; ME/W0079, 30 May 1989; *FBIS*-NES-89-095, 30 May 1989; *Khaleej Times*, 12 August 1988; *Kuwaiti Times*, 4 December 1988; *MidEast Mirror*, 5 September 1988; *Arab British Commerce*, April 1989, p. 13.

NOTES

103 *MidEast Mirror*, 24 October 1988; Arab Times, 6 March 1989; *Arab British Commerce*, April 1989, pp. 12–13.
104 See also the chronology in Chapter 7.
105 The best among these articles is *The Economist*, 29 September 1990, pp. 19–22.
106 Good coverage of developments in the oil scene in this period can be found in the *MEES* issues for the first half of 1990.
107 *MEES* issues of 26 February to 11 June 1990.
108 *MEES*, 23 July 1990.
109 *MEES*, 25 June 1990.
110 *MEES*, 16 July 1990.
111 See *MidEast Mirror*, 19 July 1990; and the transcript of Kuwaiti cabinet notes of 18 July, in the *Financial Times*, 18 August 1990.
112 *The Times*, 25 July 1990.
113 *MidEast Mirror*, 25 July 1990.
114 *Al-Ahram*, 26 July 1990; *MidEast Mirror*, 26 July 1990.
115 *MEES*, 30 July 1990; *The Independent on Sunday*, 29 July 1990; *MidEast Mirror*, 27 July 1990.
116 *Financial Times*, 3–4 August 1990; *The Observer*, 2 September 1990; *MEES*, 6 August 1990.
117 *MEES*, 6 August 1990.
118 *Financial Times*, 6 August 1990; *MEES*, 13 August 1990.
119 *Financial Times*, 20 August 1990; for reports about the other events see *Financial Times*, 4–7 August 1990; *MEES*, 13 August 1990; *MEED*, 17 August 1990.
120 *Financial Times*, 7 August 1990.
121 *Financial Times*, 8–9 August 1990; *Wall Street Journal*, 9 August 1990; *MEES*, 13 August 1990.
122 *MEES*, 13 August 1990; *Financial Times*, 20 August 1990.
123 *MEED*, 24 August 1990; *MEES*, 13 and 20 August 1990; *Financial Times*, 11 August 1990.
124 *International Herald Tribune*, 6 September 1990; *Financial Times*, 17 September 1990; *Wall Street Journal*, 19 September 1990.
125 *Financial Times*, 16 September 1990.
126 *MEES*, 27 August 1990.
127 *MEES*, 10 September 1990; *Financial Times*, 11 September 1990.
128 See the chronology in Chapter 7.
129 *The Economist*, 29 September 1990, p. 22.

NOTES

Notes to Chapter 4

1. For details see Anoushiravan Ehteshami, 'Pipelines of the Middle East: The Next Strategic Challenge?', *Gulf Report*, No. 17, January 1989, and A. Ehteshami, 'Naval Power and the Geopolitics of the Middle East', *Gulf Report*, No. 14, October 1988.
2. Interested readers can refer to Ehteshami in *Gulf Report* 14 for further background information and elucidation of the analysis that follows.
3. American, British, French, Pakistani, Moroccan, Turkish, Egyptian, Jordanian and Bangladeshi military personnel are commonly employed by the GCC states; military support personnel from France, the USSR, Jordan and Egypt are to be found in Iraq; and Iran has intermittently relied upon Syrian, North Korean, Soviet-bloc, Chinese and possibly Israeli, Turkish and Pakistani military support and technical personnel.
4. During the Kuwait crisis in the Gulf, the availability of Saudi ports on the Red Sea coast facilitated the rapid mobilisation and commitment of thousands of American, British, French, Egyptian, Moroccan, Syrian and other troops, as well as the efficient movement of huge quantities of equipment into Saudi Arabia. The well-organised and well-drilled military mobilisation scheme under America's CENTCOM was perhaps of slightly less importance.
5. For details of the Middle East defence industries see A. Ehteshami (ed.), *Defence Industries of the Middle East*, (London: Brassey's Defence Publishers/GCSS, Summer 1988). For an analysis of the Iranian arms industry see Ehteshami, 'Iran's revolution: fewer ploughshares, more swords', *Army Quarterly and Defence Journal*, Vol. 120, No. 1, January 1990.
6. The National Liberation Army was organised under the auspices of the Iranian opposition People's Mojahedin—according to NLA sources they captured 34 Chieftain and T-54 MBTs, nine Scorpion light tanks, 14 M113 and 12 BMP armoured personnel carriers, some 53 field guns and self-propelled howitzers of different calibres, two TOW anti-tank missiles and three launchers, 17 anti-aircraft guns and systems and a large quantity of mortars, handguns, and support and communications equipment. For further details see, the *NLA Quarterly*, Autumn 1988.
7. Iran's desperate reliance on Soviet and Chinese military hardware (through such intermediaries as Syria, Libya, North Korea, South Yemen, Czechoslovakia, Poland, etc.) means that even after the war ended Iran has had to approach the same countries for more and better Eastern-bloc weapons and production rights, thus, objectively, weakening long-term Western influence in Tehran. It is interesting to note that Soviet-backed Vietnam has been supplying Iran with large quantities of US-made equipment left behind after the Vietnam war.

NOTES

8 See A. Ehteshami, 'Airpower and the Missile Race in the Middle East: An Analysis', *Gulf Report*, No. 15, November 1988, and A. Ehteshami, 'IISS' 1988/89 Middle East Military Balance in Perspective', *Gulf Report*, No. 14, October 1988. More details on Iran's purchasing of MiG-29 fighters from the Soviet Union are found later in this chapter.

9 See *Gulf Report*, Nos. 14 and 15 (October–November 1988).

10 The Iraqi invasion of Kuwait ilustrates this point; Iraq's self-confidence in attacking and occupying its smaller neighbour was made possible by the size of its army and the range (and stores) of sophisticated weapons available to its armed forces.

11 The war has, however, facilitated the development and growth of Iran's domestic arms industry at a rate that was not possible under any other circumstances.

12 The windfall revenues generated since August 1990 by the increases in oil prices of some $700 million to $1 billion extra per month gave Tehran the luxury of considering the purchase of sophisticated military equipment and weapons systems purchases with ready hard currency for the first time since the revolution. The extra income also means that the Iranian government can afford to increase its military budget in the 1990s without undermining its economic reconstruction efforts, and can raise the tempo and rate of arms transfers for the next few years well beyond its original calculations and defence expenditure plans.

13 The concept of 'strategic interdependence' in the Middle East context is introduced in A. Ehteshami, *Nuclearisation of the Middle East* (London: Brassey's Defence Publishers, 1989). Basically it implies that the linkages which are created in a particular theatre receive and apply both negative and positive pressures on other theatres, and are, consequently, subject to similar pressures from them.

14 *Air International*, June 1984; *New York Times*, 7 June 1984. Latest figures indicate that at the start of the new decade, some 40 Phantoms were operational, about 70 Tigers and only 15 Tomcats. *Flight International*, 3 October 1990.

15 *Defence and Foreign Affairs Weekly*, 1 April 1985 and 11–17 August 1986; *Financial Times*, 27 August 1986; *Washington Post*, 26 August 1986.

16 *Defence and Foreign Affairs Weekly*, 2 November 1986; *Foreign Report*, 13 November 1986.

17 For details see the *SIPRI Yearbook 1980* (London: Taylor and Francis, 1980).

18 *SIPRI Yearbook* (various years); *Jane's Defence Weekly*, 19 October 1985; *Defence and Foreign Affairs Weekly*, 27 April 1986; *Armed Forces*, October and December 1985; *Flight International*, 23 February 1985.

19 *SIPRI Yearbook* (various years); *International Herald Tribune*, 30 December 1985; *Jane's Defence Weekly*, 24 November 1985; *Defence and Foreign Affairs Weekly*, 15 December 1985; *Aviation Week and Space Technology*, 3 March 1986; *Armed Forces*, January 1986.

NOTES

20 International Institute for Strategic Studies (IISS), *Strategic Survey 1973*, 1974, p. 45.
21 *Ibid.*
22 We are assuming here that the Iraqi occupation of Kuwait will prove to be a temporary measure and that, ultimately, the sovereignty of Kuwait will be restored. The fate of its ruling family, therefore, cannot be determined until the above condition is fulfilled.
23 As one observer has noted; 'The way in which Iran has co-opted the campaign against Mr. Rushdie, which erupted in predominantly Sunni communities in Britain and the [Indian] sub-continent, constitutes a direct challenge to the authority of the orthodox [Islamic] establishment and to the Saudi Arabian regime, in particular . . . '. Harvey Morris, 'The rivalry that is splitting Islam', *The Independent*, 17 July 1989.
24 In this context, it is worth noting the main points of the GCC's joint defence plan as agreed by the Council's six defence ministers in October 1981, namely to reach a realistic common procurement policy; to establish an effective GCC arms industry; to co-ordinate naval operations; to integrate air defence and early-warning systems, and to address the problem of manpower shortages within each state and for the purpose of joint action.
25 'Problems of Strategy in China's revolutionary War', *Selected Works of Mao Tse-tung—Volume I* (Beijing: Foreign Languages Press, 1967), p. 183.
26 IISS, *The Military Balance 1987–1988*, 1987, p. 238. For a commentary on the Middle East arms build-up see A. Ehteshami, 'There Are Global Military Expenditures and then there is the Middle East', *Gulf Report*, No. 16, December 1988.
27 *SIPRI Yearbook 1988* (Oxford: Oxford University Press, 1988), p. 168.
28 *Flight International*, 10 October 1990; *MEED*, 20 July, 5 October, 12 October 1990.
29 *MEED*, 5 October 1990; *Flight International*, 3 October 1990; *Nimrooz*, 28 September 1990.
30 The establishing of full diplomatic relations with Saudi Arabia and Bahrain in the Autumn of 1990 means that for the first time in many years the Soviet Union has diplomatic relations with all the Gulf states. The warming of relations between the USSR and the GCC countries, and the expansion of its ties with Iran, came at a time when Moscow was distancing itself from Iraq, its lucrative arms market and a close erstwhile Middle Eastern friend.
31 Stephen Goose, 'Armed conflict in 1986, and the Iran-Iraq War', *SIPRI Yearbook 1987* (Oxford: Oxford University Press, 1987), p. 297.

NOTES

Notes to Chapter 5

1. The new five-year development plan, launched by President Rafsanjani in 1989/90, made a total allocation of $10 billion for military purchases alone, equivalent to $2 billion per year. *SWB*, ME 20 June 1990.
2. The average figure is in fact for the 1980–88 period, but early indications show that there was little slackening in this trend after the implementation of the cease-fire agreement with Iran in 1988. IISS estimates Iraq's defence budget for 1990 to be around $13.3 billion. See *The Military Balance 1990–1991*.
3. Reports circulating in October 1990 suggest that Iran is negotiating to receive the J-8 Finback from China. The package is also known to include the further transfer of Chinese-made missiles and modern T-80 and T-89 MBTs. *Nimrooz*, 26 October 1990. Iraq has received considerably more of the J-6 and J-7 combat aircraft than Iran. Both sides are believed to have received Chinese-made Silkworm anti-ship missiles and T-59 MBTs. However, the T-69 model has only been supplied to Iraq.
4. Joint research on, and development of, this missile came to a halt well before the Iraqi invasion of Kuwait, partly as a consequence of direct American pressure on both Argentina and Egypt to prevent the transfer of further missile technology to Iraq.
5. The Tomcats of the Iranian airforce have rarely seen combat action since most of the remaining F-14s were used for their sophisticated avionics instead of their intended role as fighters, as airborne advanced radar systems and for limited electronic surveillance and counter-measures.
6. Extensive talks between British and Iranian officials in Dublin and Rome in 1989 and throughout 1990, via Britain's European partners close to Tehran and at the UN over the Rushdie affair, the freedom of the British hostages in Lebanon and the fate of Roger Cooper jailed in Iran (and of course 'exchange of views on the current Gulf crisis'), resulted in sufficient 'understandings' between the two sides for Tehran to authorise the re-opening of the British embassy in the Iranian capital on 27 October 1990.
7. But the lifting of all sanctions against Iran by the European Community in October 1990 means that from then on Tehran can buy the weapons systems it chooses from these European states, themselves desperate to minimise the impact on their domestic arms industries of the 'peace dividends' that have arisen out of the collapse of the Warsaw Pact challenge to Western security interests on their domestic arms industries by looking to lucrative export markets.
8. Even a rudimentary production line could be useful to Tehran's efforts to expand its domestic aerospace industries. The actual sophisticated fighter power required for defence and to achieve parity with the other

NOTES

two Gulf powers can continue to be imported until such time as Iran feels confident enough to opt for licensed production of modern combat aircraft. For an insight into Iranian-Israeli military relations see Samuel Segev, *The Iranian Triangle: The Untold Story of Israel's role in the Iran-Contra Affair* (New York: The Free Press, 1988); and James Adams, *The Unnatural Alliance* (London: Quartet Books, 1984).

9   A change of regime in Iraq would of course change the equation yet again: Iraq may well be weakened in relative terms, but its military machine could live to fight another round.

10 *Financial Times*, 8 December 1989; *Flight International*, 21 February 1990.

11 *The Independent*, 28 April 1990. In developing Tammuz-1, Iraq is known to have relied heavily on the experiences of its joint research with Argentina and Egypt on the Condor-2 project. The mysteries of the Iraqi 'supergun', according to French sources, can be unravelled in the context of Iraq's continuing research on rocket boosters and missile technologies. According to this view, the precision steel tubes were used as test tunnels for the testing of rocket boosters. Iraq already possessed supersonic wind tunnels and the new tunnels were intended to advance research in aeronautics with dual application; missile development and aircraft design.

12 *Jane's Defence Weekly*, 7 October 1989.

13 *Keyhan* (London), 23 November 1989; *Jane's Defence Weekly*, 13 May and 20 May 1989.

14 *ibid.*; also *Middle East Strategic Studies Quarterly* (published by Brassey's), Vol 1, No 1, 1988.

15 In 1988 Iraq announced that it had developed an anti-missile missile (the Fao-1) that was capable of destroying incoming short-and medium-range missiles. This had not reached mass production stage in 1990.

16 The delivery of 12 Italian-made missile-bearing naval vessels to Iraq in August 1990 was halted as a result of the Iraqi invasion of Kuwait. Their delivery at a later date cannot be ruled out.

17 Having said this, both Egypt and Israel have after a short pause again embarked upon acquiring more arms. Egypt has been taking delivery of some 700 surplus American MBTs from the European theatre, and Israel has been strengthening its ground-based and airborne air defence forces at a fast rate.

SELECT BIBLIOGRAPHY

Books

Abdulghani, Jasim, *Iran and Iraq: The Years of Crisis* (London: Croom Helm, 1984).

Acharya, Amitav, *US Military Strategy in the Gulf* (London: Routledge, 1989).

Axelgard, Frederick, *Iraq in Transition* (Boulder, Col.: Westview Press, 1986).

Bakhash, Shaul, *The Reign of the Ayatollahs* (New York: Basic Books, 1984).

Braun, Ursula, *Epicentre Kuwait: the international political dimension of a regional conflict*, (= *Aussenpolitik*, January 1990).

Chubin, Shahram and Charles Tripp, *Iran and Iraq at War* (London: I B Tauris, 1988).

Cordesman, Anthony, *The Gulf and the Search for Strategic Stability* (Boulder, Col.: Westview Press, 1984).

——, *The Gulf and the West: Strategic Relations and Military Realities* (Boulder, Col.: Westview Press/ London: Mansell, 1988).

Cunningham, Michael, *Hostages to Fortune: The Future of Western Interests in the Arabian Gulf* (London: Brassey's, 1984).

Davies, Charles (ed.), *After the War: Iraq, Iran and the Arab Gulf* (Chichester: Carden, 1990).

—— (ed.), *The Arab Gulf: Global Interests in the Region* (Chichester: Carden: 1991).

Ehteshami, Anoushiravan, *Nuclearisation of the Middle East* (London: Brassey's, 1989).

—— and M. Varasteh (eds.), *Iran and the International Community* (London: Routledge, 1991).

Esposito, John (ed.), *The Iranian Revolution: Its Global Impact* (Miami: Florida International University Press, 1990).

SELECT BIBLIOGRAPHY

Farouk-Sluglett, Marion and Peter Sluglett, *Iraq since 1958: From Revolution to Dictatorship* (London: KPI, 1987).

Heller, Mark, *The Iran-Iraq War: Implications for Third Parties*, Jaffee Center for Strategic Studies (JCSS) Paper No. 23 (Tel Aviv University, 1984).

Helms, Christine Moss, *Iraq: Eastern Flank of the Arab World* (Washington DC: Brookings Institution, 1984).

Hiro, Dilip, *Iran under the Ayatollahs* (London: Routledge & Kegan Paul, 1985).

——, *The Longest War: The Iran-Iraq Military Conflict* (London: Grafton, 1989).

Hufbauer, Gary C, Jeffrey J Scott and Kimberley A Elliott, *Economic Sanctions Reconsidered* (Washington DC: Institute for International Economics, 1990).

Ismael, Tareq, *Iraq and Iran: The Roots of Conflict* (Syracuse University Press, 1982).

Karsh, Efraim, *The Iran-Iraq War: A Military Analysis*, Adelphi Paper 220 (London: International Institute for Strategic Studies, 1987).

—— (ed.), *The Iran-Iraq War: Impact and Implications* (London: Macmillan, 1989).

Keddie, Nikki and Mark Gasiorowski (eds.), *Neither East Nor West: Iran, the Soviet Union and the United States* (New Haven: Yale University Press, 1990).

Khalidi, Walid, *The Gulf Crisis: origins and consequences* (Washington DC: Institute for Palestine Studies, 1991).

Khalil, Samir al-, *Republic of Fear* (London: Hutchinson Radius, 1990).

King, Ralph, *The Iran-Iraq War: The Political Implications*, Adelphi Paper 219 (London: International Institute for Strategic Studies, 1987).

Kupchan, Charles, *The Persian Gulf and the West: The Dilemmas of Security* (London: Allen & Unwin, 1987).

Litwak, Robert and Samuel Wells, *Superpower Competition and Security in the Third World* (Cambridge, Mass.: Ballenger, 1988).

Marr, Phebe, *The History of Modern Iraq* (Boulder, Col.: Westview Press, 1985).

Maull, Hans and Otto Pick (eds.), *The Gulf War* (London: Pinter, 1989).

Miller, Judith and Laurie Mylroie, *Saddam Hussein and the Crisis in the Gulf* (New York: Times Books, 1990).

Mofid, Kamran, *The Economic Consequences of the Gulf War* (London: Routledge, 1990).

Niblock, Tim (ed.), *Iraq: the Contemporary State* (London: Croom Helm, 1982).

―― (ed.), *State, Society and Economy in Saudi Arabia* (London: Croom Helm, 1982).

Nonneman, Gerd, *Iraq, the Gulf States & the War: A Changing Relationship, 1980–86 and beyond* (London: Ithaca Press, 1986).

Ramazani, Rouhollah K, *Revolutionary Iran: Challenge and Response in the Middle East* (Baltimore: Johns Hopkins University Press, 1986).

――, *The Gulf Cooperation Council: Record and Analysis* (Charlottesville: University of Virginia Press, 1988).

Safran, Nadav, *Saudi Arabia: The Ceaseless Quest for Security* (Cambridge, Mass: The Belknap Press of Harvard University Press, 1985).

Sandwick, John A. (ed.), *Gulf Cooperation Council: Moderation and Stability in an Interdependent World* (Boulder, Col.: Westview Press, 1987).

Schofield, Richard, *Kuwait and Iraq: Historical Claims and Territorial Disputes* (London: Royal Institute of International Affairs, 1991).

Wells, Samuel and Mark Bruzonsky, *Security in the Middle East: Regional Change and Great Power Strategies* (Boulder, Col.: Westview Press, 1987).

Articles

Ajami, Fouad, 'Iran: The Impossible Revolution', *Foreign Affairs*, 67, Winter 1988/89.

Axelgard, Fredrick, 'Iraq: The Postwar Political Setting', *American-Arab Affairs*, Spring 1989.

Batatu, Hanna, 'Iraq's Underground Shi'i Movements', *Middle East Journal*, 35, 1981.

SELECT BIBLIOGRAPHY

Chubin, Shahram, 'Iran and its neighbours: The Impact of the Gulf War', *Conflict Studies*, 204, 1987.

Ehteshami, Anoushiravan, 'Sinking with Iraq: Jordan and the PLO gamble on a new power balance', *International Defence Review*, 23, September 1990.

——, 'Saddam in Search of Suez', *European Affairs*, February 1991.

Farouk-Sluglett, Marion and Peter Sluglett, 'Iraq since 1986: the strengthening of Saddam', *Middle East Report*, 20/6, November 1990.

Hooglund, Eric, 'The Islamic Republic at War and Peace', *Middle East Report*, January 1989.

Hunter, Shireen, 'Post-Khomeini Iran', *Foreign Affairs*, 68, Winter 1989/90.

Karsh, Ephraim and Inari Rautsi, 'Why Saddam Hussein invaded Kuwait', *Survival*, 33/1, January/February 1991.

Nixon, Richard, 'A War about Peace', *European Affairs*, February 1991.

Nonneman, Gerd, 'Delusions of Grandeur', *The Middle East*, September 1990.

Segal, David, 'The Iran-Iraq War: A Military Analysis', *Foreign Affairs*, 66, Summer 1988.

Sick, Gary, 'Iran's Quest for Superpower Status', *Foreign Affairs*, 65/4, Spring 1987.

Stauder, Jack, 'Oil Internationalism: the crisis in the Gulf in broad perspective', *Review of International Affairs* (Belgrade), 41/975, November 1990.

Stork, Joe and Ann M Lesch, 'Why War? Background to the crisis' *Middle East Report*, 20/6, November 1990.

Strategic Studies (Journal of The Institute of Strategic Studies, Pakistan) special issue on 'Security in the Gulf: Regional and Global Aspects', 2, Winter 1988.

Wright, Claudia, 'Iraq—New Power in the Middle East', *Foreign Affairs*, Winter 1979/80.

TURKEY
USSR
SYRIA
LEBANON
Beirut
Damascus
ISRAEL
Tel Aviv
Amman
JORDAN
IRAQ
Baghdad
Tehran
IRAN
AFGHANISTAN
EGYPT
KUWAIT
Shiraz
The Gulf
SAUDI
ARABIA
Jubail
Dhahran
BAHRAIN
QATAR
Ras al Khaimah
Umm al Qaiwain
Ajman
Sharja
Dubai
Fujaira
Gulf of Oman
Abu Dhabi
UAE
Muscat
Riyadh
Red Sea
Yanbu
Jeddah
Ta'if
OMAN
SUDAN
ERITREA
San'a
Yemen
Arabian Sea
ETHIOPIA
Aden
DJIBOUTI
SOMALIA

Mahabad
Kurdistan
Mosul
Tehran
Sulaymaniya
Kirkuk
Halabiya
Sanandaj
Qom
Tikrit
Tigris
Khaniqin
Kermanshah
Sammara
IRAQ
Mandali
Zagros
IRAN
Baghdad
Mehran
Isfahan
Karbala
Mountains
Dezful
Kut
Najaf
Amara
Susangerd
Khuzestan
Ahvaz
Euphrates
Qurna
Khorramshahr
Basra
Abadan
Umm Qasr
Bubiyan
Jahra
Kuwait
Kharg Island
The Gulf
Hafr al-Batin
Khorramshahr
IRAN
Abadan
IRAQ
Shatt al-Arab
Warba
Khor Abdullah
Fao
Kuwait
Bubiyan Island
The Gulf
Bandar Abbas
Qeshm Island
Larak Island
Strait of Hormuz
Tunbs
Abu Musa

ABOUT THE AUTHORS

Iranian-born ANOUSHIRAVAN EHTESHAMI is a lecturer in Middle East politics at the University of Exeter and a frequent contributor to the newsmedia. His publications include *Nuclearisation of the Middle East* (Brassey's, 1989) and *Iran and the International Community* (co-editor) (Routledge, 1991).

GERD NONNEMAN has taught Middle East politics at the Universities of Manchester and Exeter. Born in Flanders, he worked in Iraq 1982–84, and published i.a. *Iraq, the Gulf States and the War* (Ithaca Press, 1986) and *Development, Administration and Aid in the Middle East* (Routledge, 1988).

CHARLES TRIPP is a lecturer in Middle East politics at London University's School of Oriental and African Studies. Among his publications are *Iran and Iraq at War* (with Shahram Chubin) (I. B. Tauris, 1988) and *Regional Security in the Middle East* (editor) (Gower, 1984).

INDEX*

Abadan 226
Abdullah, Prince 40
Abu Dhabi 44, 46, 78, 101
Abu Musa 44
Afghanistan 109, 117, 251
Aflaq, Michel 25
Ahl-al-Thiqa (Iraq) 32f
Ajman 44
Algeria 80, 82, 117, 248
Algiers Accord/Agreement 37, 39, 226
al-Amiri, Rashid 76
Al-Yamama 1 and 2 98f, 133
Amman Summit 52f
Anbar Space Research Base (Iraq) 135
Aoun, General 64
Arab Cooperation Council 67f, 74, 78, 82, 88, 103, 110f, 130, 236
   Alexandria Summit 68
Arab Fund for Social and Economic Development 69
Arabian peninsula 104, 110
Arabian Sea 91
Arab League 40, 46, 51, 73ff, 77–80, 82ff, 86, 88f, 107, 238f, 241 (*and following subheadings*)
   Amman Summit 52f, 232
   Baghdad Summit, 1990 72, 238
   Cairo Summit 1990 79, 239
   Charter 68
   Fez Summit 46
Arab Maghreb Union 82, 111
Arab Monetary Fund 69
Argentinia 124, 128, 135
Arms control 252ff

Asia 132
Australia 80
Austria 135
AWACS 48, 50, 101, 105
Aziz, Tariq 53, 73ff, 84f, 225, 228, 240, 242f

Bab al-Mandab 95
Baghdad Summit, 1990 72
Bahonar, Hojjatoleslam 18
Bahrain 42, 45, 48, 50–53, 55f, 60ff, 74, 101, 105, 116, 233
   relations with China 236
   relations with Iran 42, 48, 50–53, 55f, 60–63, 235
   relations with Iraq 45, 48, 50, 54f, 63, 89
   relations with Soviet Union 267
Baker, James 80, 84f, 241ff, 247, 254
   meeting with Tariq Aziz, Geneva 85, 243
Bandar, Prince 57, 234
Bangladesh 80
Bani Sadr, Abol-Hassan 18, 225f, 257
Baqir al-Sadr, Ayatollah Muhammad 225
Barzan al-Takriti 258
Basra 43, 46, 68, 70, 227f, 231
Ba'th party 24-28, 32f, 35ff, 230, 233, 236
   8th regional congress 35
   9th regional congress 36, 227
Bazargan 12, 16, 18
Beheshti, Ayatollah 18
Belgium 80, 233

*Not including Chapter 6, *Documents*.

279

INDEX

Besharati 50
Black Sea 95
Boussena 73
Brazil, 105f, 124, 128, 135ff
Britain 1, 77, 79ff, 106, 127, 130, 135, 232, 235f, 239, 241f, 246, 250, 254, 268
Bubiyan 38, 40, 44-47, 54, 58, 64f, 76
Bush, President George 78, 84, 241f
Bustan 227

Camp David 42, 109
Canada 80
Cardoen Corporation 123
Central America 251
al-Chalabi 73, 76
Chemical weapons 30, 230, 233f
Cheney, Richard 78, 241f, 247
Chile 123
China 84, 96, 102, 105, 112, 120, 122–126, 129, 131ff, 139, 239, 242, 268
CIA 229
Communist Bloc 122, 124, 132, 268
Communist Party of Iraq 27
Condor-2 Project 124, 269
Cuba 78, 84, 242
Czechoslovakia 97

Da'wa Party 27
Desert Storm, Operation 84, 86, 243, 235–250
Dezful 227
Diego Garcia 95
Djibouti 77, 95
Dubai 43f, 242

East Africa 93, 95, 114, 139
Egypt 67f, 74f, 80, 83, 89, 95f, 102, 110f, 123f, 130, 134, 138f, 236ff, 241, 269
Eraqi, Mohammadi 257
Ethiopia 95f
Europe 100, 117, 123, 126, 128, 133, 136, 252, 254

European Community 78, 80, 97, 236, 239f, 268

Fahd, Prince/King 39–42, 53, 55, 60, 67f, 74, 76, 79, 82, 239
Fahd plan on Palestine 46
Fallahian, Hojjatoleslam 11
Fao 29, 47, 49, 51, 54, 58, 230, 233
Faisal, King 40
Fazel, Iraj 5
France 77, 80f, 84f, 97, 106, 122f, 125–129, 131, 136, 228, 254, 228, 232, 234, 239, 241, 243
Fujairah 44

Gaza Strip 109
Germany 127
  West- 80, 135
Giscard d'Estaing, President 123
Glaspie, April 87, 239
Goose, Stephen 117
Gorbachev 57, 235, 241
Gulf Arab states (excluding Iraq) 93f, 101–114, 116f, 127, 130f, 137, 239ff, 243, 265 (*and following subheadings*)
  defence plan 267
  foreign policy 40–42
  relations with Iran 14f, 42, 44f, 46ff, 50–56, 58–63, 241
  relations with Iraq 38–90
  relations with United States 36
Gulf Cooperation Council:
  formation 45, 226
  and see Gulf Arab states
Gulf International Bank 69
Gulf security arrangements 15,
Gulf War *see* Iran-Iraq War, *or* Kuwait, invasion of

Habibi 18
Halabja 54, 233
al-Hamad, Yusuf 69
Hammadi, Sa'doun 64, 73
Hamd ibn Khalifa, Shaikh 55

280

INDEX

Hezbollah 5, 16
Hormuz Strait of 40, 42, 94, 235
Horn of Africa 95f
Hurd, Douglas 84, 254
Hussein, King 74, 77, 79
Hussein, Saddam *see* Saddam Hussein
Huwaiza marshes 228

Ibrahim, Izzat 53, 65, 76
IISS 106, 115
India 91
Indian Ocean 95f, 139
Indian subcontinent 114
IPSA pipeline 44, 49, 52, 58, 63, 68, 70, 78
Iran 82, 100, 102–114, 116f, 131, 134, 136, 225–237, 240–243, 250, 252f (*and following subheadings*)
 1989 cabinet 5–15
 arms procurement policy 124–128, 265, 268
 arms production 132ff, 139, 266, 268
 Bazargan government 12
 clergy in 10ff, 14, 16, 257
 constitution 4, 15, 17, 236
 Construction Crusade in 133
 Council of Constitutional Guardians 5, 257
 Council/Assembly of Experts 229, 235, 242, 257
 Defence Industries Organisation 133
 defence policy 11, 119–121, 265
 economic policy/conditions 8, 15, 235, 257, 266, 268
 Expediency Council 5, 16f, 233
 foreign policy of 14f, 257
 Hoveyda cabinet 12f
 Ideology in 8, 108
 Islamic Republican Party 231
 Majlis 4–15, 55, 120, 225, 228, 233, 237, 257f
 military in 14, 91, 103, 125, 265, 268
 Ministry of Defence and Armed Forces Logistics 121
 Pahlavi dynasty of 97, 107
 politics in 3–18
 political participation in 15, 235
 professional class in 13
 relations with Bahrain 42, 48, 50–53, 55f, 60–63, 235
 relations with Britain 4, 268
 relations with China 268
 relations with European Community 268
 relations with Gulf Arab states 14f, 42, 44ff, 46ff, 50–56, 58–63, 241
 relations with Iraq 1, 14f, 81, 84, 241f (*see also* Iran-Iraq War)
 relations with Israel 269
 relations with Jordan 243
 relations with Kuwait 14f, 46–56, 59, 61, 64, 69ff, 234f
 relations with Oman 45f, 48, 50–54, 56, 58f, 61f
 relations with Qatar 42, 46ff, 51–53, 56, 58ff, 62
 relations with Saudi Arabia 14, 41, 48f, 51, 53, 59–62, 66, 103, 113, 230, 233, 235
 relations with Soviet Union 236f, 267
 relations with United Arab Emirates 42ff, 46, 48, 50–54, 56, 58–62
 relations with United States 97, 229ff
 repression in 15f
 revolution 39
 Revolutionary Council 18
 Shah of 97, 104f, 132
 Supreme Council of National Security 4, 11, 17
 Supreme Defence Council 119
 see also Iran-Iraq War
Iran Aircraft Industries 133

281

INDEX

'Irangate' 231
Iran Helicopter Industries 133
Iran-Iraq War 1, 26, 29f, 39, 44–54,
   56ff, 83, 86f, 97, 100, 104, 108f,
   112, 114, 119ff, 127, 135,
   225–234, 240, 249ff
   cease-fire 56f, 86, 234
   Iran's capture of Fao 29, 47f
   prisoners of war issue 235, 240
   tanker war 46, 48, 52, 228, 230 (see also reflagging)
   War of the Cities 229, 233
Iraq 94, 96–105, 108–117, 130, 132,
   225–237, 240–243, 247, 249, 255
   (and following subheadings)
   aid from Gulf Arab states 44, 46, 48, 52, 63f, 69
   allied assault on 245–250
   armed forces of see military
   arms procurement 100f, 129–131, 238
   arms production 134–137, 139, 269
   Ba'th party in 24–28, 32f, 35f, 108, 230, 233, 236
      membership 24ff
      National Command 25
      Regional Command 25
      8th Regional Congress 35
      9th Regional Congress 25, 36, 227
   chemical weapons in 30, 230, 233f
   border agreement with Saudi Arabia 46
   defence 30, 129–132, 265
   economic liberalisation 37, 58
   economic conditions in 37, 86, 227
   elections 1989 27
   General Organisation for Technical Industries 134
   foreign policy of 35–38, 57, 83, 88, 103
      towards Arab world 35, 103, 109f
      towards Gulf states 35, 38ff, 57
      towards Iran 36
      towards Israel 30, 84f, 90, 241, 243
      towards Oman 39f
      on Palestine 36f, 81, 84
      towards Kuwait 33
      towards Syria 25
   hostage-taking 81, 85, 240, 242f
   ideology 24f, 27, 33, 108, 227
   invasion/occupation of Kuwait 1, 30, 35, 76–91, 104, 108f, 113f, 117, 121, 127, 131, 239–243, 251
   Kurds in 27, 29, 32, 54, 233, 250
      campaign against 30
   military in 28–32, 83f, 86, 91, 101–105, 121–124, 134, 265, 269
   Ministry of Industry and Military Production 134f
   Ministry of Mineral Resources 134
   missile capability of 30, 269 (see also military; defence)
   multi-party system, introduction of 27f
   National Assembly 23, 27, 33, 47, 81, 225, 229, 236
   oil policy of 33, 43
   patronage in 25ff, 29, 31ff
   politics in 1, 19–34, 86–89, 235, 252
   political elite 23, 33
   political parties in 27f, 235
   relations with Bahrain 45, 48, 50, 54f, 63, 89
   relations with Egypt 237
   relations with France 123, 228
   relations with Gulf Arab states 35–90
   relations with Iran 23, 30, 33, 37, 81, 89, 241f (see also Iran-Iraq War)
   relations with Jordan (Joint Military Command) 109

INDEX

relations with Kuwait 33, 39, 43–54, 56, 58, 60, 62–66, 69–76, 236, 238f
relations with Oman 39–43, 45f, 48, 50–54, 58f, 62f
relations with Qatar 43, 46ff, 51ff, 56, 58f, 63, 73
relations with Saudi Arabia 39, 42–53, 55–58, 60, 62f, 66–70, 72, 74, 76, 78ff, 82f, 89, 236
relations with Soviet Union 35, 37, 97, 122, 227, 267
relations with United Arab Emirates 39, 43f, 46, 48, 50, 52, 58ff, 62f, 71–76
relations with United States 241
Republican Guard 29
Revolutionary Command Council 53, 76, 230, 245
revolution of 1968 24
sanctions against 78–81, 84, 131, 240f, 246
security apparatus 21, 258
Shi'is in 29, 32, 250, 259
Sunnis in 29, 32
UN role in 250
see also Iran-Iraq War
Islamic Conference Organisation 61, 77f, 239
Islamic Da'wa Party 27
Islamic Development Bank 69
Islamic Front for the Liberation of Bahrain 55
Islamic Revolution Guards Corps (Iran) 11, 119, 121, 125, 133, 232
Israel 72, 90, 96, 102, 104, 110ff, 124, 128, 132, 134f, 138f, 226, 238, 240f, 243, 251, 253, 269
influx of Soviet Jews 72
Italy 77, 97, 106, 127, 234, 239

Jabir al-Ahmad Al-Sabah, Shaikh 55, 78f
Japan 80
Jeddah agreement (Gulf oil producers, July 1990) 76, 239
Jerusalem 39
Jordan 67, 74f, 77, 80, 82f, 95f, 109ff, 138, 236, 243
Jovic, General Slavo 234

Kamali, H. 8, 10
Kani, Mahdavi 5
Karrubi, Mehdi 5, 18, 237, 258
Kazerouni, Serajaddin 8
Kazzar, Nadhim 258
al-Khafaji, Isam 37
Khairallah Tulfah, General Adnan 31, 236
Khalid, King 39f
Khalifa ibn Salman, Shaikh 54
Khalkhali 258
Khamenei 3, 5, 16ff, 62, 119, 227, 229, 234, 237, 257f
designation as *Faqih* 4
Khanaqin 225
Kharg island 227ff
Khatami, Mohammed 8, 12
Khoini'a 5, 15f, 18, 258
Khomeini, Ahmad 5, 17f
Khomeini, Ayatollah 3, 16f, 45, 59, 61f, 112, 120f, 226, 229, 231, 235ff, 257
Khoramshahr 226f
Klibi, Chadli 82
Korea (North) 102, 120, 125f, 132
Korea (South) 124, 128
Kurdistan 230
Kurds 27, 29, 32, 54, 233, 250
Kurdish Democratic Party 27
Kuwait 38, 41–50, 107f, 111, 113, 116f, 229, 230f, 233, 237, 239f, 245ff, 249f, 253, 255 (*and following subheadings*)
arms transfer agreement with US 101
democracy issue in 230, 237f, 242
foreign policy of 41f
invasion/occupation of 1, 35, 76–91, 104, 108f, 113f, 116f,

283

INDEX

121, 127, 131, 239–243, 251, 265, 267
oil policy of 30, 71–74, 237f
Provisional Free Government of Kuwait 77f, 239
reflagging of tankers 49f, 52, 231f, 234
relations with Iran 46–56, 59, 61, 64, 69ff, 234f
relations with Iraq 43–54, 56, 58, 60, 62–66, 69–76, 236, 238f

Lajevardi, Ayatollah 16
Larak island 231
Lebanon 64f, 81, 96, 109, 118
Levant 93, 96, 104, 110ff, 114, 137, 139
Libya 77, 79, 82, 102, 110, 117, 126, 139

al-Majid family 31
al-Majid, Ali Hassan 259
al-Majid, Hussein Kamil Hassan 135
Majnoon 46, 54, 228, 233
Mandali 225
Mao Tse Tung 113f
al-Maskari, Hashid 54
Mauritania 77, 80, 82
McFarlane, Robert 230
Mecca riots (July 1987) 51, 232
Mehran 230
Meshkini, Ayatollah 235
Military Industries Corporation (Iraq) 134
Missile Technology Control Regime 252
Mitterrand, President 84, 123, 254
Mohtashemi, Hojjatoleslam 5, 10f, 14, 18, 258
Mojahedin 226
Montazeri, Ayatollah 3, 14, 18, 229, 235f
Morocco 80, 89
Mosul 31
Moussavi, Hussein 5, 16ff, 120, 258

Moussavi-Ardebelli 18, 257
Mubarak, President 74f, 77, 79f, 89, 238

Na'if, Prince 40, 45
National Charter for the Arab States 37f, 42f, 89
National Liberation Army (Iran) 100, 234, 265
NATO 95, 97, 240
Netherlands 233
Niblock 38
Nicaragua 249
North Africa 116, 139 (see also Arab Maghreb Union)
Nourbakhsh, Mohsen 5, 8
Nouri, Hojjatoleslam 8, 10f, 257

OAPEC 107
OECD 103
Oil 37, 43f, 46, 48f, 52f, 58, 60, 62ff, 66–69, 71–76, 78f, 83, 86, 226–230, 232, 237–241
Oman 101, 105, 112, 116 (and following subheadings)
 foreign policy 41
 relations with Iran 45f, 48, 50–54, 56, 58f, 61f
 relations with Iraq 39–43, 45f, 48, 50–54, 58f, 62f
 relations with United States 54
OPEC 49, 60, 63, 67, 71ff, 75f, 107, 237–240
 Geneva Conference July 1990 75
Osirak nuclear reactor 96, 226

Pakistan 80, 110, 124, 128, 133
Palestine Liberation Organisation see PLO
Palestine question 36, 39, 46, 81, 84, 109, 118, 242f, 251, 253f
Pasdaran see Islamic Revolution Guards Corps
Patriotic Union of Kurdistan 27
Perez de Cuellar, Javier 85, 240 243, 253

284

INDEX

PLO 77, 80, 82, 96, 109
Popular Front for the Liberation of Oman 39, 45

Qaboos, Sultan 41, 45, 50, 52, 59
Qatar 42, 46, 48, 101
   relations with Iran 42, 46ff, 51–53, 56, 58ff, 62
   relations with Iraq 43, 46ff, 51ff, 56, 58f, 63, 73
   relations with Saudi Arabia 42, 46
Quandt 40
Qutbzadeh 18

Rafsanjani, Hashemi 3, 5–15, 18, 51, 55, 60ff, 116, 119f, 235, 240, 242, 257f
   appointment as acting C-in-C 3, 233
   election as President 4, 237
Rajai, Iranian President 226
Ramazani 40
Ramadhan, Taha Yassin 49, 55, 63, 67f
Ras al-Khaimah 39, 44
al-Rashid family (Iraq) 31
Rashid Al-Maktum, Shaikh 242
Reagan, President 229
Red Sea 44, 58, 68, 70, 93f, 96, 104, 111, 265
Reflagging of Kuwaiti tankers 49f, 52, 231f, 234
Regional security structures 235, 243, 251, 254
Republican Guard *see* Iraq
Revolutionary Command Council *see* Iraq
Reyshahri, Mohammed 16, 18
Rumaila oil field 74, 76
Rushdie, Salman 3f, 61, 127, 236, 257, 268

Sabah, Al- 77
Sabah al Ahmad Al-Sabah, Shaikh 64f

Saddam Hussein 1, 19–38, 42f, 47, 53ff, 56, 62, 64, 67, 72, 75, 77ff, 81, 83, 85–90, 103, 111, 121, 135, 225ff, 230, 233ff, 238, 240–243, 245ff, 249, 258f
   vision of power 20–24, 87f, 258
   assumption of the presidency 25
Sa'd al-Abdallah Al-Sabah, Shaikh 43, 51, 65, 76
Salamcheh 55, 233
Samarra 31
Saqr, Shaikh 39, 44
Sa'ud, Al- 51, 55, 59f, 63, 79
Sa'ud al-Faisal, Prince 39, 47, 51, 55, 57
Saudi Arabia 1, 38, 93–102, 105–109, 111–114, 116, 130f, 133, 139 225, 229, 234, 238, 241f
   arms deals 91, 96, 100, 105, 116
   foreign policy 40–43, 82f, 89
   naval fleet 94
   oil policy 237, 240
   relations with China 239
   relations with Iran 41, 48f, 51, 53, 59–62, 66, 103, 113, 230, 233, 235
   relations with Iraq 42–53, 55–58, 60, 62f, 66–70, 72, 74, 76, 78ff, 82f, 89, 236
   relations with Soviet Union 241
   relations with US 116
Shakir, Sa'doun 53
Sharjah 43
Shatt al-Arab 38, 43, 70, 81, 87, 226, 236
Shevardnadze, Eduard 235
Shi'is 29, 32, 225, 237, 250, 259
Shultz, George 54, 228
Shush 227
SIPRI 116
Sirri island 230
Socotra 95
Somalia 95
South Africa 132
Southern Africa 251

285

South Asia 91, 104
Soviet Union 35f, 41, 57, 77, 83, 92, 95f, 102, 105f, 109, 111f, 114, 117, 122ff, 126f, 129, 131f, 134, 136–139, 227, 231f, 235ff, 239ff, 267
　invasion of Afghanistan 36, 42, 97
Spain 135, 230
Springborg, Robert 37
Stark, USS 49, 231
Strait of Gibraltar 95
Subiya 65
Sudan 80, 82
Suez Canal 95
Sulaimania 230
Sultan, Prince 40
Susangerd 226
Sweden 128
Swiftsword, Operation 48
Syria 25, 47, 53, 64f, 80f, 89, 102, 109–112, 117, 126, 135, 137, 139, 227, 241

Takrit 29, 31
Taiwan 128, 132
Taleghani, Ayatollah 18,
Third World 36, 85, 100, 102f, 104f, 115, 123f, 131, 137
Torkan, Akbar 121
Tulfah family (Iraq) 31
Tunb islands 44
Tunisia 80, 82
Turkey 79, 84, 94, 110, 128, 253

Umm al-Qaiwain 44
Umm Qasr 38, 43
UNIIMOG 234, 250, 252
United Arab Emirates 105, 112, 116, 237
　oil policy 71–76, 238, 242
　relations with Iran 42ff, 46, 48, 50–54, 56, 58–62
　relations with Iraq 39, 43f, 46, 48, 50, 52, 58ff, 62f, 71–76
United Nations 84, 89, 111, 230, 243, 245, 247, 249–253 (*and following subheadings*)
　role in Iraq 250
　sanctions against Iraq 78–81, 84, 131, 240f, 246
　Security Council 47, 49, 51f, 77–80, 84, 226, 228, 240, 246ff, 254
　　Resolution 582 231
　　Resolution 598 3, 51–56, 114, 120, 232, 234, 250
　　Resolution 660 77, 245, 239
　　Resolution 661 239
　　Resolution 665 240
　　Resolution 667 241
　　Resolution 670 241
　　Resolution 678 84f, 242
United States 36, 54, 62, 66, 75, 77, 79, 81, 83–87, 91, 95, 100, 104–106, 124, 128, 133f, 136, 228f, 231–234, 239f, 242f, 246, 249f, 254 (*and the following subheadings*)
　agreement with Soviet Union on Kuwait crisis 115, 239f
　Central Command 96
　relations with Iran 97, 229ff
　relations with Iraq 241
　relations with Saudi Arabia 116
　Senate Foreign Relations Committee 254f
　twin pillar policy 91, 107
　troops deployment 80, 83, 241ff
Universal Declaration of Human Rights 252

Velayati 47, 50f, 113
Vietnam 102, 105, 124ff, 249, 265

Warba 38, 40, 47, 58, 64, 76
War relief crude 44, 46, 53, 64, 66, 69f
Warsaw Pact *see* Communist Bloc
West Bank 109 (*see also* Palestine question)

INDEX

Western European Union 240

Yanbu 93
Yazdi, Ayatollah 5, 15
Yemen 74, 78ff, 82ff, 95, 109f, 117, 242f, 248
  North 67, 109, 236
  South 40, 95
  unification 238
Yugoslavia 136, 230

al-Zawawi, Qays 39, 43
Zayid, Shaikh 50, 53f, 56, 74